NICK FAWCETT

SERMON HOOKS

THEMED

IDEAS

FOR

THOSE

PREPARING

TALKS

kevin mayhew

Sermon Hooks contains material from
Daily Prayer (Kevin Mayhew, 2001).

First published in 2003 by

KEVIN MAYHEW LTD
Buxhall, Stowmarket, Suffolk IP14 3BW
E-mail: info@kevinmayhewltd.com

KINGSGATE PUBLISHING INC
1000 Pannell Street, Suite G, Columbia, MO 65201
E-mail: sales@kingsgatepublishing.com

9 8 7 6 5 4 3 2 1 0

ISBN 1 84417 090 X
Catalogue No 1500597

Cover design by Angela Selfe
Typesetting by Louise Selfe
Printed in Great Britain

Contents

The God who travels with us; Into the unknown;
Letting go; Perseverance

Introduction

What's the hardest part of writing a talk or sermon? The thing I always found most difficult during my ministry was finding an initial idea around which to construct the rest of what I wanted to say. There were many times when I fretted for several days, seeking that elusive piece of inspiration. Once I fastened on a particular analogy or illustration, the rest soon fitted into place.

This book has been put together with this in mind. Aimed at the busy minister, preacher or speaker, it presents the readings and reflections that originally appeared in my book *Daily Prayer*, these carefully revised and arranged around key themes such as 'Grace', 'Confession and forgiveness', 'Christian seasons', 'Commitment', 'Love', 'Prayer' and so on. It does not offer off-the-peg sermons or anything approaching this. Rather, it provides reflections upon a range of biblical passages which, I hope, may spark a train of thought from which a sermon or talk may develop. To help locate particular passages of scripture, I have included an index of readings and key biblical characters, which is reinforced by an exhaustive list of contents.

Eventually, every talk has to reflect our own faith and experience of God if it is to communicate effectively, but in my experience a single idea can provide the raw material from which the finished product is fashioned. It is my hope that the thoughts offered in this book may serve such an end.

NICK FAWCETT

Adversity, faith in

see also Sorrow and despair

Bouncing back

The Lord said to Moses, 'Pharaoh will not listen to you, so I will have to perform even more wonders in the land of Egypt.' Despite all the wonders Moses and Aaron showed to Pharaoh, the Lord hardened Pharaoh's heart, and he refused to let the people of Israel leave his land. (Exodus 11:9-10)

I read recently about a celebrated author whose first novel was rejected 97 times before finally being accepted for publication! That takes some doing, doesn't it? – to keep on bouncing back from disappointment after disappointment. How many of us, I wonder, would have shown anything like that same determination? It's a rare gift!

Yet that is precisely what we see in the story of Moses. Called to seek an audience with Pharaoh and demand the release of his fellow Israelites from slavery, he was to suffer repeated frustrations as his requests were either turned down flat or granted for a moment only to be denied later. It would have been hard enough for Moses to continue undeterred had he naturally warmed to the task in hand, but when we remember that every moment was an ordeal for him, so much so that his brother Aaron was needed for support, we realise the full extent of his dedication. No one could have blamed him had he washed his hands of the whole venture after the first few attempts; I suspect I would have done so in his place! Yet, with incredible resilience, he battled on until at last he achieved success. His story gives us a memorable glimpse not just of human perseverance, but also of the God who reaches out with equal devotion to his people in every place and time, determined to set them free from all that holds them captive.

Equipped for battle

Don the whole armour of God, so that you may be able to withstand the ruses of the devil. For we do battle, not with flesh and blood, but with the rulers, authorities and cosmic powers of darkness – with the spiritual forces of evil in high places. So then, take up the whole armour of God, so that you may be able to resist on that evil day, and, having done everything, resolutely still to stand. Stand, therefore, and secure the belt of truth around your waist, and put on the breastplate of righteousness. Shoe your feet with a readiness to proclaim the gospel of peace. Above all, grasp the shield of faith, with which you will be able to smother the flaming arrows of the evil one. Take also, by prayer and supplication, the helmet of salvation, and the sword of the Spirit, which is the word of God. (Ephesians 6:11-18a)

One of the biggest box office hits of recent years is Gladiator, a film that graphically depicts the fate of those who had to do battle against man or beast in the amphitheatres of the Roman Empire. Imagine what it must have been like to be one of those unfortunate individuals, pitted against a lion with only a net for protection, or against a fully armed soldier with a trident as your only weapon. What chance would you have had?

Ironically, though, in the Christian life, we can put ourselves in a similar situation, not in terms of our physical safety but of our spiritual welfare. There is so much, both within and outside us, that comes into conflict with the way of Christ. Each day brings a succession of temptations, influences, demands and pressures that threaten to undermine our faith. Little wonder, then, that the Apostle Paul, in his letter to the Romans, spoke of two selves warring within him. Yet, unlike those early gladiators, we do not need to go into battle defenceless, for, as Paul reminds us again, God has given us the resources we need to defend ourselves. Do we make time for prayer and the reading of God's word? Do we look for ways to share the gospel? Do we walk in faith and seek after truth? It is not enough to stroll casually through life trusting that God will protect us. We have a part to play, and we neglect it at our peril.

Faith in the wilderness

As Pharaoh drew near, the Israelites looked back and spotted the Egyptians coming after them. They cried out to the Lord in terror, and said to Moses, 'Was it because there were no graves in Egypt that you have brought us here to die in the wilderness? Isn't this just why we told you in Egypt to leave us alone and let us serve the Egyptians? We would rather have served the Egyptians than die in the wilderness.' 'Do not be afraid,' answered Moses. 'Stand firm, and see the deliverance that the Lord will bring you today, for you will never again see the Egyptians whom you see here today. The Lord will fight for you; you have only to keep still.' Then Moses stretched out his hand over the sea, and by a strong east wind throughout the night the Lord drove the sea back, turning it into dry land as the waters divided. The Israelites passed through the sea on dry ground, the waters forming a wall to their right and left. Then the Lord said to Moses, 'Stretch out your hand over the sea, so that the water may come back upon the Egyptians, their chariots and their chariot drivers.' So Moses stretched out his hand over the sea, and, as dawn broke, the sea returned to its place. (Exodus 14:10-14, 21-22, 26-27a)

We talk sometimes of experiencing a rollercoaster of emotions, and if ever that phrase was appropriate, it must surely be in describing the story of the crossing of the Red Sea. Imagine the ups and downs those involved must have gone through: first, suspense and excitement as they left Egypt to face an unknown but exciting future; then dismay and despondency as it became apparent that Pharaoh had changed his mind and the Egyptians were coming after them; then, sheer amazement at the sight of the waters opening before them; and then, finally, having crossed safely to the other side, an overwhelming sense of relief and exultation.

There is a lesson for us here. Life does not always go smoothly; it brings its fair share of challenges, even times when the future looks hopeless but, come what may, God is with us, in both the good and the bad. Remember that next time trouble strikes. Whatever the obstacle confronting you, God is able to lead you safely through.

God in the darkness

When it was the sixth hour, darkness fell over the whole land until the ninth hour. And at the ninth hour, Jesus cried out in a loud voice, 'Eloi, Eloi, lama sabachthani?' which translated means, 'My God, my God, why have you forsaken me?' (Mark 15:33)

How many of us are scared of the dark? Probably few of us are afraid in the sense we once were as children, yet there is still something about darkness that makes us associate it with the sinister, evil and unknown. It is not surprising, then, that if there is one thing we associate with God and one symbol used for him more than any other, it is light. 'The Lord is my light and my salvation,' says Psalm 27; 'of whom shall I be afraid?' Or again, in Psalm 36, 'With you is the fountain of life; in your light we see light.'

So we could go on, piling one text on top of another. Yet, though light may have filled our lives, there are times also when life seems dark, bleak, grim and forbidding; when even God seems far away such that we cry out in despair – times described by St John of the Cross as 'the dark night of the soul'. What do we make of moments like those? Has God no place in them? Must we face them alone? Not if the words of the gospels concerning the death of Christ are to believed, for there we read of how darkness descended on the land as Jesus hung on the cross. It seemed, even to Jesus, as though God wasn't present but the reality, of course, was different. It was there that God was supremely and astonishingly at work, offering himself for the life of the world, paying the price that would set us free. Though darkness seemed to have overtaken the world, the reality was that the light of God's love was shining brighter than ever and nothing would be able to overcome it. There are times when, for the Christian as much as any other, life seems dark and God seems far away, but never feel that God has abandoned you, for sometimes it is in the darkest moments that he is there most of all.

Going under?

The man's very words are these: 'I am worn out, O God, fit to drop. How can I hope to get through?' (Proverbs 30:1)

There are times when life gets on top of us, the pressures and demands too much to bear, and for most of us such moments are nearer than we might imagine, for who can say what tomorrow might bring? We may feel everything is under control, life running along smoothly, but one setback or disappointment can change our whole perspective, sending us spiralling into a vortex of chaos and confusion. Suddenly problems seem to engulf us from every side, sucking us in ever deeper. Most of us can survive such pressures for a time, but there comes a point when our strength gives out and we feel ourselves going under. All too many can testify to the mind-numbing, strength-sapping effect of stress and its capacity to drive us to the brink of despair and beyond.

Faith does not provide easy solutions to such times, but it does offer a resource to hold on to; namely, the knowledge that whatever we may face, nothing will finally be able to overcome God's purpose or separate us from his love. Put our trust in him and, though we may feel utterly overwhelmed, we will find his hand is there to hold our heads above the water until the storm subsides and calm returns.

Not as bad as it seems

Ahab told Jezebel everything Elijah had done, and how he had put all her prophets to the sword. Then Jezebel sent a messenger to Elijah, saying, 'Let the gods do the same to me, and worse besides, if by this time tomorrow I do not take your life as you took theirs.' Then Elijah was afraid. He arose and ran for his life, and coming to Beersheba, in Judah, he told his servant to remain there while he himself went on another day's journey into the wilderness. He sat down under a solitary broom tree, and asked God to let him die: 'It is enough; now, O Lord, take my life, for I am no better than my ancestors.' Suddenly the word of the Lord came to him, saying, 'What are you doing here, Elijah?' He answered, 'I have worked passionately for the Lord, the God of hosts; for the Israelites have forsaken your covenant, torn down your altars, and put your prophets to the sword. I alone am left, and now they want to take my life in turn.' (1 Kings 19:1-5a, 9b-10)

There's an old Arabian proverb that is a particular favourite of mine: 'All things are less dreadful than they seem.' That is the truth learned by Elijah in the story above. He had just experienced one of the high spots in his ministry, when the prophets of Baal were humiliated on Mount Carmel, but, as is so often the case, a high quickly gave way to a low. Presumably, Elijah had imagined that, following his earlier triumph, his troubles were over; that Jezebel and her prophets would have to admit defeat. Instead, he discovered that she had renewed her campaign against him with an even greater ferocity. As far as Elijah was concerned, it was him and God against the world, and he was fed up with fighting a one-man battle. God, though, had a surprise up his sleeve, for Elijah was shortly to discover that he was anything but alone – that, in fact, there were seven thousand people in Israel who had not bowed the knee to Baal.

There is a continuing message in this for us today. In the Church, we can feel up against it, struggling to keep the doors of our buildings open, demoralised by lack of members, disheartened by the limited impact of our efforts. As individuals, we can feel we are ploughing a lonely furrow, or simply find that life is getting on top of us. Through the experience of Elijah, God is saying, 'Don't be dismayed; all things are less dreadful than they seem.' However isolated you may feel, he has not left you to carry the load alone. Seen or unseen, there are others playing their part and working for his kingdom. Seen or unseen, he is always there to strengthen, to support and to see us through.

Rising to the challenge

Following the death of the Lord's servant Moses, the Lord spoke to Moses' assistant, Joshua son of Nun, saying, 'My servant Moses is dead. Now advance with all the people of Israel and cross the Jordan into the land that I am giving them. I will readily give to you everywhere that you set foot, as I promised to Moses. From the wilderness and the Lebanon as far as the great river, the river Euphrates, all the land of the Hittites and on towards the Great Sea in the west shall be your territory. Nobody will be able to withstand you all the days of your life. Just as I was with Moses, so I will be with you; I will not fail or forsake you. Be strong and of good courage; for you will lead this people to take possession of the land that I swore to their ancestors to give them.' (Joshua 1:1-6)

Anyone who has ever been hillwalking will know the experience of thinking one is nearing the summit, only to find, as one gets closer, that there is another stretch to climb . . . and another . . . and another! However far we progress, there is always that little bit further to go.

So it proved, in a rather different sense, for Joshua and the people of Israel following the death of Moses. After years of wandering in the wilderness, they had finally arrived at the border of the Promised Land, their long journey at last over. Or was it? A closer inspection revealed that others already occupied the land they thought was reserved for them. The task of making it their own had only just begun. No wonder Joshua, the newly chosen leader of Israel, felt overwhelmed by the sudden responsibility thrust upon him. His was the onerous challenge of rallying a people reeling from disappointment and inspiring them to new levels of enthusiasm and endeavour. Alone, he couldn't have done it; but he wasn't alone, for God had promised to be with him wherever he went. He goes on making that promise to us today – to anyone and everyone willing to serve him, however great a challenge such service may involve.

Set free from fear

Though an army encamp against me, my heart shall not fear; though war rise up against me, yet will I be confident. Do not be afraid of sudden calamity, or of the storm that strikes the wicked; for the Lord will be your confidence and will keep your foot from being caught. Even though I walk through the darkest of valleys, I fear no evil; for you are by my side; your staff and your crook continually there to reassure me. (Psalm 27:3; Proverbs 3:25-26; Psalm 23:4)

Of all the destructive forces at work within us, few, I believe, are more powerful than fear. I don't mean the fear we all feel sometimes when confronted by danger, but rather that dull nagging anxiety that can creep into our lives almost unnoticed and then slowly take over. Such fear saps us of energy, drains us of self-confidence, and robs us of enthusiasm. At its most extreme it can result in inexplicable feelings of panic, even complete breakdown.

It is hardly surprising, then, that our natural instinct is to run away from our fears, and to stifle as best we can any such feeling within us.

This, though, is a recipe for disaster. The only way to conquer fear is to confront it, in the knowledge that with God on our side nothing can finally harm us. We have his assurance that, whatever we may face, he will be there to see us through and set us free.

Call of God

Getting the message

The Lord called Samuel, and he answered, 'Here I am', and ran to Eli, saying, 'You called me. I'm here.' But Eli said, 'I didn't call; lie down again.' So he went and lay down. The Lord called Samuel again, and he got up and went to Eli once more, saying, 'Here I am, for you called me.' But he said, 'No, I didn't call, my son; lie down again.' At this time, Samuel had not yet come to know the Lord, and the word of the Lord had not been made known to him. The Lord called Samuel a third time, and once more he got up and went to Eli, and said, 'Here I am. You did call me.' Then Eli realised that the Lord was calling the boy, so he told Samuel, 'Go and lie down; and if he should call again, say, "Speak, Lord, for your servant is listening."' So Samuel went and lay down in his place. (1 Samuel 3:4-9)

What would have happened to Samuel, I wonder, had it not been for Eli? Would he finally have realised that the voice he heard was God calling him, or would he have gone on for ever imagining it was someone else speaking to him? It's an interesting thought, and one that highlights the ongoing problem of recognising God's voice. Many people believe themselves called to something when it is patently clear to others that they are mistaken. Equally, there are some who appear manifestly called by God yet who, for reasons best known to themselves, cannot or will not believe it. Samuel's story reminds us that even the greatest spiritual leaders are by no means always certain when God is speaking to them. Equally important, they remind us that it can take a third party to help us recognise God's call. Sometimes others can see what he is saying to us more clearly than we can see it ourselves.

The inescapable call

The word of the Lord came to Jonah, son of Amittai, saying, 'Go straightaway to Nineveh, that mighty city, and speak out against it; for their wickedness is an affront to my eyes.' But Jonah set off instead to Tarshish, wanting to escape from the presence of the Lord. (Jonah 1:1-3a)

In 1916 a law was passed in Britain making it compulsory for all unmarried men between the ages of 18 and 41 to enlist in the army and fight in the First World War. Not long after, married men were included too. In 1941, during the Second World War, women were compulsorily conscripted for the first time. The practice of conscription was only abolished in this country in 1962, a change in the law for which I personally give thanks.

How does all this compare with the story of Jonah? At first sight, there seem to be clear parallels – it almost looks as though God conscripted Jonah – but this is to misunderstand the story. God's call is not like that, for he will never compel us to do something against our will. What he will do, however, if he has a particular purpose for us, is keep on calling for as long as it takes us to respond. We may attempt to deny his call – thrusting it to the back of our minds, making excuses, convincing ourselves that we have misunderstood – but we will not find peace that way, for God will go on challenging us, day after day, year after year. The option is always ours to resist, as resist some do, but if God has chosen us for a particular task, then we will find that ultimately we cannot escape that call.

The unwelcome call

The word of the Lord came to me, saying, 'Before I formed you in the womb I knew you, and before you were born I consecrated you; I appointed you to be a prophet to the nations.' Then I answered, 'Ah, Lord God! I don't know how to speak. I'm only a boy.' But the Lord responded, 'Do not say you're only a boy; for you will go to those I send you to, and you will speak to them the words I give you. Do not be afraid of them, for I will watch over you and protect you; you have my word.' (Jeremiah 1:4-8)

What would we give to have the faith of Moses or Samuel, Elijah or Isaiah? How much easier it would be to serve God then. How much clearer our path would be. Have you ever felt like that? If so, think again, for when you read the biblical accounts of God calling people to service, almost always the initial response is the same: not delight but dismay, not pleasure but panic, not thanksgiving but fear. Look closer, and it's hardly surprising, for, as we shall see later, the things God called these people to do were onerous to say the least, nine times out of ten guaranteeing a less than enthusiastic reception. Few if any of those called considered themselves suited for the job, and most would have ducked it given the chance. Yet God was to equip each one to meet the task set before them.

We too may find ourselves facing challenges we believe beyond us, God's call a disturbing experience rather than the joy-ride we might have hoped for. But, if we are ready to respond, then we, like those before us, will discover that when God asks us to do something, he gives us the resources we need to finish the job.

Christian festivals

see also Time: The fullness of time

First Sunday of Advent

Be prepared

As for times and seasons, my friends, there is no need to write to you, for you are well aware that the day of the Lord will come upon you as a thief in the night. Just when people are saying, 'Relax, all is well', destruction will strike them as labour pains grip hold of a pregnant woman, and no one will escape. You, though, my friends, are not in the darkness such that the day should overtake you like a thief, for you are all children of light and of the day rather than of night and darkness. So, then, do not sleep like others, but be watchful and clear-headed. Those who sleep, do so in the hours of darkness just like those who get drunk, but since we are of the day let us remain clear-headed, putting on the breastplate of salvation through our Lord Jesus Christ, who died for us so that, whether we wake or sleep, we shall live together with him. (1 Thessalonians 5:1-10)

'Be prepared' – two words that all Scouts, past or present, will have indelibly printed on their minds. In theory, they should never be caught short, ready instead to respond to every eventuality. But life, of course, has a habit of catching us on the hop, and although that can be a problem, it is also a blessing. Imagine how dull life would be if we could know everything that was going to happen and had exhausted life's ability to offer new horizons and experiences.

It is not just life, however, that can surprise us but, above all, God. Take, for example, his coming to the world in Christ. For years, the people of Israel had looked forward to his coming, yet when the moment arrived many failed to see it. They thought they understood what God would do and were unprepared for anything else. The words of Paul to the Thessalonians suggest that we can do much the same. At first sight, Paul seems concerned simply with the return of Christ, but that is to miss the point, for he goes on to stress that we do not know when that day will be, or what it will involve. We should live each day in a sense of expectation, recognising that God is at work in a host of ways, constantly able to surprise us. Do that and whenever Christ comes we will be ready to meet him. Strictly speaking, we can't be prepared for the unexpected, but we can be open to the possibility that God may speak to us and work through us in ways we have not even begun to imagine. Be prepared!

Second Sunday of Advent

Believing the impossible

An angel of the Lord appeared to [Zechariah], standing on the right-hand side of the altar of incense. On seeing him, Zechariah was awestruck and paralysed by fear, but the angel said to him, 'Don't be frightened, Zechariah, for your plea has been heard. Your wife Elizabeth will bear you a son, and you are to call him John. He will bring you joy and gladness, and many will rejoice at his birth, for he will be great in the eyes of the Lord. He will turn many of the people of Israel to the Lord their God, and he will go out in the spirit and power of Elijah to turn the hearts of parents to their children, and those who have gone astray to the wisdom of the righteous – to prepare people so that they are ready for the Lord.' Zechariah said to the angel, 'How can I know this is true? For I am an old man, and my wife also is getting on in years.' The angel replied, 'I am Gabriel. I stand in God's presence, and he has sent me to tell you this good news, but now, since you have not believed my words, which in due course will be fulfilled, you will be struck dumb, rendered mute until the day these things happen.' (Luke 1:11-15a, 16-20)

'Impossible! It can't be done!' That was the response of Zechariah to the news that his wife Elizabeth was to give birth to a son. Whether she was beyond childbearing years is not clear, but there is no doubt that any hopes the couple might have had of her conceiving were long since gone. They were reconciled to their disappointment, so to be told that a child was to be born to them after all must have seemed too good to be true. From a human point of view, it was a perfectly understandable response, but here we are talking about God. That is what Zechariah failed to account for, and that is what made all the difference, for with God all things are possible.

Do we believe that? There will be times when we find God's promises hard to accept; times when we look at our life or the life of the world and feel that both are beyond redemption. Humanly speaking, that again is perfectly understandable, but once more it fails to account for God – the God who lived and died among us in Christ, raising him from the tomb; the God who has repeatedly shown that nothing is beyond him, however much it may seem beyond us!

Third Sunday of Advent

Preparing the way

The angel said, 'Don't be frightened, Zechariah, for your plea has been heard. Your wife Elizabeth will bear a son, and you are to call him John. He will turn many of the people of Israel to the Lord their God, and he will go out in the spirit and power of Elijah, to turn the hearts of parents to their children, and those who have gone astray to the wisdom of the righteous; to make ready a people prepared for the Lord.' (Luke 1:13, 16-17)

Watch any star or celebrity in concert, and, almost certainly, they will have a supporting cast. Turn to the first two chapters of the gospel of Luke, and you will find something rather similar. The chapters are concerned primarily with the birth of Jesus, but there's another birth entwined with his, another character who figures prominently in his story, and that, of course, is John the Baptist. In fact, John is given a mention in the early chapters of all four gospels, so, clearly, his role was important, but what exactly was that role and what can we learn from it?

The answer is very simple: 'to make ready a people prepared for the Lord.' This was John's task: to prepare the way of Christ; not in the sense of being a warm-up act, but rather as one who would get people ready to welcome Jesus when he came. For John that was to mean speaking out concerning the kingdom Christ would bring. It meant also following a distinctive lifestyle to reinforce his message. It meant pointing away from himself and towards Jesus. The lesson for today could hardly be clearer. We need to echo John's example in our own lives. Like him, we are called to prepare the way of Christ so that others today may meet him for themselves.

The forgotten person?

He was in the world, and the world owed its existence to him, yet the world did not recognise him. He became part of what was his own, and his own people did not accept him. (John 1:10-11)

Have you finished writing and posting your Christmas cards? If you haven't, then you'd better get a move on if you want to ensure that they will be delivered before Christmas Day. Yet, even when you've posted the last one, you can just about guarantee an unexpected card will arrive from someone you've completely forgotten about. Embarrassing, isn't it!

That person, though, may not be the only one you forget about, for contrary to what we might expect, we can forget, also, about Jesus! We may sing about him, read about him and hear about him time and again, yet fail actually to stop and meet him. We can be so busy with our festivities, even our carol services and celebrations, that we miss out on the personal encounter that Christmas offers. Instead of offering a welcome, the doors of our lives are firmly barred. Instead of going in heart and mind to Bethlehem, we stay wrapped up in our own little world. Instead of receiving the greatest gift ever offered to humankind, we find ourselves asking why it hasn't quite felt like Christmas. Don't let that happen to you. Whatever else, don't forget the one who Christmas is ultimately all about and don't forget to respond to him.

Fourth Sunday of Advent

Magnifying the Lord

Then Mary said, 'My soul magnifies the Lord, and my spirit exults within me in God my Saviour, for he has looked on the lowliness of his servant. From now on and for all time, people will call me blessed, because the Mighty One has done great things for me. Holy is his name!' (Luke 1:46-49)

When I was a child I was given a magnifying glass; not just any old magnifying glass, but one so powerful that when I looked through it I could see things in enormous detail. I can still remember how it opened up a whole new world that I had never imagined existed before. A moss-covered wall near my home became a thick and lush jungle, and the tiny ant crawling through it a terrifying monster rampaging through the undergrowth. Everywhere I looked, I saw things in a different light and on an altogether different scale.

What, you may ask, has all that to do with the song of Mary? The clue is there in that opening line: 'My soul magnifies the Lord.' The expression is an old-fashioned one, so much so that many newer translations have altered it, but, in so doing, they have lost an important part of what it is saying. On one level, it is talking simply about God, but, on another level, it is also about Mary and the way God had taken on a new significance in her life. Suddenly, a new world has opened up for her – a world in which she glimpsed God's greatness and goodness as never before, recognising that he was actively involved in her life and the life of the world. For Mary, of course, the circumstances were special, yet the coming of Christ, and his coming again to each one of us through his Spirit, means that we too can taste that joy and experience a similar sense of wonder. Advent calls us, then, in turn, to catch sight of the awesomeness and sovereignty of God, so that we might thrill to his presence and join with Mary in declaring: 'My soul magnifies the Lord, and my spirit exults within me in God my Saviour.'

'Who, me?!'

Now in the sixth month the angel Gabriel was sent by God to a town in Galilee called Nazareth, to a virgin engaged to a man named Joseph, a member of the house of David. The virgin's name was Mary. Approaching her, he said, 'Greetings, you who have been highly favoured. The Lord is with you.' She was bewildered by his words, and contemplated what such a greeting might mean. The angel said to her, 'Don't be frightened, Mary, for you have found favour with God. You will conceive in your womb and bear a son, and you will give him the name 'Jesus'. He will be great, and will be called the Son of the Most High, and the Lord God will give him the throne of his ancestor David. He will reign over the house of Jacob for ever, and his kingdom will never end.' Mary said to the angel, 'How can this be, since I am a virgin?' The angel answered, 'The Holy Spirit will come upon you, and the power of the Most High will rest over you, so that the child you will bear will be called the Son of God, for with God nothing is impossible.' Mary responded, 'I am the Lord's servant. Let it be to me just as you say.' (Luke 1:26-35, 38)

Surely God can't use me? How often have we echoed that response of Mary when God has asked something of us? The response is all the more vociferous when what God is asking involves sacrifice on our part. Yet if Mary's initial response is perfectly understandable, how then do we account for her compliance with God's wishes just a few moments afterwards? The answer is simple – she measured what was being asked of her not against her own resources but against God's. So it was that she offered acceptance – no doubt still confused, still wondering quite why she had been chosen, but ready to let God use her as he saw fit.

This story of Mary calls for a similar response from us today. We warm to accounts of the birth of Jesus, we celebrate his life and ministry, we give intellectual assent to the lordship of Christ, and we may be fascinated, even moved by it all, but God wants more. He wants us to be changed: our lives turned around, our very self re-created through his grace. He wants us to become part of his people and to use us in the work of his kingdom. 'Who, me?!' we may say – and that, of course, brings us back to where we started: to the quiet, trusting response of Mary to God's call. It is a response that resounds across the centuries, speaking loud and clear today; as also does the answer God gave her: 'Yes, you!'

Who? Them!

This is what happened concerning the birth of Jesus Christ. While his mother, Mary, was engaged to Joseph, but before they lived together, she became pregnant, through the Holy Spirit. Being a good man unwilling to expose her to public disgrace, Joseph planned to end the engagement quietly. However, just when he had made this decision, an angel of the Lord appeared to him in a dream and said, 'Joseph, son of David, do not be afraid to take Mary as your wife, for the child conceived within her is from the Holy Spirit. She will bear a son, and you are to call him Jesus, for he will save his people from their sins.' All this took place to fulfil what the Lord had spoken through the prophet: 'Look, the virgin will conceive and bear a son, and they will call him "Emmanuel", which means, "God is with us".' After waking from his sleep, Joseph did as the angel of the Lord had instructed, taking Mary as his wife, but he had no sexual relations with her until she gave birth to a son; and he named him Jesus. (Matthew 1:18-25)

If there's one thing harder than accepting that God can use you, it's accepting he can use others, especially when those 'others' are close to us. We think we know all about them, and, almost certainly, their faults and weaknesses are clearer to us than to most people. Any suggestion that God has singled them out for a special purpose is often met with more than a raised eyebrow. When those faults are writ large, then it's all the harder to believe.

What must it have looked like then, to Joseph, when Mary broke the news that she was expecting, only to tell him in the next breath that the child she carried was not the result of some illicit liaison but had been conceived by the Holy Spirit? How would you have responded in his shoes? A little scepticism was perfectly understandable. Yet Joseph, like Mary, was willing to let God overturn his preconceptions; ready to accept that God should use this girl he thought he knew in the most remarkable of ways. The circumstances in this case were, admittedly, unique, but the principle holds nonetheless for us all. We need to be open to God working through those we might least expect him to; and, above all, through those we are so close to that we mistakenly imagine we know everything there is to know about them. It may be that it is time to think again!

Christmas

It *is* you!

There were shepherds in that area, living in the fields and keeping watch over their flock during the night. Suddenly, an angel of the Lord appeared to them, and the glory of the Lord shone around them, and they were overcome with terror. However, the angel said to them, 'There's nothing to be frightened of; for see – I am bringing you good news of great joy that is for all people: today a Saviour has been born to you in the city of David, who is Christ the Lord. Let this be a sign to you: you will find a child swaddled in strips of cloth and lying in a manger.' All at once, there was with the angel rank on rank of heavenly beings, praising God and saying, 'Glory to God in the highest heaven, and peace on earth among all on whom his favour rests!' (Luke 2:8-14)

Do you remember the advertising campaign, some years ago now, which preceded the launch of the National Lottery? It caused quite a controversy at the time: a giant hand hovering over the rooftops of a town before finally a finger reached down to single out one household as the lucky winner of the coveted jackpot, backed up by the words, 'It could be you!' The suggestion was that the hand of providence might one day select us to receive a fortune. Did you take the bait? Many have, and a number of people have become millionaires as a result, but the majority of participants will have spent a considerable amount of money with little if anything to show for it.

Contrast that with the events of Bethlehem that we are preparing once again to celebrate. Here was the promise not of money on earth but of riches in heaven; a prize not merely for this life but for all eternity – the greatest gift ever offered. Yet this was no lottery, dependent on the whim of fate. There was no question of it *could* be you if you happened to get lucky. The message of the angels, the evangelists and countless generations of faith since is quite simple, 'It *is* you!' The promise of God in Christ – his gift of new life with everything that means – is not reserved for the exclusive few, nor dependent on any quirk of chance. It is ours for the taking, waiting simply for us to claim it – for you, for me, for everyone!

Making room

It happened at that time that Caesar Augustus issued a decree that a census should be taken of the entire world. This was the first such census and occurred while Quirinius was governor of Syria. All, therefore, went to be registered, each to their appropriate town. Joseph, being of the house and family of David, went from the Galilean town of Nazareth to Judea, to the city of David called Bethlehem, to be registered with his fiancée Mary, who was expecting a child. While they were there, she went into labour and gave birth to her first-born son. She swaddled him in strips of cloth, and laid him in a manger, because there was no room for them in the inn. (Luke 2:1-7)

Anyone who has ever commuted by train to London will know all about the problems of making room. Carriages are already full to over-flowing as the train pulls into another station heaving with yet more people. Or you may have travelled to the coast on a bank-holiday weekend looking for somewhere to stay, only to see the same sign in every window: 'No Vacancies'. The situation must have been a little like that in Bethlehem on the night of Jesus' birth. People of the house and line of David had come from across Judea to be enrolled as part of the Roman census, cramming into every house, guest room and inn. We can scarcely imagine what Mary and Joseph must have gone through as they searched desperately for somewhere to stay overnight.

That experience, of course, was a symbol of things to come: Jesus found no room in the hearts of many throughout his ministry and continues to find no room in the hearts of many today. We may imagine that we are different; that we have opened the door of our lives and welcomed him in, but let's not be complacent about it. The truth is that most of us only half-open the door, at best. We allow Jesus access to certain areas of our life but keep other areas ring-fenced. We make room when it suits us, but at other times give him our divided attention if any at all. It is easy to fool ourselves that such a response will do, when, in reality, Jesus is knocking at the door, still asking to come in.

One with us

The Word became flesh and lived among us, such that we have seen his glory: glory as of a father's only son, full of grace and truth. (John 1:14)

Despite its message of joy and celebration, Christmas is a time of mixed emotions, meaning different things for different people. For some it will indeed be a time of celebration, bringing family get-togethers, parties, the giving and sharing of presents, the laughter of children, feasting and merriment. For others, by contrast, it will bring pain. It may be the memory of a loved one who has recently died that hurts, or of an earlier bereavement around Christmas. It may be the recollection of bygone years before children grew up and left home to start a family of their own. It may be the burden of sickness, disability or terminal illness. Or it may be the continuing suffering of countless millions across the world facing the ever-present reality of poverty, homelessness, hunger and disease. Many will have little, if anything, to celebrate, in worldly terms. Christmas may be a time of joy, but not everyone will be rejoicing.

Yet it is precisely here that we glimpse the true wonder of the Christmas message, for at its heart is the proclamation that God became flesh, taking on our humanity. In other words, he understands what we are going through, whatever it might be. He doesn't just sympathise with our pain and sorrow; he empathises. He doesn't stand aloof from the daily round of life, for he has shared in it himself and is involved in our human situation. Christmas is a time of joy, but it is not just for the joyful; it is a time of celebration but it is not reserved for those who are celebrating. It is a time of good news for all, whether they laugh now or weep, rejoice or despair. God has entered our world so that, whatever we face now, we know that he is with us in it, and that his love will finally bring joy and blessing to all.

Seeing for ourselves

When the angels had departed and returned to heaven, the shepherds said to each other, 'Let us go, then, to Bethlehem and see this event that has taken place, which the Lord has made known to us.' (Luke 2:15)

I learned something interesting recently. Apparently, many people claim that the artist, Picasso, was left-handed; to the extent that several websites dedicated to left-handedness cite him as a celebrated example of such. The truth, however, is that he was right-handed, as can be proven by an examination of the photographic and historical records. What was it, then, that caused so many people to think otherwise? The answer is that they took someone else's word as fact; assuming that what they were told had to be right. It's an understandable mistake, for we often have nothing but hearsay to go on, yet we need to be alert to the dangers, for ultimately there can be no substitute for first-hand experience. Until we have seen the truth of something for ourselves, either by witnessing it or testing its veracity, we cannot categorically say that we know something.

That is just as true when it comes to knowing God. We need to learn from the example of the shepherds, who, when told the good news that the Saviour had been born, went to find out for themselves. 'Let us go, then, to Bethlehem,' they said, 'and see this event that has taken place, which the Lord has made known to us.' We may have been taught about faith as a child; we may have been brought up in a Christian home; we may have sat in church and shared in countless services; we may even know the Bible back to front – it makes no difference. What matters is that we have met with Christ; that we have put our faith in him and discovered in practice the truth of his words and the reality of his presence.

Don't let your faith rest on someone else's experience, on what others have told you about Christ – turn to him, open your life to his love, and let the gospel be true for you!

Something worth hurrying for

So they came with haste, and found Mary and Joseph, and the baby lying in a manger. (Luke 2:16)

If you were to be told in church on Sunday that a wealthy philanthropist was in the street outside handing out wads of cash, how much time would you waste after the service before you went to find out if it were true? The chances are that you'd be out of the church like a shot the moment the final hymn had ended – if not before! Again, if you were out walking and spotted an excited cheering crowd ahead of you, rushing towards something, you'd probably quicken your pace, eager to see what was happening. Some things in life are worth hurrying for. So it was for the shepherds after hearing the news of the birth of Christ. It's only a small detail, but it's an important one: 'they came with haste'. Why? Because the news they'd heard was exciting, breathtaking, wonderful; news they and their people had been waiting so long to hear – almost too good to be true! There was no question of waiting until the next morning and then casually strolling down to Bethlehem after they'd knocked off work. This was news that had to be investigated at once, not something that could be postponed.

Do we, I wonder, still feel that sense of excitement at the Christmas message? Do we still marvel at what God has done for us in Christ? Do we still catch our breath in wonder at the miracle of the Saviour's birth – God made flesh? Do such things still capture our hearts and fire our imagination, not just at Christmas but also day after day and week after week? We may have responded; we may have discovered the truth for ourselves long ago – that doesn't matter: the message of Christmas is still one to get excited about!

The start of it all

At the start of it all was the Word, the Word being God as well as with God. He was there in the beginning with God, all things coming into existence through him and nothing existing without him. What has come into being in him is life; life that is light for all people. That light shines in the darkness, the darkness having been unable to extinguish it. He was in the world, and the world owed its existence to him, yet the world did not recognise him. He became part of what was his own, and his own people did not accept him. To all, though, ready to receive him and believing in his name, he gave the right to become God's children – children born not of blood or any union of the flesh, nor of any human desire, but of God. The Word became flesh and lived among us, such that we have seen his glory: glory as of a father's only son, full of grace and truth. (John 1:1-5, 10-14)

There is something unusual about the Gospel of John. Unlike Matthew and Luke, John does not start with Mary or Joseph, nor does he refer to Bethlehem, a stable or a manger; in fact, there is no mention of a Christmas story at all. Unlike Mark, he does not start with the ministry of Jesus either, though he soon moves on to this. He takes us instead to the dawn of time and the events of creation, reminding us of God's sovereign will active at the beginning of it all. Despite everything that would frustrate him and deny his love, says John, God's gracious purpose was being worked out from the start, the living Word later to be embodied in the Word made flesh. For John, then, the coming of Christ is not God's attempt to make up for a ghastly mistake; it is the natural expression of a love constantly at work, revealed in history, declared through prophets, and finally lived out in flesh and blood. John's testimony calls us to reflect on all God has yet to do in the light of everything he has already done.

A time for rejoicing

How lovely on the mountains are the feet of the herald who proclaims peace, who brings good news, who announces deliverance and who says to Zion, 'Your God reigns!' Listen! Your watchers lift up their voices and together they sing for joy. (Isaiah 52:7-8a)

Some years ago a prominent newsreader bemoaned the fact that only bad news seems to make the headlines. Sadly, nothing much seems to have changed; daily bulletins are still dominated by news of another riot, murder, disaster or tragedy somewhere in the world.

The seasons of Advent and Christmas, however, remind us of another kind of news, for the events they speak of were marked from the very start by a mood of rejoicing. When Mary and Elizabeth met for the first time since Mary became pregnant, Elizabeth exclaimed: 'The moment I heard you call in greeting, the child in my womb leapt for joy' (Luke 1:44), and Mary's response was to joyfully proclaim 'I rejoice with all my heart because of God my Saviour' (Luke 1:47). So it was to continue after the birth of Jesus, as angels appeared to shepherds with the message, 'See – I am bringing you good news of great joy that is for all people: today a Saviour has been born to you in the city of David, who is Christ, the Lord' (Luke 2:10b-11). Finally, when the wise men at last reached their destination and entered the house where Mary and Joseph had taken lodging with their child, 'they were overwhelmed with joy' (Matthew 2:10). This is not to say that sorrow was at an end – the slaughter of children in and around Bethlehem ordered by Herod was to show this was far from the case. Yet, within the trouble and pain of the world, the tragedies and trials that beset us all, God had brought joy that nothing finally could overcome – good news that we continue to celebrate today.

First and Second Sunday after Christmas

A costly response

Simeon blessed them and said to Mary, [Jesus'] mother, 'This child is destined for the fall and rise of many in Israel, and will be a sign that many will speak against, revealing their inner thoughts – and a sword will pierce your own soul too.' (Luke 2:34-35)

How much will you be spending on Christmas this year? Probably a lot more than you might think. Not only will there be presents to buy, which themselves represent a sizeable expense, but there will also be the Christmas dinner, boxes of sweets and chocolates, perhaps a few bottles of wine, not to mention Christmas cards, a tree, decorations and all the other odds and ends that go to make up what we see as a traditional Christmas. There's no doubt about it, Christmas is becoming an increasingly costly time, to the point that some people pay into a Christmas kitty each week so as to spread the expense over a year.

There was, however, another cost involved in the very first Christmas, which perhaps we can sometimes overlook. We see it partly in the response of Mary to God's call; her willingness to surrender her body to God's will. That alone, alongside the joy and privilege, entailed making a sacrifice, for life from that moment was never to be the same again. Yet it went further than that, for just a few days after the birth of her son there were to come those words of Simeon warning of a sword that would pierce her soul; words that must have cast a lengthening shadow across her life as Jesus inexorably took the way that led to the cross. It was Mary's willingness to accept the cost of service, as well as the rewards, that made possible God's gift of life. How willing are we to accept the cost of discipleship, in turn?

The God who comes to us

I have come to bring light into the world, so that everyone who believes in me will not remain in darkness. (John 12:46)

There was a time when, should you feel too unwell to get to your local surgery, a doctor would come and see you. Not any more, or at least not as was once the case. There are some circumstances, of course, when a doctor will still come but the usual procedure out of hours is to get yourself to a duty doctor who will deal with your problem. The onus is on the patient to go because, quite simply, there aren't enough doctors to come.

We can tend to think of God in a similar sort of way – as one we have to go to, with the responsibility on us to make the first approach. Look, though, at the nativity stories in Matthew and Luke, or the opening verses of John's Gospel, and a very different picture emerges. Running through them all, like a common thread, is the message that it is God who first comes to us. He came to Zechariah, then Mary, then Joseph, and then to the shepherds out in the fields – the approach always at his initiative. He came bringing his word of promise, challenge, joy and hope, offering his love and his gift of new life – and so he continues to come today. Before we yet know him, before sometimes we even know our need, he draws near, reaching out in welcome, extending his grace. Yes, Christmas calls for a response, but it is not finally about us coming to God; it is, above all, about him coming to us.

Keeping faith

There was a man called Simeon in Jerusalem who was upright and devout, eagerly awaiting the consolation of Israel, and the Holy Spirit was with him. The Spirit had disclosed to him that he would not taste death before he had seen the Lord's Messiah. Led by the Spirit, Simeon entered the temple; and when Jesus' parents brought in their child to honour the customs of the Law,

Simeon cradled him in his arms and praised God, saying, 'Master, now let your servant go in peace, according to your promise. With my own eyes I have seen the salvation you have prepared before all the world – a light that will reveal you to the Gentiles and bring glory to your people Israel.' The child's parents were stunned at these words concerning him. Then Simeon blessed them and said to his mother Mary, 'This child is ordained to be a sign that many will reject; one through whom the inner thoughts of many will be revealed and even your own soul will be pierced. Many in Israel will stand or fall because of him.' (Luke 2:25-35)

It is not just faith in ourselves that can take a knock as the years go by; it is faith in God as well. As another natural catastrophe strikes, another country is plunged into violent conflict, another friend dies of cancer, or another person is raped, mugged or murdered, it is hard to reconcile the harsh realities of life with the picture of a loving and merciful Father. The fact that society as a whole generally dismisses any talk of God makes it all the harder to keep on believing, harder to withstand the drip-drip effect of scorn and scepticism or sheer disinterest.

Yet the example of Simeon, and of the prophetess Anna whose story follows his, urges us to keep trusting, confident that God is at work and that, in the fullness of time, his will shall be done. Both Simeon and Anna had the courage to stay true to their faith despite outward appearances. Have we?

RSVP

To all, though, ready to receive him and believe in his name, he gave the right to become God's children – children born not of blood or any union of the flesh, nor of any human desire, but of God. (John 1:12-13)

RSVP – four letters that we put on an invitation to a special event, asking people to indicate whether or not they accept. It's a way of politely asking the recipient not to put the invitation away and forget about it, or to delay their reply until the very last minute, but to respond as soon as possible.

There is a sense in which we see something similar in the events of the birth of Christ, and indeed throughout his life and ministry. First, it was Mary, asked to respond to God's word pronounced by Gabriel, and her response was swift and unreserved: 'I am the Lord's servant. Let it be to me just as you say' (Luke 1:38). Next, it was Joseph, challenged to think again about breaking off his engagement, his response equally prompt: 'After waking from his sleep, Joseph did as the angel of the Lord had instructed, taking Mary as his wife' (Matthew 1:24). Then, it was the shepherds, told that a Saviour had been born to them in Bethlehem, and from them too there was no hesitation: 'They came with haste, and found Mary and Joseph, and with them the baby, lying in a manger' (Luke 2:16). Finally, there were the wise men, seeing the star in the east and immediately following it: 'They knelt down and paid him homage. Then, opening their treasure chests, they offered him gifts of gold, frankincense, and myrrh' (Matthew 2:11). The coming of Christ was an invitation to respond, and it is an invitation that God continues to extend today – to you, to me, to everyone. It's no good just receiving it and then putting it away; no good thinking we can put off a decision until some other time, for God is asking you, as he asked so many all those years ago and as he has asked so many since: RSVP.

Something worth sharing

Having seen it, they shared everything they had been told concerning the child, and all those who heard them marvelled at what the shepherds said. (Luke 2:17-18)

If I were to say to you the words 'made for sharing', what words would you automatically insert before them? The chances are that you would think of that old advertisement, 'Quality Street, made for sharing'. Today, though, I have something very different in mind: the word 'Christmas'. You will see some logic in this straightaway, for Christmas is traditionally a time for sharing cards, presents and good wishes. It is a time also when families come together and share in a way that may not be possible during the rest of the year. For Christians, it is also a time for sharing in worship: nativity, candlelight and carol services.

Yet, special and important though all those are, we see in the example of the shepherds something more important still. 'When they had seen him, they spread the word' (Luke 2:17). Think about that for a moment, and then ask how far it is reflected in your life. Having seen Jesus, their instinctive response was to want to share it – to tell others the good news, to make sure that they too heard about what God had done. This wasn't something to keep to themselves, an event staged solely for their own benefit. In the words of the angel, it was 'news of great joy for all people'. I've no doubt we will share much this Christmas, and hopefully what we give will bring those nearest and dearest to us great joy, but will we share the greatest gift of all? Will we communicate what we have experienced of God's gift in Christ? 'Christmas, made for sharing' – is that how you see it?

Think about it

Mary stored these things up in her heart, pondering what they might mean. (Luke 2:19)

Still waters, we are told, run deep. They also have another quality: the ability to reflect. Both those qualities, though in a somewhat different sense, are amply evident in the example of Mary at the birth of Jesus, and we do well to ponder them. It must have been an exciting night for her, that night Jesus was born. For a start, there was the natural euphoria of giving birth and of holding her child close for the first time, but, alongside that, there was more. There was the memory of Gabriel, telling her that this child was the Son of God, and then, as if to confirm it, the coming of shepherds, no doubt blurting out their story of angels praising God and directing them to where a Saviour, the Messiah, had been born. She could so easily have been swept along by the tide of events, carried away by it all in such a way that she scarcely gave a thought to what was happening, but she didn't – she stored these things up in her heart, pondering what they might mean. In other words, she looked deeper, beneath the surface, and she reflected on what God had done in her life. She made time to consider and to understand.

Do we do that today? Christmas is an exciting time for us too, though for different reasons. It's an occasion for partying and celebrations, for family reunions and get-togethers, for giving and receiving, laughing and making merry. And why not? – those all bring some welcome happiness in the bleakness of winter. Yet, how many of us pause to reflect on what it's ultimately all about, on what we're celebrating and why, on the thing God has done for us that gives the season its name. Make time for fun and celebration, but, above all, make time to think and reflect on the true meaning of Christmas, for then you will truly find something worth getting excited about.

A time for worship

All at once, there was with the angel rank on rank of other heavenly beings, praising God and saying, 'Glory to God in the highest heaven, and peace on earth among all on whom his favour rests!' (Luke 2:13-14)

What words should you use to address the Queen, another member of the royal family, a Lord or Lady, or even the Archbishop of Canterbury? Do you know? I don't – and the chances are, if I were to be introduced to anyone so eminent, I would clam up completely, unsure quite how I ought to respond. You may feel a little like that when it comes to responding to what God has done in Christ. 'I want to respond,' you might say, 'but how?' To answer that in full would take many pages, but one response stands out above all others in the Christmas stories, and that is an instinctive outpouring of worship.

When Zechariah regained the power of speech, the first thing he did was to praise God. When Mary realised the full wonder of what God had done for her, she burst into joyful song. When the shepherds had been to the stable and seen the child in the manger, they returned, glorifying and praising God for everything they had heard and seen. When Simeon and Anna saw Mary and Joseph bringing Jesus into the temple, they immediately cried out in praise. When the magi reached the house where Jesus was, they fell down and worshipped him! For each one there could only be one response to the coming of Christ, one response that would do: to offer their worship in glad and joyful praise. Of course, there's more to our response than that, for worship leads on to service and witness in a wide variety of ways, but this is where it starts – in recognising what God has done, in joyfully acknowledging his greatness and in humbly offering our grateful worship.

Epiphany

A careful search

Herod secretly summoned the wise men and ascertained from them exactly when the star had appeared. Then he sent them to Bethlehem, saying, 'Go and search carefully for the child; and when you have found him, bring word to me, so that I, in turn, may go and offer homage.' (Matthew 2:7-8)

Familiarity, it is said, breeds contempt, and if ever there is a danger of that it must surely be in relation to the Christmas message. We know the story so well – too well – having heard it so many times that we no longer take in sometimes what we are hearing. We listen to the words of scripture and sing well-loved carols, but they wash over us, no longer firing our imagination as they once did.

It is worth reflecting occasionally on those words of Herod to the magi as he sent them off to Bethlehem. The situation, of course, is different, in that they were seeking someone they had not yet met, encountering Jesus for the first time, but Herod's words are nonetheless just as appropriate for those of us today who have known and followed Jesus for as long as we can remember. 'Go and make a careful search for the child.' Do that, not just today but every day, and what we find may still surprise us.

Wise men still seek him

Following the birth of Jesus in Bethlehem of Judea during the reign of King Herod, magi arrived in Jerusalem from the east, saying, 'Where is the one born king of the Jews? For we saw his star rising in the east and have come to pay our respects. As they entered the house they saw the child with his mother Mary, and, falling down in worship, they offered him their treasures: gifts of gold, frankincense and myrrh. (Matthew 2:1-2, 11)

There's a pithy little saying often still displayed around Christmas time on church noticeboards, car windscreens or suchlike. The words? 'Wise men still seek him.' And, of course, that's perfectly true, for there are many today, just as there have always been, who still search in vain to find faith. It's not that they don't want to believe – quite the opposite – but there is so much in the world they cannot make sense of, so much that seems to contradict the God of love preached in the Christian faith. It would have been easy for the wise men to give up on their search, not least when they arrived in Bethlehem to find that no one had any idea who or what they were talking about. Could there have been some mistake? Had their journey been a waste of time? Yet they kept on searching and trusting until, finally, they came to the place where the child lay.

We, too, will reach our destination if we have the courage to keep on seeking. If we persevere on the journey, we will find our questions answered and the confusion resolved as we glimpse for ourselves the wonder of God revealed in Christ.

Shrove Tuesday

A positive response

If you died with Christ to the spirits underlying the universe, how is that you behave as though you still belong to the world? Why do you give in to rules stating, 'Hands off, don't taste, not to be touched'? Regulations like these are concerned with perishable goods and are simply conventions rooted in human instructions and institutions. They may look astute in terms of advancing self-imposed godliness, modesty and mortification of the flesh, but they are useless in preventing decadence. If, then, you have been raised to new life with Christ, pursue the things of heaven, where Christ is ensconced at the right hand of God. Focus on what is above, not on the things of this world. (Colossians 2:20–3:2)

Tomorrow will be Ash Wednesday, the first day of Lent. What does the season mean to you? What sort of ideas does it conjure up in your mind? For many, it is associated with giving something up: an opportunity, perhaps, to kick that unwanted habit, go at last on that long-intended diet, or deny oneself those unnecessary extra luxuries. All such acts of discipline have their place, as the teaching of Jesus concerning taking up our cross makes clear, but they give a very one-sided view of Lent, for, if anything, it should be about taking something on; committing ouselves, in the words of Jesus, to going the extra mile.

That doesn't mean taking work on for work's sake, or looking for extra duties, demands and responsibilities. Rather, it is about resolving to follow Christ more faithfully, determined to give him our whole-hearted discipleship. It might mean more disciplined devotion, perhaps more practical service, maybe more effective witness or possibly the offering of previously unused gifts. Whatever it is, it is more than giving something up; it is primarily giving something back to the one who gave us his all. Consider today what Christ has done for you; then ask what you can do for him, and use Lent as an opportunity to respond.

Lent

Consequences

The stubborn get their just deserts; likewise the good get what they deserve. The simple believe anything but the wise think before they act. The wise are circumspect and avoid evil, but the fool acts without thought, discarding moderation. The hot-blooded act foolishly, and the conniver is despised. The simple are dressed up with folly, but the wise are crowned with understanding. (Proverbs 14:14-18)

In recent years, a fascinating school of thought has gained ground in scientific theory centred around so-called 'chaos theory'. The proposition behind this is that something as tiny as the fluttering of a butterfly's wings in Australia could have far-reaching consequences in Europe, or that a pebble falling in a Saharan oasis might ultimately influence conditions on the Antarctic ice-sheet.

How true the theory is remains to be demonstrated, but it is certainly indisputable that many actions have consequences far greater than we might expect. An angry word, an error of judgement or a split-second moment of carelessness can set in motion a catastrophic chain of cause and effect. Before we act, we need to think about where our action may lead. Above all, in our response to God – whether we obey his commandments and follow his guidance – we need to consider the consequences: for us, for others and for him. Lent offers us the opportunity to pause and reflect on both what we do and why.

A glimpse of glory (Transfiguration)

Six days after this, Jesus took Peter, James and John up on to a lofty mountain with him, where they were alone together, removed from all, and there Jesus was transfigured before them. His garments gleamed a dazzling white, such as no fuller on earth could ever whiten them; and alongside Jesus, in conversation with him, appeared Moses and Elijah. (Mark 9:2-4)

I've never found the story of the Transfiguration an easy one to understand. It calls to mind the words in *Alice in Wonderland*: 'curiouser and curiouser', or the claims of a certain soap powder to wash whiter than white. Yet the strangeness of the incident should not blind us to its underlying message. This was no sensational sideshow designed to dispel doubts among the inner circle of disciples. On the contrary, it was a glimpse of the extraordinary in what had seemed an ordinary moment, a blossoming of faith leading to a deeper vision. At least that's how I read it. The three disciples are walking with Jesus, listening to his words, reflecting on his ministry, and, suddenly, it's not just a mountain they ascend but a spiritual peak – a high spot in which the reality of who Jesus is dawns on them. They discern, albeit fleetingly, that he is the fulfilment of the law and the prophets, represented by Moses and Elijah. They realise he is sent from God, dazzling in his splendour. They catch a brief vision of Christ in all his glory. Life would never be quite the same for them again, for this is the moment in which faith came of age, their old picture of Jesus exposed as hopelessly inadequate.

We can imagine, in our turn, that, having committed ourselves to Christ, we are well advanced along the path of faith, but we should never underestimate the power of Jesus to surprise us. The message here is similar to that of Peter's confession of Christ – namely that our knowledge of Jesus and our understanding of his glory will never be complete until this life is over and we meet him face to face. Until then, let us make time to be alone in his presence – to listen, hear and reflect – so that perhaps we too may glimpse a little more of his awesome wonder.

Taking stock

Assess yourselves to check that you are living in the faith. Test yourselves to make sure. Do you not realise that Jesus Christ is in you? – assuming, of course, that your faith is not a sham. (2 Corinthians 13:5)

The very mention of the two words in our title today is enough to send a shiver down some people's spines. For them, stocktaking conjures up images of mad panic and frenetic activity; hours counting and recounting, scouring warehouses and checking manically through computer records, wondering just how so much has gone missing. For any business, however, taking stock is essential, not only in checking against theft and fraud but also in assessing how well and in what areas the firm is succeeding.

We do well to apply the same principle to ourselves as Christians, as the words of Paul to the Corinthians powerfully remind us. 'Examine yourselves,' he says, 'and see whether you are living in the faith.' In other words, stop and take stock; make time for a long hard look at your life, some serious soul-searching. Don't just muddle through. Don't assume that everything is automatically ticking along as it should be. Don't imagine that once you've set out on the road of Christian discipleship you can leave it to take care of itself. Nothing could be further from the truth. It's all too easy to get lost along the way: to take a false step here, a wrong path there, until instead of making progress you're slipping backwards, unsure of where you're going and why. How far have you honoured the vows you once made? How far have you lived up to your commitment? How far have you achieved the things you once set out to achieve? In short, what have you made of your life? Stop and take stock. You may not like what you find, but at least you will know where you stand and, with God's help, have the chance to do something positive before it's too late to put matters right.

A thorough examination

Assess yourselves to check that you are living in the faith. Test yourselves to make sure. (2 Corinthians 13:5a)

The older we get, the more it pays to keep a check on our health. That's not to say we should become morbid hypochondriacs; simply that we should keep an eye out for problems so that we can seek help to put them right before they take hold. If that is true medically speaking, it's true also when it comes to our spiritual health, for that can equally suffer as the years go by. Complacency, disillusionment or sheer weariness are all conditions that can steal up on us, sapping our faith of its natural vitality. Just as with our physical well-being, we need to be alert to the signs, regularly making time to examine ourselves.

Traditionally, Lent is such a time, calling us to reflect on our discipleship and to ask if everything is as it should be. None of us is perfect, of course, and the last thing God wants is to encourage a spirit of negative self-criticism. Rather, he wants us to conduct an honest self-appraisal, and then to seek his gracious help in bringing inner healing and renewal. The cure does not lie solely in us, any more than self-help remedies are the answer to every physical ailment. It lies in recognising something is wrong and seeking help from the one who alone is able to give us wholeness. If we are willing to admit our need, he will do the rest.

Palm Sunday

Changing our tune

As he rode, people carpeted the road with their cloaks. Then, as he started the descent from the Mount of Olives, the whole multitude of the disciples began loudly and joyfully to praise God for the mighty deeds they had seen, saying, 'Blessed is the king who comes in the name of the Lord! Peace in heaven, glory in the highest heaven!' Some Pharisees in the crowd said to him, 'Teacher, rebuke your disciples and tell them to stop.' He answered, 'I tell you this, if they were to keep silent, the very stones would shout out.' As he caught sight of the city, he wept over it, saying, 'If only you recognised this day the things that make for peace! Instead, though, they are hidden from your eyes!' (Luke 19:36-42)

It was only a children's story but it made the point well. 'Who will help me sow my seed?' asks the chicken. 'Not I,' comes the answer. 'Who will help me reap the harvest?' 'Not I,' comes the answer again. 'Who will help me grind the flour . . . knead the dough . . . bake the loaf? 'Not I . . . not I . . . not I.' Then, finally, the all-important question: 'Who will help me eat the bread?' and, immediately, a change of tone: 'Me! Me! Me!' It is an illustration, of course, of the fickleness of human nature, our friendship and loyalty so often depending on what's in it for us.

So it was on that first Palm Sunday as Jesus entered Jerusalem to the acclaim of the crowds; only this time the story is in reverse. 'Who will welcome me as king?' his actions seemed to be saying, and the answer was 'Me!' Who wants to share in the kingdom of God?' and again the answer is 'Me!' Yet, just a few days later when the crunch question comes – 'Who will follow the way of the cross?' – the response from many is so very different: 'Not I!' – or, to put it more accurately, 'We have no king but Caesar. Crucify! Crucify! Crucify!' Palm Sunday is a day that challenges us concerning our loyalty, asking how ready we are to follow when faith is demanding and the going gets tough. Thank God, it is also about the one who, however often we may change our tune, stays faithful to us to the point of death.

Maundy Thursday

Look both ways

During supper, he took bread, and having given thanks he broke it and gave it to them, saying, 'Take this; it is my body.' Then he took a cup, and, giving thanks to God, he handed it to them; and they all drank from it. Then he said, 'This is my blood, the blood of the covenant, shed for many. I tell you the truth, I will not drink of the fruit of the vine again until that day when I drink it new with you in the kingdom of God.' (Mark 14:22-25)

There's a piece of advice we will all have received many times as children: 'Look both ways.' I refer, of course, to learning to cross the road, and to the advice of the Green Cross Code: 'Look right, look left, look right again.'

In a sense, Maundy Thursday invites us to do something very similar, only this time we are called to look not left and right but to the past and the future, and to the difference those make to the present. As Paul reminds us in his letter to the Corinthians, our sharing in the Lord's Supper is to serve as a constant reminder to Christians, calling to mind his suffering and death. Yet it was not all solemnity, for there was also a message of hope; a hint of joy to come in his words, 'I will not drink of the fruit of the vine again until that day when I drink it new with you in the kingdom of God.' Here, then, is a call to look backwards and forwards, to remember and to anticipate. It is a message not just for Maundy Thursday, nor simply for each time we break bread and share wine, but for each day and every moment. We are called to live, here and now, in the light of what God has done and what he promises to do.

Good Friday

He was dead

Since it was the day of preparation for the Passover, the Jews did not want dead bodies left on the cross during the Sabbath, especially because Passover Sabbath was a day of special import, so they asked Pilate to have the legs of those who had been crucified broken and their bodies removed. Accordingly, the soldiers broke the legs of the first and then the second of those crucified with Jesus, but when they came to Jesus, they saw he was already dead so they did not break his legs. Instead, one of the soldiers pierced his side with a spear. (John 19:31-34a)

Some animals, when faced with danger, make use of a cunning trick. Instead of running or standing up to fight, they play dead, thus confusing their attacker, which is only interested in live prey. To hear some people talk, you might imagine that the crucifixion involved a similar trick. Maybe Jesus wasn't dead, after all, some suggest; perhaps in the coolness of the tomb he regained consciousness, and was subsequently whisked away by his followers under cover of darkness.

It's far-fetched, I know, but some people will believe anything rather than have their preconceptions challenged. The idea of resurrection simply goes against everything they believe or experience. Yet, one look at the Gospels – and at the Gospel of John in particular – leaves us in no doubt about the truth. Jesus was dead, a spear thrust into his side to make doubly certain. He was laid limp and lifeless in a tomb, and a stone rolled against the entrance. Humanly speaking it was over, the end of a wonderful ministry and an unforgettable man. He had shared our life; he had shared our death. If the story was to continue, it was out of human hands – it was down now to God.

A straight choice

The passers-by hurled insults at him, shaking their heads and saying, 'So, then, you who would destroy the temple and build it in three days: come down from the cross and save yourself!' The chief priests and teachers of the law joined in mocking him with similar taunts. 'He saved others,' they said, 'but he cannot save himself! Let this Messiah, the king of Israel, come down now from the cross, so that we might see and believe.' (Mark 15:29-32a)

'Many a true word is spoken in jest', so we say, and if you need convincing of that, take a look at the taunts faced by Jesus on the cross. 'He saved others, but he cannot save himself!' – words of mockery and derision aimed at adding to the suffering already experienced by Jesus, and you can imagine his tormentors smirking, chuckling, congratulating themselves on their own wit. Make him eat his words, they thought; now let's see how smart he is!

Yet, if they had but known, they could not have spoken more profoundly, for those words give voice to the stark choice faced by Jesus and the love he showed in taking the path he did. Could he have saved himself? Of course he could. Not only could he have steered well clear of Jerusalem in the first place, but for someone who had healed the sick, stilled the storm, fed the multitude, even raised the dead, to come down from the cross was nothing, positively straightforward by comparison. Yet to do that would have been to go back on his mission and deny his calling; for it was only through his accepting suffering and death that he could open up the way to life for others. It was a straight choice, an 'either/or' rather than 'both/and' situation, and he chose to save us rather than himself. 'He saved others but he cannot save himself.' How wrong they were, yet how right!

Easter

Better than expected

That same day, there were two going to a village called Emmaus, about seven miles from Jerusalem, and they were discussing everything that had happened. As they conversed and talked together, Jesus himself drew near and walked with them, but somehow their eyes did not recognise him. He said to them, 'What was it you were discussing together as you walked?' They halted, look- ing dejected. Then one of them, called Cleopas, answered, 'Are you the only one visiting Jerusalem not to know the things that have happened there over recent days?' 'What things?' he asked. 'The things about Jesus of Nazareth,' they replied; 'a prophet mighty in word and deed before God and all the people; how our chief priests and leaders handed him over to be sentenced to death and then crucified him. We had hoped that he was the one who was going to redeem Israel.' (Luke 24:13-21a)

How often do plans work out as well as you hoped? There may be the odd occasion when they measure up to expectations, but, in my experi- ence, our grand designs and dreams rarely yield in practice what they promise in theory. More often than not, hopes have a habit of falling horribly flat.

A similar sense of anticlimax, though infinitely more intense, was felt by the two disciples walking back along the Emmaus Road, their mood summed up in those plaintive words: 'We had hoped that he was the one who was going to redeem Israel.' For a time, they had dared to imagine that the promised day of the Lord had dawned, but their hopes had been dashed – another case, so it seemed, of reality not measuring up to expectations. Read on, though, and it's a different story; for suddenly, as they broke bread with this stranger, they realised who he was – not just the redeemer of Israel but the risen Lord, back from the grave, victorious over sin and death. Here, in miniature, is one of the great truths of the gospel: that Jesus does not simply fulfil our hopes but far exceeds them, offering joy and peace, hope and strength beyond anything words can begin to express. Thanks be to God!

Beginnings from endings

Mary stood beside the tomb, sobbing. As she wept, she peered again into the tomb and saw two angels clothed in white sitting where the body of Jesus had previously been lying, one at the head and the other at the feet. They asked her, 'Woman, why are you crying?' She answered, 'They have taken away my Lord, and I have no idea where they have laid him.' Having said this, she turned round and saw Jesus standing there but she did not realise who it was. Jesus said to her, 'Woman, why do you grieve? Who are you looking for?' Imagining he was the gardener, she replied, 'Sir, if you are the one who has carried him off, tell me where you have put him, and I will take him away.' Jesus said to her, 'Mary!' Spinning round, she exclaimed, 'Rabbouni!' – the Hebrew for Teacher.
(John 20:11-16)

At first sight the story of Mary Magdalene in the garden is a little puzzling. How is it that, having been told Jesus has risen, and then seeing him face to face, she doesn't realise who he is? Yet is that really so strange? She'd watched as he drew his last breath on the cross, she'd seen him carried limp and lifeless into the tomb, she'd witnessed the stone being rolled across, and, understandably, she was convinced that it was all over, his life irrevocably extinguished. Anybody who has faced the apparent finality of the death of a loved one will understand those feelings.

Yet slowly the truth dawned: from that ending had come a new beginning, a beginning not just for Jesus but for her and everyone. Joy, hope, purpose, love, which had all been buried with Jesus in the tomb, came leaping back to life; the future that a moment before had seemed so empty was suddenly brimming over with promise. That is the truth of resurrection not just for Mary but also for us all. It does not only speak of life beyond the grave; it tells us that from what looks to be the bleakest of endings God is able to bring new beginnings beyond our wildest dreams.

From defeat to victory

He is not here; he has risen! (Luke 24:5b)

'Oh well, that's it,' he said. 'No point in watching any longer.' And it genuinely looked like it. We'd allowed our son to stay up late that night to watch Manchester United in the European Cup Final but, with the disappointment increasingly evident in his eyes, we were beginning to wish we hadn't. Just a few seconds left – no, actually into injury time – and the German supporters were already saluting their team, the engraver poised over the trophy that was already decked out in their team's ribbons . . . and then it happened: a goal from nowhere, scenes of wild jubilation, and the game heading for extra time. But what was this? Another attack . . . a corner . . . a goal! From the jaws of defeat, Manchester United had snatched victory!

Unbelievable? Well almost. Yet not half so extraordinary as the event nearly two thousand years earlier, when three women made their way solemnly to their master's tomb. There were tears in *their* eyes too; not just of disappointment but utter devastation, for the one who had been the centre of their lives and on whom they had pinned all their hopes was dead; cruelly murdered on a cross. There was no hope of him coming back; it was over, finished. Until suddenly, there was the tomb . . . empty . . . a stranger telling them Jesus had risen . . . and the Lord himself standing before them, greeting them as he'd greeted them so often before. Defeat had been turned to victory; a victory not just for them but for us, and one we share in not simply by proxy but first-hand – for it means new life for all, new beginnings, new hope – the assurance that whatever we might face, nothing can stand between us and the love of God in Christ. Unbelievable, yet true!

The God who cannot be kept down

The following day – in other words, the day after that of Preparation – the chief priests and the Pharisees congregated before Pilate and said, 'Your excellency, we recall how that deceiver said while he was alive, "After three days I will rise." Will you, then, order that the tomb be made secure until the third day? Otherwise his disciples may come and steal him away, and tell the people, "He has been raised from the dead" – a final deception that would be worse than the first.' Pilate said to them, 'You have a guard of soldiers; go and make it as secure as possible.' So they went and made the tomb secure by sealing it with a stone and leaving a guard in charge. (Matthew 27:62-66)

When my daughter was a baby she had a wonderful inflatable toy called 'Bopper Bear'. No matter how hard or how often you knocked it over, it would always bounce back up again. I don't know if Kate enjoyed it, but I did!

There is something of that idea in the story of the resurrection, for we see there a supreme demonstration of the God who cannot be kept down. The enemies of Jesus had conspired together, determined finally to do away with him, and as they cut him limp and lifeless from the cross, sealing him in a tomb, they must have been convinced they had succeeded. Even then, they placed a guard outside the tomb, just to make sure. They were leaving nothing to chance. Yet, it didn't matter, for the next day what did they find but the stone rolled away and the tomb empty, their worst fears realised. How could it be? What could have happened? These are good questions, which anyone who disputes the resurrection still needs to answer. Hatred had done its worst, but the love of God could not be kept down. Christ was risen! It's as true today as ever; ultimately there is nothing and no one that can frustrate the will of God. Though many may still try and sometimes seem to succeed, ours is a God who will finally triumph, and who gives us the victory in turn.

Making waves

We always thank God, the Father of our Lord Jesus Christ, because we have heard of your faith, and your love for all the saints, springing from the hope stored up for you in heaven that you heard about in the word of truth, the gospel that has come to you. Just as it has been bearing fruit and growing in the whole world, so, from the moment you first heard it and truly understood the grace of God, it has been bearing fruit among you. (Colossians 1:3-6)

From when he was a little boy, my son loved throwing stones into water – the bigger the better, since it made all the more exciting the resultant splash. Not that it needs a big stone to have a profound effect – just a tiny pebble tossed into the centre of a pool sends ripples radiating inexorably outwards until they reach the bank.

In a sense, the same could be said of the life, death and resurrection of Christ. It all began so quietly, in a stable in Bethlehem and a baby lying in a manger, and, even at the height of his ministry, the majority of the world's population would have been oblivious to his existence. What could one man hope to achieve through his life, death or even resurrection? In global terms, it was a drop in the ocean – but what a drop, for still today the ripples of Christ's coming are reaching outwards! Who would have believed two thousand years ago that the gospel would still be changing lives and the Church continuing to grow? It was beyond his enemies' worst nightmares and greater than his followers' wildest dreams. Yet that is the nature of our God; the God who, in his sovereign power, plunged himself into the pool of human history in such a way that the world would never be the same again.

A second chance

When they had breakfasted, Jesus said to Simon Peter, 'Simon, son of John, do you love me more than these?' He said to him, 'Yes, Lord, you know that I love you.' Jesus said to him, 'Feed my lambs.' He said to him a second time, 'Simon, son of John, do you love me?' He answered, 'Yes, Lord, you know that I love you.' Jesus said to him, 'Look after my sheep.' He asked him a third time, 'Simon, son of John, do you love me?' It wounded Peter that he asked him a third time, 'Do you love me?', so he responded, 'Lord, you know everything; you know that I love you.' Jesus said to him, 'Feed my sheep.' (John 21:15-17)

Which of us haven't at some time wished we could have a time over again; that we could undo some thoughtless or angry word, some rash commitment or unwise judgement, or some careless mistake? If only we could have a second chance, an opportunity to put right the past!

If anyone longed for that it must surely have been Peter; for he must have felt helplessly and hopelessly burdened by past mistakes. The memory of his denial of Jesus – not once, not twice, but three times – must have haunted him without respite. What wouldn't he have given to undo those moments? Only, of course, he couldn't – or could he? For suddenly, here was Jesus asking, not once, not twice, but three times: 'Do you love me?' It took a while for the message to sink in, his initial reaction one of pique, but finally, I suspect, the truth dawned – for each time he'd denied him, Jesus was offering the opportunity to make amends, to put the past behind him and start afresh. No, we cannot put the clock back as such, and, yes, sometimes, in terms of others at least, we have to live with the consequences of our mistakes, but with God the opportunity is always there to move forward from what *has been* towards what *shall be*. We need only to acknowledge our faults and be truly sorry for resurrection to begin once again, here and now.

Truth will out!

Some of the guards went into the city and told the chief priests what had happened. After the priests had called together the elders, they formulated a plan to give a generous bribe to the soldiers, telling them, 'You must say this, "His followers came during the night and made off with him while we were sleeping." If the governor gets to hear of this, we will reassure him and keep you out of trouble.' So the guards took the money and did as instructed.
(Matthew 28:11-15a)

Truth will out, we are told, and so it repeatedly proves. There may be occasions when deceit goes unnoticed, but falsehood has an uncanny habit of being exposed; of weaving a web that finally traps the very one who spins it. We may suppress the truth, we may twist and distort it, but it is hard to keep it hidden for ever, as the death and resurrection of Christ make crystal clear. His enemies stopped at nothing to get their man, cynically employing false witnesses to secure the verdict they were looking for. Similarly, when they heard news of the empty tomb, they turned once again to deceit, slipping a backhander to the guards in a desperate bid to hush up events. They did all they could to stifle the truth, but it was no good, for first one person, then another, then another still, and so on in perpetuity, met with the risen Lord and knew the truth for themselves.

There is here both challenge and promise. On the one hand, there is a warning that deception will be uncovered however hard we try to conceal it; that all things will finally come to light. On the other hand there is assurance that right will triumph; that God's purpose will prevail. So we put our trust in Christ – the way, the truth and the life – knowing that his love is sure and his mercy dependable, now and always.

Too good to be true?

Returning from the tomb, they related everything to the eleven and those gathered with them – it was Mary Magdalene, Joanna, Mary the mother of James, and other women with them who told it to the Apostles – but their words seemed like a foolish fancy, and they did not believe them. (Luke 24:9-11)

Do you know the hymn 'Can it be true?' It's not sung today as often as it used to be, which is a pity, for it asks a question central to Easter that many stumble over. The question is essentially this (though the hymn puts it more poetically): Can it be true that Jesus lived and died and rose again? Most people have no problems with the first two of those – that Jesus lived and died. But when it comes to resurrection it's a different matter. Quite simply, for many people it seems too good to be true. It's almost as though the very fact that the idea is so special, by definition disproves it. We're just not used to good news like that. It's the stuff of daydreams, not for hard-headed realists of the twenty-first century.

The funny thing is that it wasn't the stuff for hard-headed realists of the first century either. When the women who'd gone to the tomb burst in on the disciples with the news that Christ had risen, their words, so we are told, seemed like a foolish fantasy, or, as the New International Version of the Bible so graphically puts it, 'like nonsense'. These were no credulous romantics waiting to swallow any old story; they were down-to-earth individuals, utterly convinced that it was all over; that Jesus was dead and buried. Yet, each came not just to believe but also to know that he was alive and with them again through his Spirit; such knowledge sufficient not just for them to recommit their lives to him but gladly to die in his service. It may have seemed too good to be true, but they were soon to discover that it wasn't. Have you discovered that too?

The Sunday after Easter

Still good news

The eleven disciples went to the mountain in Galilee that Jesus had directed them to. On seeing him, most worshipped him, though a few doubted. Then Jesus appeared, instructing them, 'I have been given complete authority in heaven and on earth, so go and make disciples among all people, baptising them in the name of the Father, Son and Holy Spirit, and instructing them to observe everything I have decreed. And never forget that I am constantly by your side, to the very end of time.' (Matthew 28:16-20)

Which of us haven't at some time wished we could have a time over again; that we could undo some thoughtless and angry word, some rash commitment or unwise judgement, or some careless mistake? Do those lines sound familiar? They may well do, for I used them a few pages earlier in this book. Like most things, when you've heard them once, you've heard them enough! The great wonder of Easter, by contrast, is that we can hear its message again and again, yet it goes on being as true and relevant today as it was yesterday, and as it will continue to be tomorrow and the next day, ad infinitum.

How different that is from most modern-day news headlines, as I was reminded the other day when lifting carpets in the course of redecorating. Beneath these were newspapers dating back three years or so, yet the events emblazoned on the front pages seeming curiously trivial, filled with the names and faces of yesteryear. Not that you have to go back years for that to be true; in our high-tech media age, even *yesterday's* news is old hat. The good news of the resurrection is different. Why? Because it continues to change lives in the present, each day offering hope and new beginnings to believers across the world. Easter Day may be over, but we cannot consign the message it proclaims to the past. It is still good news, today and every day!

Ascension Day

The complete picture

Coming together, they asked him, 'Lord, is this the time when you will restore the kingdom of Israel?' He replied, 'It is not for you to know the time or seasons that the Father has laid down by his own authority, but you will receive power when the Holy Spirit comes upon you and you will be my witnesses both in Jerusalem, and all Judea and Samaria, and to the ends of the earth.' Having said this, and while they were watching, he was lifted up, and a cloud hid him from their sight. While he was going and they were staring into the sky, suddenly two men clothed in white stood next to them. They said, 'Men of Galilee, why do you stand staring into the sky? This Jesus, who has been taken from you up into heaven, will come in the same way that you saw him go.' (Acts 1:6-11)

There are few things worse than reading a book and finding that a page is missing. It's worst of all when it's the last page. Few of us would even start to read a book if we knew it would be cut short, yet, with Jesus, we sometimes do something very similar, celebrating his resurrection, and the gift of his Spirit at Pentecost, but virtually overlooking his Ascension. One reason for this, perhaps, is that our account of the Ascension is caught in a time-warp, reflecting the cosmology of days gone by. God is seen as 'up there' and so Jesus is portrayed as vanishing up into heaven, the disciples staring stupefied into the sky. Such language serves to obscure the underlying message of Ascension as surely as the cloud hid Jesus from the Apostles' sight.

Yet, if the details of what happened are a mystery, the significance is clear enough. This was a watershed moment for the Apostles when they realised, for the first time, the full magnitude of who Jesus was. They had followed him during his ministry, believing him to be the Messiah; they had rejoiced at his resurrection, greeting him as the risen Lord; but now they recognised that he was the Son of God, the King of kings and Lord of all. Don't forget Ascension Day! Above all, don't forget what Ascension Day means, for it reminds us that Jesus is greater than words can begin to express, sovereign over all. It gives us the complete picture, without which our faith is infinitely the poorer.

Pentecost

A gift for all

When the day of Pentecost dawned, they were gathered in one place. Suddenly, a sound like the rush of a mighty wind came from heaven, filling the house where they were sitting. After that, tongues of fire appeared which divided, so that a tongue rested on each of them. They were all filled with the Holy Spirit, and began to speak in various tongues, as the Spirit enabled them. This is what was spoken of by the prophet Joel: 'In the last days, God declares, I will pour out my spirit on all people; your sons and daughters will prophesy, your old men will dream dreams, and your young men will see visions. I will pour out my Spirit even on male and female slaves in those days.' (Acts 2:1-4, 16-18a)

Have you stayed in the Hilton hotel, owned a Rolls-Royce or dined with the Queen? I haven't, and I very much doubt I ever will. Some things in life are reserved for the select few, while the majority of us have to make do with more run-of-the-mill facilities and occasions. The people of the Old Testament believed that this was true of the Spirit of God, convinced that it was a rare and special gift which only a privileged elite would experience. There was no way in the world they would be filled by that Spirit; such an honour went to those like Gideon, Samuel, Isaiah, Ezekiel and others of similar stature. For the rank and file, God would always be one step removed, access to him mediated by priest and temple. The words of the prophet Joel, wonderful though they sounded, must have raised more than a few eyebrows when first spoken, for they postulated an entirely new relationship with God.

Yet that is the relationship experienced by the Apostles on the so-called day of Pentecost, and it is a gift offered to us in turn. God is not remote and detached, but can be experienced as a living reality within – encouraging, teaching, empowering, guiding – ever at work in our lives. There is no favouritism with God. One privilege is for us all to enjoy: the inner presence of the Holy Spirit – surely the greatest privilege there can be!

Standby Christians

Jesus drew near and said to them, 'All power in heaven and earth has been given to me. Go, then, and make disciples of all people, baptising them in the name of the Father, the Son and the Holy Spirit.' (Matthew 28:18-19)

Did you know that the power used to keep televisions and electrical appliances in the UK on standby for just one day would be sufficient to provide electricity for a small town? It's a sobering thought, isn't it, all that power going to waste, achieving nothing.

Perhaps equally sobering is the thought that we as individual Christians and, together, as a Church, might be guilty of wasting a different sort of power – the power of God. 'You will receive power,' said Jesus, 'when the Holy Spirit comes upon you.' What he envisaged there was the power of the Spirit so flowing through us that we shall make a difference to the world we live in, changing lives through our work and witness. Some, of course, do just that, but, all too often, our efforts are devoted simply to keeping our own affairs ticking over. We look to our own journey of discipleship, our own relationship with Christ, and no further. As churches, we look inwards rather than outwards, concerned with servicing our plethora of committees, maintaining the fabric and supporting church events. Instead of surging out, God's power becomes trapped in an internal loop. It is as though we are put on standby, rarely if ever used for the purpose we were designed for. If the power stored in all those appliances on standby could meet the needs of a town, so the power at our disposal could meet the needs of the world, if only we had the will and courage to release it.

Trinity Sunday

A glorious mystery

Now there are various gifts, but the same Spirit; various ministries but the same Lord; different types of service but the same God working through all of them. (1 Corinthians 12:4-6)

Mention Advent, Christmas, Holy Week or Easter to most Christians, and you will see a sparkle in their eyes, for these are well-loved festivals that speak in innumerable ways. Mention Trinity Sunday and you are more likely to witness a blank expression or complete lack of interest. It is an occasion that few people warm to, and one that in many nonconformist churches passes completely unnoticed. Why? You only need to look at the so-called Athanasian Creed to find out the answer. It goes like this: 'I believe in God the Father incomprehensible, God the Son incomprehensible, God the Holy Spirit incomprehensible' and so on, at great length. For many the word 'incomprehensible' sums up both the Creed and the ideas about God it is trying to express. When it comes to the doctrine of the Trinity, we are out of our depth, struggling with concepts that baffle us, for how can it make sense to talk of three persons who are at once wholly distinct yet wholly one? It is, indeed, incomprehensible.

Yet that is the whole point, the very reason why Trinity Sunday is so important, for it reminds us of a truth we cannot afford to forget: that God is beyond the human intellect, defying expression, greater than we can ever conceive. We encounter him as a loving Father who is yet sovereign over all; as a human being who lived and died among us yet rose again and is exalted at the Father's right hand; and as an inner reality that fills us with peace, joy, hope and power. We cannot explain how the pieces fit together but we know that they do, for we have experienced the truth for ourselves. If we imagine that we have solved the mystery and that the full wonder of God is firmly in our sights, then it is time to think again, for the truth is that we have lost sight of him altogether.

All Saints' Day

All Saints

Remember your leaders, those who spoke the word of God to you; consider the outcome of their way of life, and imitate their faith. (Hebrews 13:5)

In 1492, as we will all have learned at school, Christopher Columbus set off from Spain in the Santa Marìa, sailing west on a journey that he hoped would take him around the world to India. His crew were terrified, convinced that, since the earth was flat, they would eventually fall off the edge to their deaths. Of course, nobody fell off anywhere, the ship eventually reaching what came to be known as the West Indies. The destination may have been other than intended, but the voyage proved conclusively that the world was not flat at all but round. Once done, many followed the same journey, and a thriving trade route was soon established. As so often in life, it took someone to show the way; someone to convince the doubters of what could be done.

That, for me, takes us to the heart of All Saints' Day, a day that celebrates those who have gone before us in faith, and whose Christian discipleship has inspired subsequent generations. It's not about holier-than-thou men and women adorned by a halo, such as we might see in a church stained-glass window, but about ordinary people like you and me whose lives serve as an extraordinary example. Remember such people, take note of their way of life, and learn from them, for they have shown what can be done and what God waits to do, here and now, in your life today.

Remembrance Sunday

Lest we forget

We have heard for ourselves, O God, our predecessors have told us the deeds you performed in their time, how in bygone days you saved us from our enemies. (Psalm 44:1, 7a)

'Do you remember the time we came here before?' asked my mother. I racked my brains, trying to recall it, but it was no good; the occasion was clean forgotten, as though it had never been. We do remember many things, of course, but we forget many others, as probably all of us can testify from bitter experience. Points we ought to remember have that infuriating habit of disappearing from our minds just when we need to recall them most, and so we resort to such props as a knot in a hankie or a memo-board in the kitchen, hoping that these may jog our memory.

Such, increasingly, is the rationale behind Remembrance Day. Every year, the number of those who lived through one or both of the two World Wars diminishes, yet for that reason the occasion becomes more rather than less important. We have only to witness the horrors of

Bosnia, or the continuing violence in the Middle East and so many other parts of the world, to realise that things haven't changed as much as we might like to think. Some even dare to suggest that the horrors of the Holocaust never actually happened, thus dismissing, at a stroke, the suffering, terror and anguish experienced by so many millions. The fact is that we cannot afford to forget the past. Remembrance Day does not glorify war but rather recalls the price of peace, reminding us of the evil and inhumanity that people can stoop to, and the sacrifice so many made to ensure that such tyranny did not triumph. It purposely thrusts such things back into our consciousness – lest we forget.

Commitment

see also Discipleship: Journey of discipleship; Faith

Continuing in the faith

From that time, many of his followers turned back, no longer walking with him. (John 6:66)

Looking through the bargain section of our free paper, I was struck by certain items that kept reappearing: musical instruments, golf clubs, fish tanks and so on. It didn't need much imagination to work out why these were for sale: each had clearly been bought by someone in a fit of enthusiasm, eagerly anticipating an exciting new hobby, only for the novelty to wear off and the new 'toy' to be discarded. Having started, many found they couldn't continue.

That, I'm afraid, is true of many who commit themselves to Christ. They start out bursting with similar enthusiasm but, as soon as the first flush of excitement fades, they quickly lose interest. No, I am not just talking about others; such a scenario can be as true of us as anyone. We may think we are just as committed as we used to be, yet in reality simply be going through the motions, our faith taking us nowhere. Like the followers of Jesus mentioned in John's Gospel, we may have turned back so that we no longer walk with him. The initial act of commitment is easy; it's when the cost of discipleship and level of commitment required become clear that the real test comes. I'm reminded of the catchphrase immortalised by Magnus Magnusson in the TV quiz *Mastermind*: 'I've started, so I'll finish.' That's what faith is all about, what it means to be a disciple of Jesus. Can we honestly echo those words?

The courage of our convictions

The administrators and satraps plotted together and then sought an audience with the king. They said to him, 'O King Darius, live forever! The administrators, prefects, satraps, counsellors and governors of the kingdom are all of the opinion that the king should pass and enforce a royal law decree that anyone caught praying, whether to God or man, over these next thirty days – unless, of course, it's to you, O king! – will be thrown into a den of lions. Now, O king, institute this law and sign a decree, so that it is irrevocably binding according to the law of the Medes and the Persians, which cannot be revoked.' So King

Darius signed the decree. Daniel knew full well that the decree had been signed, but he followed his usual practice, going to his house, in which the upstairs windows faced towards Jerusalem, and there kneeling three times a day in prayer to offer praise to God, just as he had always done. The plotters came and found Daniel praying and asking God for help. (Daniel 6:6-11)

The story of Daniel in the lions' den must be one of the best known in the whole of the Old Testament; a tale that has been told and retold across the centuries, delighting countless generations. It is a classic example of good conquering evil; a victory against all the odds. But, of course, it needed the faith and courage of Daniel for that triumph to happen, his willingness to make a stand for the things he believed in, never mind the consequences. Today, thankfully, times are very different; there is little chance of us being fed to the lions, not literally anyway! Yet we need people of Daniel's stature as much as ever; people ready to risk all in the cause of truth, ready to hold firmly to their principles despite every attempt to sway them. Have we even a fraction of that courage and commitment?

Declaring our loyalties

Anyone who is ashamed of me and my words, the Son of Man will be ashamed of in turn when he comes in his glory and the glory of the Father and the holy angels. (Luke 9:26)

It's several years since I last watched Southend United, my hometown football team, in action. The reason is very simple – the journey from Somerset is simply too long and expensive to contemplate. That's not the only factor, however. I could have gone to watch Southend play Exeter, Torquay or Bristol Rovers – all relatively near to where I live – but one experience has put me off: the memory of the last away-match I attended. It was against Swindon Town during Southend's best-ever spell in their history; the club pressing, believe it or not, for a place in the Premier League, and I was there with my brother Julian to cheer on the team. Frustratingly, though, it was Swindon who scored first, and as an almighty roar erupted around us, we realised to our horror that we were entirely surrounded by home supporters. Another goal, another roar, and we nervously struggled to hide our disappointment. Eventually, Southend managed to score, but our instinctive whoop of delight died in our throats as a thousand malevolent stares bore down upon us. Discretion proved the better part of valour! We weren't ashamed of the team – far from it – but we were afraid to declare our loyalties, worried about the possible repercussions.

How often is the same true of our relationship with Christ? We sit quiet when we ought to speak up; we turn a blind eye when we ought to make a stand; we compromise our convictions when we ought to stay true. With a football team it's understandable, no club, however special, worth risking one's safety for, but can there be any such excuse with Jesus? The cause is far greater and any danger is a thing of the past. Can we ever justify failing to declare our loyalty to him?

A faith to die for

Full of the Holy Spirit, [Stephen] gazed into heaven and saw there the glory of God with Jesus standing at his right hand, and he said, 'Look, the heavens are open, and I can see the Son of Man standing at God's right hand.' Then, crying out with a mighty roar of rage and shutting their ears to his words, they fell upon him with one mind. They cast him out of the city and stoned him, and as they stoned him he called out in the name of Christ, saying, 'Lord Jesus, receive my spirit.' Then, falling on his knees, he cried out in a voice all could hear, 'Lord, do not hold this sin against them.' And, having said this, he fell asleep. (Acts 7:55-58a, 59-60)

Nearly 400 years ago, the world of medicine was plunged into controversy by an English physician, William Harvey, who contradicted established wisdom by suggesting that blood is pumped from the heart to the lungs, back through the heart and then out via the arteries before returning to the heart through the veins. The theory was spot on, but at the time it aroused a storm of protest from medical, scientific and religious 'authorities'. At around the same time, Galileo caused yet greater consternation with his hypothesis that the earth orbits the sun rather than vice versa. So shocking was this considered that he was forced to recant and put under house arrest for the remainder of his life. Each of these two men, however, continued with their work, refusing to sacrifice their beliefs despite intolerable pressures.

There are parallels here with the story of Stephen, the first Christian martyr. On trial for his faith, it must have been tempting to tone down his message, even opt for secret discipleship, for he knew well enough the consequences should he refuse to back down. Yet, instead he spoke out boldly, conscious that many would take their lead from him. Had he and others like him given in and denied their faith, who can say where the Church would be today – whether indeed the gospel message would have died an early death back in Jerusalem. It is unlikely that any of us will ever be called upon to die for our faith but how ready are we to live up to it in a sceptical and sometimes hostile world?

The folly of faith

Having left the prison, they entered the house of Lydia, and having seen and exhorted their fellow Christians there, they went on their way. (Acts 16:40)

What do you think of today's reading? It's a bit dull, isn't it – hardly the stuff to capture the imagination or stir the spirit. Think again, for in this almost incidental remark concerning Lydia welcoming the disciples into her home there lies an action of astonishing faith, courage and commitment. Lydia was a seller of blue cloth; in other words, a woman who, against the odds, had made it in the world of Roman business selling the fabric worn by the highest officers in the land. It couldn't have been easy to succeed in the world of her time and one whiff of something untoward could have brought all she'd built tumbling down over her head. Yet, when Paul and his companions came preaching the gospel she responded immediately, confessing her faith and seeking baptism, never mind that Christians were already facing persecution for their faith. If that wasn't enough, a short while later Paul became embroiled in a public row concerning a young slave girl; a dispute that led to him being hustled with his colleagues before the civic authorities, committed to prison, and finally expelled from the town.

Now do you see the message in these verses? Despite all this, knowing the risks, she opened her home gladly to the Apostle and his friends. In the eyes of the world, it must have seemed madness and I am sure many among her friends must have upbraided her for her folly. They were wasting their breath, for Lydia had discovered in the folly of the gospel the power of God.

Fully committed?

Your hearts must be fully committed to the Lord our God, to live by his decrees and obey his commands, as at this time. (1 Kings 8:61)

If you were at the ground of a football team riding high in the Premiership, or enjoying an extended run in the FA Cup, the chances are that you would hear a jubilant chant from the fans along the lines 'We'll support you evermore!' If you were watching a team in mid-table, having just drawn a cup match that they should have won, you'd no doubt hear a few jeers and catcalls from increasingly disgruntled spectators. If you were watching a team at the bottom of the table enduring yet another 6-0 thrashing, you probably wouldn't hear much at all, because most of the 'fans' would long since have deserted the club and stayed at home. True commitment is hard to find; most of us are fair-weather supporters.

Sadly, that's often also the case when it comes to our commitment to God – a truth reflected in those words of Solomon above. He spoke at a time of celebration, the people of Israel having excitedly gathered to dedicate their new temple, and, understandably, spirits were high and the enthusiasm of the crowd contagious. It was easy at such a time to make bold declarations of faith and sweeping promises of loyalty, but Solomon knew how easily those could be forgotten once people returned to the routine business of life. The danger is just as real today. Many start out as Christians, bubbling over with enthusiasm, full of everything God has done for them and everything they plan to do for him, only to lose interest when life doesn't quite work out as expected. Once the first flush of faith has faded, the novelty is over and the initial excitement of conversion has passed, discipleship doesn't hold the attraction it once did. It's easy to start out on the journey of faith and to walk it when all is going well, but are we ready to follow even when it proves costly or demanding? Are we truly committed?

For God's sake

Whatever your task, do it for God's sake rather than anyone else's, knowing that you will receive an inheritance from the Lord as a reward. (Colossians 3:23)

'For God's sake, stop doing that!' 'For Christ's sake, get it right!' How often have we heard words like those? The name of God or Christ is frequently invoked in such ways, yet the irony is that those who tend to invoke it have little or no religious faith, using it instead as an expression of exasperation to underline their feelings. The Apostle Paul uses the idea in a very different sense, urging us to see everything we do as literally done for God's sake. He is not just talking about 'religious' activities but every aspect of life: our work, rest, interests and relationships, our thinking, speaking and doing – each of them offered as a gift to God.

That is a message we would do well to consider, for we tend to compartmentalise life into the sacred and secular to the point that the two barely meet. We also tend to see some people as specially called to religious vocations and others as engaged in less spiritual activities. I don't think Paul would have been happy with such a dichotomy. For him, whatever we do should be sacred, consecrated to God as part of our daily discipleship. It may catch the eye, it may not, but that's not important. What matters is that we live each moment in such a way that all we do is truly done for God's sake.

Learning to say no

I deemed it necessary to send to you Epaphroditus – my brother, co-worker and fellow-soldier, and your messenger sent to minister to me in my need – since he has been pining for you all and troubled that you heard about his illness. He was indeed so ill that he came close to death, but God had mercy on him, and not only him but me also, sparing me yet another sorrow. I therefore readily sent him to you, so that you may rejoice at seeing him again and I may be less anxious. Welcome him, then, in the Lord with all joy, and treat him with respect, because he risked his life for the work of Christ and came close to death in order to offer service to me that you were unable to provide. (Philippians 2:25-30)

It was the church AGM and we'd reached the point every member dreads: a couple of posts had yet to be filled causing the minister to pronounce those dreaded words, 'Any volunteers?' Needless to say, the posts went unfilled! Ask for a volunteer when a job needs doing and the chances are you'll be wasting your time. Paradoxically, if you ask someone face to face, there's every prospect of a different response, for when we're put on the spot it's surprisingly hard to say no; in fact, some of us find it virtually impossible. It may be a cliché but it is also true that 'if you want something done, ask a busy person'.

What the saying fails to add is that the extra task taken on may just prove to be the straw that breaks the camel's back. If you are the sort of person who takes on ever more jobs, responsibilities and demands, even when you're already flagging under the strain of others, take note. Paul's words afford us a glimpse of Epaphroditus, a man who quite clearly took on too much and nearly paid for it with his life. He learned the hard way that we all have our limitations beyond which it is foolhardy to push ourselves. It may seem the Christian thing to say yes, but if that causes our health to suffer, endangering the happiness of our loved ones and preventing us from fulfilling our responsibilities as we would want to, then perhaps it's time we learnt to say no. All of us can do something; none of us are called to do everything!

An outer veneer

You who yearn for the day of the Lord are fools, for what will that day actually mean to you? It will be darkness, not light; as though you have fled from a lion only to be met by a bear; or taken refuge in a house only to be bitten by a snake as you rest a hand against the wall. That is what the day of the Lord will be like: unrelieved darkness, night with no prospect of dawn. I loathe and reject your festivals, and take no pleasure in your sacred rituals. Bring me your animal sacrifices and cereal offerings if you must – I will not accept them; I want nothing to do with the atoning sacrifices of your fatted animals. Take away from me the clamour of your songs; I will not listen to the tune of your harps. Instead, let justice cascade down like a mighty river, and righteousness like an inexhaustible stream. (Amos 5:18-24)

It looked a nice piece of furniture, nice enough, in fact, to take me in completely. I imagined it was solid wood, built to last, but time was to prove otherwise. Before long, the thin layer of veneer began to peel away, exposing the cheap chipboard beneath and, eventually, the whole surface cracked beyond repair.

Furniture is not the only thing that can superficially look the part; the same can be equally true of people. As Amos so powerfully observed, outwardly our practice of religion may be exemplary, yet this may mask a profound failure to serve God. He wasn't just talking about those who hide dark secrets behind a respectable public face but warning also of the danger of fine-sounding words that are belied by actions, of ostentatious show concealing a hollow interior.

Playing our part

Once sufficient time has been allowed for the fruit to develop, the farmer immediately sets to with the sickle, because the time for harvest has come. (Mark 4:29)

Every would-be gardener will have experienced the disappointment of planting seeds only for a few spindly shoots, or even nothing at all, to come up from them. Why does this happen? It may be we forget to water them or water them too much. It may be that we planted them in the wrong place or at the wrong time. It may be that we overfed or underfed them. And so we could go on. Although it is God, ultimately, who gives growth, there are times when he both needs and expects a helping hand. He could go it alone if he wanted to, but he invites us to share in his creative purpose, to be a part of his ongoing activity in human history. On the one hand, this is an awesome privilege; on the other, it is a daunting responsibility.

Before deciding that everything can be safely left in God's hands, consider an alternative possibility; maybe he's already done his bit and is depending on you to do yours!

A question of sovereignty

If you openly acknowledge that Jesus is Lord and wholeheartedly accept God raised him to life, you will be saved. (Romans 10:9)

For some time now, one topic has come to dominate political debate across the spectrum as few others before it: the issue of European Monetary Union. Should we sign up to a single currency or shouldn't we? It is a vexed issue, guaranteed to stimulate lively debate, the thrust of which will invariably revolve around the question of sovereignty: are we to be answerable to Europe or to ourselves, and will joining make any difference either way? For my part, like many others, I'm undecided, my heart telling me one thing but my head another.

Few people like giving up their sovereignty, but there is a sense in which, as Christians, we have to do just that, for coming to faith involves decisions concerning not national but ultimate sovereignty. Who is Lord of our lives? Who is the one finally in control? Whom do we answer to? To say Jesus is Lord is not just a formal expression, like an oath we take before being admitted to some secret society. It is an acknowledgement that Jesus has first place in our lives. It is a pledge to devote time and energy in the service of his kingdom. Yes, we declare it with our lips, but we need to back that up in our lives. How many of us can honestly say, 'Jesus is Lord', and point to our lives to prove that we mean it?

Secret disciples?

Joseph of Arimathea – a disciple of Jesus, albeit secretly because of his fear of the Jews – asked Pilate for permission to take away the body of Jesus. Pilate consented; so he went and removed the body. Nicodemus, who first came to Jesus by night, accompanied him, bringing with him a blend of myrrh and aloes, about a hundred pounds in weight. They took the body of Jesus and bound it, together with the spices, in linen cloths, following the burial custom of the Jews. (John 19:38-40)

Our first reaction, reading of Joseph of Arimathea and Nicodemus asking for the body of Jesus, is that it was too little, too late. It was well intentioned, undoubtedly, but what use to Jesus was it now? If they'd stuck their necks out earlier, how different things might have been. Yet is such an interpretation fair? Certainly open commitment from the start would have been better, but which of us would have acted differently in their place? To publicly declare allegiance to Jesus would have involved considerable risk. For the ordinary people to follow him was bad enough in the eyes of the Jewish authorities; for a Pharisee it was unthinkable!

Many generations of Christians since have felt forced by persecution to be secret disciples: witness the catacombs of Rome or the story of Christians in the Soviet bloc before the demise of communism. For us, there is no such excuse. We have freedom of speech, freedom of conscience and freedom of belief. It's conceivable that we might suffer discrimination due to our faith but it's unlikely to be anything worse. Yet how many of us are up-front about our faith, proud to acknowledge it, ready to nail our colours firmly to the mast? Or, to put it another way, how many of those we regularly have dealings with have any inkling that we are Christians or any idea of what our faith means to us? At least Joseph and Nicodemus had some reason to be secretive. Have we?

The slippery slope

Demas, in love with this present world, has deserted me and gone to Thessalonica. (2 Timothy 4:9)

How often have you started something full of enthusiasm, only to wonder a little later just what it is you have taken on? It may have been a job round the house, an interest, a hobby, a responsibility – the list is almost limitless – but, whatever it was, we believed at the time that we'd see it through with undiminished energy. Nine times out of ten, the bubble soon bursts. Another job, another interest, another hobby, another responsibility, and suddenly the old is discarded in favour of the new.

The same, sadly, can all too easily happen with faith. How many have started the course only to turn back, professed faith in Christ only to lose interest in anything to do with him? The commitment is real enough at the outset but, for a variety of reasons, it is undermined. Make no mistake: none of us is immune to the same befalling us. We all have our weak spots; we can all grow cold. That which began as a joyful privilege can end up as an empty duty, before finally petering out into nothingness. Don't let what happened to Demas happen to you.

Taking hold of Christ

I want to know Christ, and the power of his resurrection, and the fellowship with him that comes through sharing his suffering, even identifying with his death. Not that I have yet received these or been made perfect, but I follow Christ so that I may take hold of them, even as Christ has taken hold of me. (Philippians 3:10, 12)

It may be a cliché but the old saying is true nonetheless: it takes two to tango. It's true in our human relationships and it's true in our relationship with God in Christ. He will not let go of us, but he needs us to take hold of him if we are to stand firm. We warm to that first truth, but find the second rather harder, don't we? We mean to stay close, but somehow we drift away, disentangling our hand from his to follow our own path and pursue our own interests. Christ is still there, reaching out, ready to respond the moment we ask him, but if we will not hold on then we limit what he can do. It goes further than that. The joy of faith, the peace of God, the hope of eternal life can all be lost so easily, not because they are taken away but because we lose our grip on them, intent on grasping other pleasures. Don't leave it all to him: each day take hold afresh of Christ and make him yours as you are his.

A time to decide

No one can serve two masters, for they will either hate the one and love the other, or cling to the one and spurn the other. You cannot simultaneously serve God and this world. (Matthew 6:24)

One of the things I have never succeeded in doing is learning to swim. I've tried many times, having had lessons in school and later in life as an adult but, though I've come close, I've never quite mastered it. The reason is simple enough – I try to keep a foot in both camps. Whereas I should trust myself completely to the water, I insist on keeping one foot firmly on the floor and the result is that I neither sink nor swim. I know I should leap out in faith but somehow I just can't bring myself to make that decisive step. The same, of course, can be true of life. To change the metaphor, there are times when sitting on the fence or hedging our bets means that we end up achieving nothing.

It is even truer when it comes to faith, as Jesus made plain in those often-quoted words from the Sermon on the Mount. We may like to think we can play it both ways, but there comes a point when we can't. This doesn't mean that we should live as reclusive eccentrics, still less that we should dismiss the very real joys this world has to offer. What it does mean is that when life throws up difficult choices, as it assuredly will, we have to be clear about our priorities; about who or what we are serving. Compromise, in an attempt to secure the best of both worlds, and we may end up securing neither.

Truly committed?

Come to him, a living stone rejected by mortals yet chosen and precious in God's sight, and, like living stones, allow yourselves through Jesus Christ to be built into a spiritual house, a holy priesthood offering spiritual sacrifices acceptable to God. (1 Peter 2:4-5)

As mentioned earlier, I like to think of myself as a supporter of Southend United Football Club. In my mid- to late-teens I watched them play most weeks, my home being just a couple of minutes' walk from the ground and, although I moved away from the town twenty-five years ago, I still follow the team's fortunes with interest. Indeed, I have even taken to looking up the club's official website to catch the latest match report or news. Sadly, though, I haven't watched the team play for many years, and that, I'm afraid, exposes my 'support' for what it is – an empty illusion. The truth of the matter is that I'm inter-ested in Southend rather than a supporter, for support needs to show itself in action. Unless I am there on the terraces, cheering on the players or contributing to the club's finances through paying at the turnstiles, my so-called support means precious little.

The parallel between this and nominal discipleship is not hard to spot. Many of us claim to be Christians, but when was the last time we darkened the door of a church, turned the pages of a Bible, approached God in prayer or expressed our faith through practical service? Yes, we may tune in to the occasional TV *Songs of Praise* or 'God slot' on the radio, but if that's as far as it goes, then something is wrong. I'm not saying that you have to go to church to be a Christian, or that there is a certain lifestyle that must be rigidly adhered to in order to be counted such – therein lies the road to bigotry, hypocrisy and legalism. What I am saying, as much to myself as anyone, is that being a Christian – that is, belonging to Christ rather than simply being interested in him –

must necessarily make a difference to the way we live. If that isn't the case, then it's time we asked ourselves if we're actually Christians at all.

With all we have

What then, O Israel, does the Lord your God ask of you? Simply to fear the Lord your God, to follow in all his ways, to love and serve him with all your heart and soul, and, for your own good, to observe the Lord's commandments and decrees that I am giving you today. (Deuteronomy 10:12-13)

I watched the University Boat Race recently – a gripping battle in which both teams fought to the last. What always catches my eye in such encounters is not just the rowers but also the Cox in each boat. They seem superfluous at first sight, an extra weight that the crew could well do without, yet their role is vital. As well as keeping the strokes synchronised, they also encourage the crew to greater effort, summoning every last ounce of energy from them. Their job is to ensure that all the team don't just give a little but their all.

So it should be when it comes to loving God. Our relationship with him is not one we can breeze in and out of; not simply a vague feeling of thankfulness and adoration, nor merely a matter of the intellect, recognising that God deserves our worship. We are called to love God with all we have – body, mind and soul. It involves the will and the heart, acting on impulse and dogged determination, joyfully responding and actively seeking. Our prayers, our hymns and our worship talk a lot about loving God, but what do we actually mean by that? Is it simply pious sentiment, or are we committed to giving everything to make the relationship really work?

Working it out for ourselves

You must work out your own salvation with fear and trembling, recognising that God is at work in you so that you will be able to understand and accomplish his good purpose. (Philippians 2:12)

Are you good at crossword puzzles? I used to have a whole book of them and, in my few spare moments, much enjoyed tackling them. But I discovered I have a fundamental weakness: I can't resist looking at the answers! The result was that I finished each crossword in good time but rather defeated the object of the exercise in the process! When it comes to learning something, there is a similar danger. A child can use a calculator to work out a complicated sum but this will do nothing to further his or her understanding of mathematics. A parent can help children with their homework, yet if they do the work for them, they are ultimately doing a disservice. To appreciate and understand something, we need to work it out for ourselves.

That surely is the point of Paul's words to the Philippians. He is not saying we can earn our salvation or find a way to achieve it through our own ingenuity. Rather he wants to stress the importance of working at our relationship with God, of growing each day in our faith, of striving to become more like Christ. We depend on grace but that does not excuse us our part. Learn about God parrot fashion, consider ourselves a Christian because we know about Jesus and have heard something of the gospel, and we will discover eventually that we have learned very little. Salvation involves commitment to an ongoing relationship and, in that sense, it is something no one else can do for us – we must work it out for ourselves.

_____ Confession and forgiveness _____

see also Grace

Confessing

Acknowledging our mistakes

I will get up and go to my father, and I will say to him, 'Father, I have sinned against heaven and before you; I no longer deserve to be called your son; regard me instead as one of your hired hands.' (Luke 15:18-19)

'Someone who has committed a mistake and doesn't correct it is committing another mistake' – so said Confucius. He was right, wasn't he? Attempt to cover up some error of judgement or pretend it never happened and, before we know it, one thing leads to another until a situation spirals horribly out of control. Yet, true though we realise that to be, we continue so often to do precisely that: making excuses for our behaviour, sweeping our mistakes under the carpet or dismissing them as unimportant. It takes courage to admit we've done wrong and to seek forgiveness. We manage it sometimes with God, though even there we are probably more selective than we might think, there being some things we are loath to admit even to ourselves.

When it comes to others it is infinitely harder, especially when it means facing up to someone we have wronged. Many prefer to brazen it out rather than lose face, even though that may mean adding one mistake to another. Is it enough simply to confess our sins to God, or does true confession need to involve acknowledging our mistakes and saying sorry to those we have sinned against? It's a more costly and demanding path for, unlike with God, we have no guarantee of being forgiven, yet it is often the only way to healing and reconciliation. Do we have the fibre to admit our mistakes, even when it involves embarrassment and humiliation? Are we ready, where necessary, to put our hands up and to candidly confess, with no excuses or reservations, 'I was wrong'?

A changed life

A certain young man accompanied him, wearing nothing but a linen cloth. They grabbed hold of him, but he wriggled out of the cloth and ran off naked. (Mark 14:51-52)

Who was the young man who ran off naked into the night at the time of the arrest of Jesus? That question has fascinated scholars across the years and although no definitive answer has been given, the general consensus of opinion favours John Mark, the writer of the gospel in which this enigmatic character is mentioned. It's an intriguing thought, isn't it – both heart-warming and inspiring to think that someone so desperate to disassociate himself from Jesus could, in the space of a few years, become the writer of what most regard as the earliest of all the gospels, eagerly testifying to his faith in the risen Christ.

If the conjecture is right, was this, I wonder, the first time that Mark had faced up to the incident? If so, it seems he still couldn't bring himself to come clean completely, yet he wanted to testify to what for him must have been the most marvellous truth in the already unforgettable gospel message: the fact that Jesus had changed him, turning his life inside out and upside down. The same testimony, together with a similar sense of wonder, can equally be ours! No one is outside the transforming power of his saving love and no mistake is beyond his forgiveness. He is constantly at work in the lives of all who will receive him, to redeem, renew and restore. Whoever you are, Jesus can change you!

A clean breast of it

Happy is the one whose wrongdoing is forgiven, whose faults are covered. Happy is the one to whom the Lord ascribes no guilt, and in whose spirit there is no pretence. While I remained silent, my body grew weary with my constant groaning, for day and night your hand weighed heavily upon me; my strength dried up like sap in the heat of summer. Then I acknowledged my sin and did not conceal my guilt from you; I said, 'I will confess my disobedience to the Lord', and you absolved me from my guilt and sin. (Psalm 32:1-5)

In the mid-1990s, an issue came to dominate British politics – the question of sleaze. Scarcely a week went by, it seemed, without some sordid scandal emerging about an MP or public figure; so much so that this matter in large part contributed to the humiliating defeat of the Conservative government in 1997. Countless prominent people have had cause over the years to wish they had come clean when they could, rather than have their guilty secrets splashed out later on the front pages of the tabloids. The reason they keep quiet, of course, is that they are afraid honesty might jeopardise their careers.

Fear can similarly come to rule our lives. The stakes involved may not be quite so high, but we hesitate to admit to past errors or present indiscretions for fear of losing face, endangering a relationship, or causing hurt to others and embarrassment to ourselves. At the time, sweeping a mistake under the carpet may seem an attractive option. It is only later that we learn how wrong we are, as guilt eats away at our conscience and the fear of being found out nags away at the back of our minds. Saying sorry is never easy and can prove costly, but it is also the only way to resolution and reconciliation. Refusing to admit our mistakes may ultimately prove more costly still.

Excuses, excuses

The Lord God called to the man, and said to him, 'Where are you?' He answered, 'I heard your footfall in the garden, and I was ashamed because I was naked, so I hid myself.' He said, 'Who told you that you were naked? Have you eaten from the tree I told you not to eat from?' The man said, 'The woman you gave me as a companion, she gave me fruit from the tree, so I ate it.' Then the Lord God said to the woman, 'What have you done?' The woman said, 'The serpent misled me, and I ate.' (Genesis 3:9-13)

Are you good at admitting your mistakes? I wish I were. To hold up one's hand and candidly admit one has done wrong is a rare gift, taking courage that few of us possess. Our natural reaction is more like that of Adam and Eve, frantically trying to justify our actions. 'It wasn't my fault,' we claim. 'I was forced into it. My hands were tied.' Deep down, though, we know that the responsibility to choose is ours, no one else's. We are all answerable for our own actions. It isn't easy to admit our mistakes, but until we learn to do that, they will hang heavy upon us, impinging on our relationships with those we have wronged. Acknowledge our errors, and we pave the way to forgiveness and a new beginning.

Learning to say sorry

If you are bringing a gift to the altar and, when you get there, you remember that someone has something against you, leave your gift before the altar and, before anything else, make your peace with that person; then come and offer your gift. (Matthew 5:23-24)

There is one word that, could we learn to use it more often, has the power to change the world, but it is probably one of the hardest words to say. I refer, of course, to that little word 'sorry' – a word apparently so simple, yet one that sticks in the throat as few others do. We can mean to say it and even look for the opportunity to do so but, when the moment comes, so often we are unable to spit it out. The reason I suppose is our reluctance to lose face, our unwillingness to admit publicly our fallibility. Yet, although some might see saying sorry as a sign of weakness, it actually requires great humility and immense strength of character. If only more of us had the courage to give it a go.

Papering over the cracks

This is what the Lord said to Jeremiah: 'Go down at once to the potter's house, and there I will speak to you.' So I went down to the potter's house, and there I found him working at the wheel. Occasionally, one of the vessels he was shaping from the clay was spoiled in his hands, and then he would start again and rework it into another vessel more to his liking. (Jeremiah 18:1-4)

Anyone who has ever wallpapered an old house will be well acquainted with that sinking feeling that comes on surveying one's handiwork the next morning. No matter how thick the paper you put on in an attempt to hide the various lumps and bumps in the plaster, such blemishes always succeed in showing through. Take the wall I papered the other day. I had spent considerable time filling and sanding until arriving at what I thought was a relatively smooth finish. A good-quality blown vinyl would, I reckoned, make it look good as new. How wrong I was!

Something very similar is often true in life. We attempt to cover over our weaknesses rather than tackle and eradicate them. We know all is not as it should be, but we vainly imagine that, through our own efforts, we can make the best of a bad job. The truth is that we can't. What my wall needs is replastering. What we need is remaking, and only God can achieve that. Don't paper over the cracks. Don't settle for a ham-fisted make-over. Acknowledge before God what's wrong with your life, and let him put right what you can't start to tackle yourself.

Recognising our faults

He told a further parable to some who were so convinced of their own right-eousness that they looked down dismissively on others. 'Two men went up to the temple to pray, the first a Pharisee and the second a tax collector. The Pharisee, standing aloof, prayed like this, "God, I thank you that I am not like other people – corrupt, deceitful, adulterous – or even like this tax collector.

I fast twice weekly and tithe all my income." But the tax collector, standing at a distance, could not even bring himself to lift his eyes to heaven, but rather beat his breast, saying, "God, be merciful to a miserable sinner like me!" Mark my words, it was this man rather than the other who went home at peace with God; for all who laud their own virtue will be humbled, but those who humble themselves will be exalted.' (Luke 18:9-14)

During my student days, I worked for a time in a factory. The work was dull but the camaraderie among the workers was fun and, although their language could be a little ripe at times, the majority were good-hearted people whose company I enjoyed. Then a woman there asked me about my long-term plans and, when I told them of my intention to enter the ministry, her face fell. 'What do you want to do that for?' she said. 'It will ruin you!' For this lady, the Church was synonymous with narrow-minded, holier-than-thou bigotry.

Was she right? Not entirely, no – generalisations only contain half a truth at best – but it's disturbing, isn't it, that someone can gain this impression of Christianity? Many, justified or otherwise, would echo her sentiments – a fact we would do well to reflect on. I'm sure we all like to think of ourselves as the humble sinner seeking repentance but we need to ask, honestly and prayerfully, are we guilty sometimes of being more like the smug, complacent Pharisee?

It won't wash

Nothing is hidden that will not be revealed; nor is there any secret that will not come out into the open and be known by all. Cleanse me from my secret faults. (Luke 8:17; Psalm 19:12)

Do you know what the term 'Greenwash' means? I didn't until recently. Apparently, it's a term used to describe the efforts of large industries and corporations to present their products as environmentally sensitive, even when they may be anything but. Have you noticed, for example, how virtually every detergent you buy today is labelled eco-friendly, how every foodstuff is farm-fresh, how every packaging is recycled and recyclable? Such claims are not necessarily groundless, many firms having done much to clean up their act, but green labels and marketing have become useful promotional tools in the hands of some who are less than scrupulous.

However, faceless corporations are not the only ones who dress things up; we all do it. We each have a public face we wear for the world and each of us seek to present ourselves in the most flattering light, putting the best gloss possible on those less-desirable aspects of our character. It's understandable that we should and, to a point, we can get away with it when dealing with people – but not with God. It is useless being anything other than honest with him, for he discerns the thoughts of our heart, the attitudes and motives that lie behind our actions. We may think we're being straight with him, but are we really? The image we have of ourselves is one thing; what God sees may be quite another.

Forgiveness of God

The God of mercy

The scribes and Pharisees escorted a woman into the crowd who had been caught committing adultery and, setting her before Jesus, they said to him, 'Teacher, this woman was caught red-handed in the act of adultery. Now, in the law Moses commanded us to stone women like her, so what do you say we should do?' They said this to trap him, so that they might have some accusation to level against him. Jesus crouched down and wrote with his finger in the dust, but since they persisted in questioning him, he straightened up and said to them, 'If any of you are without sin, then you be the one to hurl the first stone at her.' He bent down once more and again wrote in the dust. Hearing his words, they melted away, one by one, starting with the oldest, until he was left alone with just the woman before him. Standing up again, he asked her, 'Woman, where are they? Has no one condemned you?' She said, 'No one, sir.' Then Jesus said, 'I do not condemn you, either. Off you go, and from now on do not sin again.' (John 8:2-11)

There's a wonderful old hymn, all too rarely sung nowadays, which begins 'There's a wideness in God's mercy', and which continues, in a later verse: 'But we make his love too narrow by false limits of our own; and we magnify his strictness with a zeal he will not own.'

How true those words are. We tend to assume that God will judge us in much the same way that we so readily judge others. Surely even *his* patience has its limits! Yet, the astonishing message at the heart of the gospel is that God is altogether different from us, his attitudes, goodness and forgiveness on a level we find hard to comprehend. Never labour under a burden of guilt. Never imagine that you have committed some unforgivable sin. Whereas we are swift to point the accusing finger, even at ourselves, the nature of God is always to have mercy.

Past put behind us

The people said to Samuel, 'Intercede before the Lord your God for us, your servants, so that we may not die; for we have compounded our many sins by the evil of demanding a king for ourselves.' Samuel said to the people, 'Do not be afraid. Yes, you have done evil, but don't let that deflect you from honouring the Lord. Rather, serve him with all your heart. Do not experiment with false gods that can neither profit nor save, for they are useless. For his sovereign name's sake, the Lord will not cast you off, because it has pleased him to make you his own people.' (1 Samuel 12:19-22)

Have you ever made a mistake that you have rued ever since? It is a rare person indeed who has no regrets, but the question is, how do we respond to them? Two wrongs, we are told, don't make a right, yet all too often our response to one mistake is to make another, until life ends up spiralling out of control.

The situation underlying our reading from Samuel was much like that, the people of Israel in danger of abandoning their trust in God and going their own way. On the surface, there is nothing so terrible in their so-called 'mistake'; what was wrong, after all, in asking for a king? The answer lies in the thinking behind their request; namely, their desire to follow the way of the world rather than the way of God. They preferred an earthly ruler that they could see and touch, however fallible he might be, to a heavenly ruler who seemed remote and isolated. Now, having seen their mistake, they felt God must surely have abandoned them, but they came to Samuel with one last desperate plea, and his reply offers an enduring message as applicable today as it was then. Yes, you made a mistake, he tells them, but in God's eyes, it's over and done with, already forgotten. Don't dwell on the past; look forward to the future and make the most of the present. God doesn't brood over what's been and gone, but puts it behind him. If he can do that, isn't it time we did as well?

Under the carpet

Hatred stirs up strife, but love covers over all offences. (Proverbs 10:12)

Sweeping things under the carpet – it's not a good idea, is it? Whether we're speaking literally or metaphorically, attempting to keep something hidden rather than tackling it head on only stores up extra trouble in the future.

So, how do we make sense of the words above? At first sight, they seem to suggest love does something much like this, sweeping our mistakes from public view, but this is only half the story. Leave it there, and our faults would always be lying beneath the surface, waiting to be dragged out and used against us at any time. Love is different – it not only covers over our offences but does away with them so completely that when the carpet is lifted there is no trace to be found. Such love is rare in human relationships – few of us, however devoted we may be, are able to forgive and forget – but that is the love God has for us, and the love he calls us to show to others in turn.

As white as snow

Come now, let us talk this through together, says the Lord: though your sins are like scarlet, they will be as white as snow; though they are red like crimson, they will become like wool. (Isaiah 1:18)

Are you the sort of person who dreams of a white Christmas? I am. Yes, I know snow can be a nuisance and a hazard, but I just can't help myself. There's something magical about the way a heavy snowfall transforms the world into a picture postcard scene, like something from a Christmas card or a fairy story. It doesn't last, of course. Before long, it's churned up into piles of slush and muddy footprints, but for a few moments all the greyness and ugliness of winter disappear.

For me, that idea is echoed in those unforgettable words of the prophet Isaiah. We all know that our lives are not what they could and should be, that there is so much which prevents us from being the people that God intended. Yet, says the prophet, with God's help things can change, not by our own efforts but through his grace. If we are ready to turn to him and admit our mistakes, he is ready to forgive and wipe the slate clean. No doubt, we will soon muddy the picture again, just as with that fresh fall of snow, but this time it is different, for the offer is always there to start again, however often we may fail.

Why did I do it?

I do not understand why I act as I do. For I end up doing the things I hate rather than the things I want to do. I do evil instead of the good I wish to do. Now if I do what I don't really want to do, it must be the sin within me rather than me personally that does it. I find it to be a law that whenever I intend to do good, evil is there as well, for, while deep within I delight in the law of God, I see a different law in my body that battles with the law of my mind, holding me captive to the law of sin that dwells in my members. What a wretched man

I am! Who will deliver me from this body of death? Thanks be to God through Jesus Christ our Lord! (Romans 7:15, 19-25)

Why did I do it? How often have you asked yourself that question? Time and again, just like the Apostle Paul, we find ourselves doing exactly the opposite of what we intended. The reasons, of course, are many and varied: greed, envy, lust and pride, to name but a few. Yet why is it that we struggle sometimes to control these, no matter how much we long to? That is a much deeper question, which people will answer in different ways according to their perspective on life. For Paul it pointed to the essentially fallen nature of humanity: what some might term original sin; what others would simply call human weakness. We could debate the issues involved for the rest of our days and still not exhaust them. We could struggle to overcome our faults with every fibre of our body, yet be no nearer success at the end than at the beginning.

Thankfully, as Paul reminds us, we can also spend the rest of our days, and those beyond, at peace with God and ourselves, for what *we* cannot deal with has been decisively dealt with by *him* through his living, dying and rising among us in Christ. No wonder Paul ended his outburst of frustration in an outpouring of praise: 'Thanks be to God through Jesus Christ our Lord!'

Forgiving others

Learning to forgive

Peter approached him and said, 'Lord, how often should I let someone sin against me and still forgive them? As many as seven times?' Jesus said to him, 'Not seven times, but, I tell you, seventy-seven times.' (Matthew 18:21-22)

How hard it is to say sorry when we've made a mistake. To do that means swallowing our pride, overcoming our embarrassment and laying ourselves open to a possible rebuff. It is far easier, though far less satisfactory, to keep our head down and wait for the hurt to subside. But if 'sorry' can be the hardest word to say, there are three words, directly related, which can be even more difficult to mean: 'I forgive you.' We may be happy enough to say that; we may want to mean it and genuinely believe that we do, but to really forgive someone in the true sense of the word is a rare gift indeed. All too often a past mistake is dredged up again in the heat of anger; an error which we considered long-since forgotten suddenly thrown back in our face. Probably each of us is as guilty of doing that as any.

With God, it is different. When we confess our sins and are truly sorry, they are put behind us, over and done with. There will be no going back to them later, no dragging them up to use against us; it is as if they never were. That's the good news. The bad news is this: God wants us to show that same level of forgiveness to others. It's a lot to ask and we will probably always finally fail, but if we are serious about discipleship we need to try. If God can forgive us, who are we not to forgive in turn?

A second chance

A few days later, Paul suggested to Barnabas, 'Let's pay a return visit to every city where we have announced the word of the Lord, to see how the believers are getting on there.' Barnabas wanted to take John Mark with them, but Paul felt it inappropriate to take someone who had deserted them in Pamphylia and failed to accompany them in their work. A sharp disagreement ensued, as a result of which they parted company; Barnabas took Mark with him and sailed to Cyprus, while Paul, having chosen Silas, set out on his journey, commended by the believers to the Lord's grace. He went through Syria and Cilicia, affirming the work of the churches there. (Acts 15:36-41)

'Once bitten, twice shy', we sometimes say, and so it was for the Apostle Paul. He'd set off on the first of his missionary journeys with Barnabas and John Mark as his trusted companions, these two clearly those he especially looked to for support, encouragement and inspiration. Mark, though, had found the going tough; so tough, in fact, that midway through their itinerary, he felt compelled to call it a day, no longer able to cope with the endless demands and privations. It was an understandable reaction from a young man at the end of his tether, but for Paul it was unforgivable. In his view, Mark had jeopardised his God-given mission, and he was in no mood to make allowances.

Barnabas was different. Whereas Paul felt unable ever to trust Mark again, he was ready to give him a second chance.

I can't help feeling that Paul should have known better; after all, hadn't he once been given a second chance himself, enabling him to start a new life? Like Mark, like Paul, like every Christian, we too have been given not only a second chance but as many chances as it takes; God's love and patience is never exhausted. Unlike Paul, are we ready to give those who have let us down a second chance?

Turning the other cheek

You have heard that it was said, 'An eye for an eye and a tooth for a tooth.' Yet I say to you, do not resist an evildoer, but if someone strikes you on the right cheek, offer the other cheek too. (Matthew 5:38-39)

An eye for an eye and a tooth for a tooth – that is the rule we find in the Old Testament, and it is one some feel we should still live by today, not least the proponents of corporal and capital punishment. Most of us prefer a less extreme kind of justice, based, in theory at least, on reform and reintegration rather than retribution. Should *we* be the one wronged, however, the desire for revenge would probably not be so far beneath the surface as we might like to think. What would we give to get our own back in such circumstances? If the chance were to present itself there is every possibility that we might just take it.

The law of Christ is different. It does not rule out some kind of retribution, for to do that would be to deny any kind of justice or morality in the universe, but it tells us to leave such matters in the hands of God. The best way to respond is with love, not hatred; to meet evil with good and inhumanity with compassion – a way exemplified by Gordon Wilson who, in November 1987, amazed the world by publicly forgiving the terrorists whose bomb at Enniskillen injured him and killed his daughter Marie. His humble Christian witness over the ensuing years, and that of others like him, has stirred hearts and quickened consciences, in no small part paving the way for new initiatives towards peace. I'm not sure that I could do what he did, for I know if someone harmed me or, worse still, my loved ones, the desire for vengeance would be overwhelming. Yet I know too that such a response leads only to an endless cycle of violence and hatred that ultimately destroys all. It is the Gordon Wilsons of this world who help us to glimpse the logic of the way of Christ.

Creation

Stewardship of creation

The call to conserve

The earth is the Lord's and everything in it, the world and all those who live in it. In his hand are the innermost parts of the earth, and the mountain peaks belong to him. The sea is his, for he made it, and his hands shaped the dry land. (Psalm 24:1; Psalm 95:4)

An article in *The Ecologist* magazine a while ago offered a perspective on the story of Noah's flood that I had not considered before. It was nothing revolutionary: based simply on the observation that God commanded Noah to take two of every living creature into the ark. What was the reason for that? The truth, it was argued, is that not only humankind but the whole of creation matters to God. It is not ours to exploit willy-nilly, as we sometimes seem to imagine; he has a place in his heart for everything he has made. Do we as Christians take that seriously? We may think we do, but how many of us show it in the way we live.

There seems little doubt that the world today is in the grip of a growing ecological crisis. Sadly, the response from the Church has typically been muted, one Christian even suggesting to me that such matters should not concern us since our future is in heaven rather than on earth. I, for one, cannot accept such a simplistic response. Indeed, I wonder sometimes if those who call us to wake up to our environmental responsibilities, whether they be Christian or otherwise, are the true prophets of our time. If the earth is the Lord's, as we claim, then do we not owe it to him to take care of it, if not for our sakes then for his?

Caring for creation

The heavens extol the glory of God; the firmament testifies to his handiwork. Each day witnesses eloquently and each night communicates knowledge, without need of speech, language or any other voice. Their music pervades all the earth; the words of their mouth reach out to the furthest parts of the world. (Psalm 19:1-4)

Across the years, few things have spoken more powerfully of God's presence than the wonder of nature. Take the words of the poet William Wordsworth:

The sun, above the mountain's head,
a freshening lustre mellow
through all the long green fields has spread,
his first sweet evening yellow.

Books! 'tis a dull and endless strife:
come, hear the woodland linnet,
how sweet his music! on my life,
there's more of wisdom in it.

And hark! how blithe the throstle sings!
he, too, is no mean preacher:
come forth into the light of things,
let Nature be your teacher.

One impulse from a vernal wood
may teach you more of man,
of moral evil and of good,
than all the sages can.

From *The Tables Turned*

All this is not to idealise nature, for there is much within it that is harsh and even ugly. Yet this can never detract from the loveliness of so much around us: the awesomeness of the stars at night, the simple yet exquisite beauty of a bird singing or a bud bursting into bloom, the evocative smell of the sea or scent of a wild flower. These speak not just of the wonder of this world but also of the splendour of God. We need to thank him for such treasures, but, more than that, we need to recognise our duty to safeguard these for future generations. Ecological responsibility in an age of global warming and unprecedented environmental exploitation is not just an optional extra – for the Christian it is central to faithful discipleship.

Stewards of creation

The Lord is a great God, a great king over all gods. In his hands are the depths of the earth, as well as the hills and valleys. The sea is his, he made it, together with the dry land, fashioned by his hands. Come! Let us prostrate ourselves in worship, let us kneel before the Lord who made us, for he is our God and we are his people, the flock that he shepherds. (Psalm 95:3-7a)

One of the first acts of George W. Bush, on his accession to the US presidency, was to cancel American support for the Kyoto agreement on greenhouse gases and climate change. Given his record as a state governor, it was pretty much par for the course, yet even the most hardened observers must have caught their breath at the stunning cynicism of his actions. The world today is facing intolerable pressures, and the threat of ecological catastrophe is all too real, yet the richest country in the world, responsible for well over half of all greenhouse gas emissions, saw fit to turn its back on the most important international agreement on the environment so far negotiated.

The reason? Money. And there, in a nutshell, is the issue at the heart of environmental change. Most of us claim to be concerned about the environment, yet we baulk when it comes to paying more for a truly green product. We say we abhor waste, yet make little effort to recycle rather than throw things away. We wring our hands over pollution, yet we think nothing of hopping into the car rather than walk or cycle. If we really believe that this is God's world held by us in trust, can we ever justify such carelessness? As Christians, we not only need to add our voices to the mounting calls for a sensible stewarding of creation; we also need to live in such a way that we give a lead through our actions. To fail in that is to betray the responsibility God has placed into our hands.

Glimpsing God in creation

Open our eyes

Look at the birds of the air; they do not sow or reap or store away in barns, and yet your heavenly Father feeds them. Are you not much more valuable than they? See how the lilies of the field grow. They do not labour or spin, yet I tell you that not even Solomon in all his grandeur was clothed like one of these. If that is how God clothes the grass of the field, which is here today yet tomorrow is thrown on to the fire, will he not much more clothe you, O you of little faith? (Matthew 6:26, 28-30)

You may recall that a while back 3-D pictures were all the rage. Open virtually any magazine or newspaper, it seemed, and you would be confronted with a curious pattern of dots and colours, which, we were told, would reveal a wonderful three-dimensional image when focused on in a particular way. Could you ever see it? I never did. That's the thing about sight; we don't all see things in quite the same way. An old saying puts it well: 'Two men looked out through prison bars; one saw mud, the other saw stars.' I like that. Where one sees ugliness another sees beauty, where one sees despair another sees hope. That's not to say that everything is subjective; rather that on occasions we need to have our eyes opened to the wonder of something before we appreciate it.

That is what Jesus was saying to the crowd gathered to hear his teaching: look properly at the ordinary things of life – something as commonplace as a flower in the meadow – and you will see God's hand behind it. To the eye of faith, life takes on a completely new dimension, speaking not just of the beauty of this world but also of the loving purposes of God. Let our prayer each day be that he might open our eyes to glimpse a little more clearly his presence all around us.

Daily life,
——— finding and serving God ———

Finding God

The word of the Lord came to Nathan: Go and tell my servant David, 'This is the word of the Lord: Are you the person to build a house for me to live in? Down to the day I brought Israel up out of Egypt, I have never lived in a house, but have journeyed in a tent and a tabernacle. Wherever I journeyed with Israel, did I ever ask any of those I appointed as leaders to shepherd my people Israel: "Why haven't you built me a house of cedar?"' (2 Samuel 7:4-7)

Where do we find God? The answer, of course, is everywhere. Yet, though we know that to be true, we can act sometimes as though the reality is otherwise. We treat 'church' as if God is especially present there; as if meeting together gives us special access in a way no other situation can offer. It is an understandable mistake, for in worship we set time aside for God and so may well be particularly conscious of his presence, but, as those fascinating words of Nathan to David show us, this runs the risk of getting things back to front.

David wanted to build a glorious temple in Jerusalem where people could go to honour God. His motives were laudable enough, but as Nathan reminded David, the scheme overlooked the fact that God could never be tied down to one place, he having constantly travelled beside his people through all the ups and downs of their history. Wherever they had been, whatever they had faced, he had been there with them. For the Israelites, his presence was symbolised by the Ark of the Covenant that they carried with them; for us today it is experienced yet more closely through the indwelling of the Holy Spirit. Where do we find God? In church, certainly; in times of quiet prayer and reflection – then too; but he is also present throughout our lives, involved in every aspect of every day. Wherever we are, whatever we experience, he is there, waiting to meet us!

Idle hands

I passed by the field of one who was lazy, by the vineyard of someone with no sense; and I saw that it was all overrun with thistles; the ground strewn with weeds, and its stone wall in ruins. I took careful note of what I saw; I looked and received instruction. A quick doze, a brief nap, a little folding of the hands to rest, and poverty will come upon you like a thief, and want like a brigand. (Proverbs 24:30-34)

For some people the very thought of hard work makes them go weak at the knees, to the point that they keep on putting it off, ad infinitum. Others simply get stuck in, and in no time at all the job gets done. Most of us are probably somewhere in between. We do what's expected of us – most of the time anyway – and perhaps just occasionally, if we're feeling especially virtuous, we do that little bit extra; yet somehow there's always a few things left undone, just enough to niggle away in the back of the mind and disturb our peace. We know we've got to do it, but we just can't summon up the enthusiasm. We realise it will have to be done eventually, yet we invariably succeed in putting it off one more day.

Is it worth it? We may buy ourselves a little time – an evening together away from the children, an all too rare morning lie-in, an afternoon on the beach, but the thought of that unfinished job is always there, haunting us like some tantalising spectre. The longer we leave it the worse the prospect becomes and the less we feel inclined to do it. If we are not careful, we slip into a self-perpetuating downward spiral, achieving ever less as we prevaricate all the more. The warnings of Solomon in the book of Proverbs may seem somewhat over the top, but beware, the danger may be more real than you think.

Unsung disciples

Jesus sent Peter and John, with the words, 'Go and make ready the Passover meal so that we might share it together.' They replied, 'Where would you like us to prepare it?' 'Listen,' he answered, 'the moment you enter the city you'll be met by a man carrying a water jar. Follow him into the house he enters and say to the one who owns the house, "The teacher says, 'Where is the room where I can share Passover with my disciples?'" He'll lead you to a spacious and furnished upstairs room. Get things ready there.' They did as he asked, and everything worked out just as he said, so they prepared the Passover celebration. (Luke 22:8-13)

'First, I'd like to thank my wife and family for their faithful support; then, there's my manager, my agent, my friends . . .' We've all heard speeches like that, haven't we? Whether it's an Oscar winner, a sports personality having just won a prestigious event, an author awarded the Booker prize, or any other celebrity achieving recognition in their chosen field, the routine is much the same. And why not, for each of us, famous or otherwise, have people to whom we owe much; those who have helped make things possible. The speeches may often be boring, even embarrassing to listen to, but they nonetheless give well-deserved thanks to those behind the scenes.

There are no such speeches associated with Jesus in the days leading up to the cross, but there are hints of at least two people who played such an incognito role. The first was the owner of the colt upon which Jesus rode into Jerusalem. It only needed the disciples to say, 'The Lord needs it', for him gladly to let it go. The second was the owner of the upper room in which Jesus and the Apostles shared the Last Supper. Again, we have no idea who he was, but he also played his part in allowing Jesus to use his room in this way. These two shadowy individuals remind us that we can offer service in simple, practical ways that are no less valuable than 'spiritual' contributions. Our gifts may not be those that catch the eye, and it may be that we prefer it that way, but that does not mean we have nothing to offer. All of us have a part to play in God's kingdom and all have something to contribute in the service of Christ.

Daily relationships

see also Love: Loving others

Anger

Dealing with anger

Give vent to anger, yet do not sin; never let the sun set on your anger, thus making room for the devil. (Ephesians 4:26-27)

Few of us never lose our temper. For those cursed with a short fuse it can be a common occurrence, whilst for those of a more phlegmatic disposition it may be something of a rarity, but all of us have our threshold where something snaps inside and we fly into a rage.

There is, of course, a place for anger, as Jesus showed on more than one occasion during his ministry. Confronted with evil and injustice, actions or attitudes that prevent people from living life to the full, it is not only natural but necessary. Yet more often than not anger is sparked by very different motives – wounded pride, frustration, intolerance, an unwillingness to face the truth, or simply misunderstanding. It doesn't take much to send the blood rushing to our heads, but it can take a great deal to put right the consequences of one moment's madness.

Disagreements

Agreeing to disagree

I beg Euodia and Syntyche to share a common mind in the Lord. And yes, I ask you, my trustworthy colleague, to help them both, for they struggled with me in the cause of the gospel, alongside Clement and my other fellow-workers, each of whose names is in the book of life. (Philippians 4:2-3)

When were you last involved in an argument? Probably more recently than you care to remember. What begins as a healthy disagreement invariably seems to develop into a full-blown quarrel. At times this may have good cause, but just as often it is about something futile, and the issues so hotly disputed are of little or no importance. What had come between Euodia and Syntyche we are not told, but it is clear that daggers were drawn and others were inexorably being drawn into the conflict. Sadly, once a quarrel starts, it develops a life of its own; the smallest of details magnified out of all proportion until the initial difference of opinion is lost behind a mountain of real or imagined slights. How many families have been divided, friendships broken and feuds started through the most trivial of disagreements? A quarrel is easy to start and hard to end – far better to avoid it in the first place.

Living in peace

How good and pleasant it is when kindred live together in unity! It is as fragrant as oil poured over the head and running down upon the beard, running down the beard of Aaron and over the collar of his robes. It is like the dew of Hermon falling on the mountains of Zion. There the Lord grants his blessing, life for all eternity. (Psalm 133)

There are few things sadder, yet more common, than a divided family. Yet it is something we see over and over again: husbands who no longer speak to wives; children who have fallen out with their parents; brothers, sisters, cousins, nephews, aunts and uncles, each disowning the other and refusing to have any further dealings with them. As if that isn't sad enough, invariably the cause of such bad feeling is something trivial, blown up out of all proportion over the years because of an unwillingness to meet and resolve the issue. Unchecked, the poison festers, feeding on itself and destroying the lives of all concerned.

Whether a dispute such as this or something more complex lies behind Psalm 133, I do not know. The reminder this simple psalm gives, however, of the importance of living together in harmony is one we would all do well to consider, whether at the level of our immediate family or the family of the Church. The relationships we are intended to enjoy in both are special; we simply cannot afford to waste them.

Encouraging, supporting and enabling

Being there

Judas and Silas, being prophets themselves, encouraged and built up the fellowship there. After they had been with them some time, the believers sent them back in peace to those who had sent them. However, it seemed right to Silas to remain there. Similarly, Paul and Barnabas, and many others, remained in Antioch, teaching and preaching the word of the Lord. (Acts 15:32-35)

If I said the names 'Paul' and 'Silas' in the same breath, which one would you immediately recognise? The answer, of course, is Paul, the celebrated Apostle who did so much to further the gospel during the early days of the Church. We can overlook the fact that for many of his missionary journeys he was accompanied by Silas, but though we might forget the contribution Silas made, Paul never did.

What was it, then, that made Paul value Silas so much? For one thing, Silas may have acted as his scribe, recording his letters as he dictated them. For another, he clearly had gifts in his own right, regarded as a leader of the Church among Christians back in Jerusalem. Perhaps, though,what stood out above all else was, quite simply, his willingness to be there when needed. Whatever Paul came up against, he knew that Silas would be ready to face it with him. Imprisoned, beaten, attacked, insulted, it made no difference – he remained a friend in need, someone to lean on in moments of crisis. Never underestimate that gift, for it is one of the most precious there is, and one that each of us can show in our turn. It may not seem much – simply being there – yet for someone going through the mill it can mean more than any words or action.

Encouraging others

Joseph – a Levite and Cypriot by descent – who had been nicknamed Barnabas by the Apostles, meaning 'Son of Encouragement', sold the land that he owned and laid the proceeds at the Apostles' feet. (Acts 4:36-37)

When we read the pages of scripture, hear dramatic stories of testimony, or meet sparkling Christians, it's hard sometimes not to feel a little daunted. Few of us have eye-catching gifts and it is unlikely that any contribution we may make will hit the headlines. That's why stories like that of Barnabas are so important. He wasn't one of the Apostles, nor one whose name has gone down in history for stunning signs and wonders, but I suspect had you taken a poll among the early Christians as to who in the Church meant most to them, Barnabas would have been one of the leading contenders to come out on top. Why? Because he had that most precious of gifts: the ability to encourage. In the verses above, it was through his generosity. In Acts 9:26-27 we see it through his trust, introducing the newly converted Paul to the Apostles when others still doubted his conversion. In Acts 15:36-39 he did it again, this time bringing encouragement to John Mark, giving him a second chance when Paul felt it too risky. We see it, yet once more, in Acts 11:23-24, where we read, 'when he arrived and saw the evidence of the grace of God, he was glad and encouraged them all to remain true to the Lord'. His was an unsung gift but a vital one; the sort that releases all kinds of gifts in others.

Are we the sort of people who encourage others, or do we discourage instead: seeing difficulties, highlighting weakness, stifling enthusiasm? There is no excuse: we may not possess show-stopping gifts but all of us, without exception, can offer a ministry of encouragement.

Sharing the load

Bear one another's burdens, and so fulfil the law of Christ. (Galatians 6:2)

To say it was heavy was an understatement: it was like a lead weight – a suitcase crammed full to overflowing as I set off to the railway station to catch the train back to college. Unsurprisingly, the handle could not cope. A hundred yards up the road and it came off in my hand, the case crashing down and bursting open, spilling the contents everywhere. How glad I was, having stuffed everything back in again and bodily wrestled with the load for the rest of the journey, to be offered a helping hand by one of my fellow-students as I lugged it up to my room. Such a weight was too much to carry by myself and I learned never to try it again.

Few people avoid carrying a burden of some sort. It may not be a physical load but it is no less difficult to bear for that. The weight of guilt, fear, sorrow, despair, anxiety and pain, to name but a few examples, can be equally crushing and far more so. We cannot shoulder such burdens for others, much though we might sometimes wish we could, but we can share them, not least through listening and showing we care. To be there to share the load in such a way means more than we might imagine.

Thinking of you

Tychicus will pass on all the news about me; he is a much-loved brother, a faithful minister, and a fellow servant in the Lord. I have sent him to you with one aim in mind: to let you know how we are and to encourage your hearts through him. He will come with Onesimus, that faithful and beloved brother from among your own ranks. Together, they will let you know what's been happening here. Aristarchus, my fellow-prisoner, greets you, as does Mark, Barnabas' cousin, about whom you have been instructed – if he comes to you, welcome him. Similarly, Jesus, also known as Justus, sends you greetings. (Colossians 4:7-11a)

How often have you promised to write to somebody and then not done so; or assured a friend that you will pray for them, only for it to slip your mind? If you are anything like me, you will have done so more times than you care to remember. Such forgetfulness is perhaps understandable but it is also regrettable, for it does us all good to know that someone is thinking of us. I remember receiving a letter several years ago from an old friend whom I had not seen since student days. What prompted her to write I have no idea, but it was heartwarming to know that the experiences we had shared at university so long before still meant something. No doubt, we can all testify to similar experiences, when an unexpected card, letter or phone call brought us encouragement and inspiration.

The Apostle Paul recognised how much it meant for someone to stay in touch, as his many letters in the New Testament illustrate. He wrote for a variety of reasons, but his chief concern was simply to let those churches he had been instrumental in setting up know that he was thinking of them. However difficult their circumstances may have been, however severe a time of testing they were facing, he wanted them to know that they were not alone. How far do we make a point of remembering those we can no longer be present with in the flesh? More important, how often do we let those people know we are thinking of them? We talk often in high-flown language about love, fellowship and service without actually doing much to make these real. Staying in touch with someone and showing we care is a very simple yet meaningful way of putting such words into practice.

Behind the scenes

Give my greetings to Mary, who laboured so hard on your behalf. Greet Urbanus, our fellow-worker in Christ, and my beloved friend Stachys. Greet Apelles, who has proven himself in Christ. Greet Tryphena and Tryphosa, those women who have also worked so hard in the Lord. Greet my dear friend Persis, who has toiled in so many ways for the Lord's sake. Greet Rufus, chosen in the Lord, and his mother, who has been a mother to me, too. Greet Asyncritus, Phlegon, Hermas, Patrobas, Hermes and the brothers with them. Greet Philologus, Julia, Nereus and his sister, and Olympas and all the saints with them. (Romans 16:6, 9-10a, 12-15)

How often do you read the credits at the end of a film or television programme? The answer is probably never; most of us switch off our attention the moment the action has ended. Those credits, however, remind us that more people are involved in a production than simply those who appear onscreen. Producer, director, camera crew, musicians, make-up department, lighting technicians and numerous others – all play a part in perfecting the finished article. Bear that in mind when you come to the lists of names, such as the one above, that typically end the letters of Paul. The temptation is to skim through these – particularly given the tongue-twisting nature of some of them! – yet that is to miss an important point. The people referred to may not have gone down in history as spiritual giants, yet their contribution was nonetheless vital.

These, if you like, were Paul's backroom staff; those who encouraged, supported, nurtured or worked alongside him behind the scenes. Paul may have made the headlines but, without their tireless involvement, he couldn't have functioned as he did.

We do well to remember how easy it is to overlook those working in the background. Unglamorous tasks such as cleaning, catering, cooking, washing-up, preparing the minutes, arranging flowers and so on – do we ever show our appreciation for such things? All too often, we take them for granted when a word of thanks would mean so much. Conversely, you may be one of those undertaking such work. If so, never underrate the part God has called you to play, for it is as important as any other. We all have different gifts and different roles – let's remember to value them all.

Envy

The folly of envy

Who is wise and discerning among you? Show by the quality of your life and works a sensitivity stemming from wisdom. If your hearts are filled with sourness, envy and selfish ambition, do not take pride in it and flout the truth. Such wisdom is not God-given, but is earthly, secular and fiendish, for where there is envy and self-centred ambition there will correspondingly be turmoil and evil of every kind. (James 3:13-16)

When I was training for the ministry, a certain poster was in vogue among my college colleagues. It was a cartoon depicting four cows in adjoining fields, each leaning over a fence to munch the grass in their neighbour's field. And the caption? Well, there was no need for one, was there? It delightfully illustrated that old saying about the grass always being greener on the other side, and, illusory though that greener grass may be, it is so true of the way we think. Instead of being content with what we have we just can't help looking jealously at those around us, eyeing up their latest acquisition, their comfortable lifestyle, their beautiful house, and wishing it was ours. A daily bombardment of advertising wards off any possibility of us coming to our senses.

Occasionally, of course, the grass *is* greener, in material terms anyway. But if we allow ourselves to get sucked into the whirlpool of envy, then the quality of our lives will spiral downwards, for in time it will poison our perception of everything.

Friendship and loneliness

A friend in need

Ruth said, 'Do not urge me to turn back and abandon you. Wherever you go, I will go; wherever you stop, I will stop; your people will be my people, and your God my God. Where you die, I will die and be buried. In God's name, I swear that not even death will part me from you!' (Ruth 1:16-17)

What kind of friend are you? Are you the sort who can be depended on in a crisis, or the fair-weather variety, swift to vanish into the night the moment there is any suggestion that commitment might cost you something? Naturally we all like to think we're the former – true, loyal, trustworthy – but ask yourself honestly: how many people are there you would be willing to make sacrifices for?

For the Christian, not only should friendships possess a special quality, but the very concept of friendship has been widened by Jesus to include those both near and far, those we are close to and those who will always be strangers. To demonstrate such friendship is hard indeed and few will get anywhere near it, but today we are reminded of the devotion of Ruth who, centuries before Christ, showed herself to be a friend in need. What is God saying to you about your service to others through her example?

Will you be my friend?

Only Luke is with me. (2 Timothy 4:11a)

What would you say is the greatest social problem of our time? Homelessness? Poverty? Unemployment? There can certainly be no denying the pain each of these causes, but let me suggest another problem, equally widespread and involving immeasurable pain. I speak of loneliness. We live in a world today where people are crying out for companionship, and I don't just mean the elderly or housebound, though for these the problem may be most acute. It is true of people from all walks of life and all ages, condemned to increasing isolation in an ever more fragmented society. For some this means the agony of scarcely meeting another human being from week to week; for others the equal, if not more intense, pain of feeling utterly alone, even when part of a crowd.

So how should we respond? If we are lonely, perhaps we need to reach out to another in friendship and break the ice – it may well be that the other person is equally as lonely as us. If, on the other hand, we know someone is lonely, perhaps we can do something to help. It needn't take much: a word of greeting, a solicitous phone call, even a cheery wave can mean the world to someone crying out for human contact. Whoever you are, try reaching out the hand of friendship – the results might surprise you.

Honesty and integrity

Do as you would be done by

Laban had two daughters, the oldest called Leah, and the younger, Rachel. Leah had appealing eyes, but Rachel was both attractive and elegant. Jacob fell for Rachel, and so he said, 'I will give you seven years' service in return for your youngest daughter Rachel.' Laban answered, 'I'd rather give her to you than any other man. Stay and work for me, certainly.' So Jacob served his seven years for Rachel, and such was his love that they seemed just a few days. Then Jacob said to Laban, 'I've honoured my pledge. Give me my wife for I want to sleep with her.' So Laban invited everyone in the region and staged a banquet. That evening he took his daughter Leah and brought her to Jacob, and they slept together. When dawn came, he realised it was Leah! (Genesis 29:16-23)

Your sins, we are told, will find you out. Is that true? It was for Jacob. While it is hard not to feel sorry for him being duped so outrageously on his wedding day, there is a delicious irony in his being hoodwinked in much the same way as he had cynically deceived his father to filch the blessing intended for his brother Esau. Whether Laban had decided on a little restorative justice or whether we glimpse here God's sense of humour, I'm not sure. It would be wrong to draw simplistic conclusions from this, for much of the time cheats seem to prosper, corruption reaps handsome rewards and evil goes unpunished. Nonetheless, here is ample support for that old proverb, 'Do as you would be done by.' Jacob's experience offers a salutary reminder that there is accountability in this life as well as the next. If we spin a web of deceit, the chances are that we will end up getting caught in it ourselves.

Cruel to be kind

Well-intended are the wounds inflicted by a friend, but effusive are the kisses of an enemy. (Proverbs 27:6)

'Be truthful, now – what do you think?' How many times have you been asked a question like that? And the chances are, when it came, your heart sank, for you knew full well that the judgement you were being asked to make would cause upset, if not outright offence. The truth can hurt. Few find it easy to be honest in awkward situations like those, and fewer still relish facing home truths about themselves.

Yet sometimes we need people with the courage to do just that if we are to see ourselves as we really are and so find the spur we need to rectify our faults. In the words of the Greek philosopher Socrates: 'Think not those faithful who praise all thy words and actions, but those who kindly reprove thy faults.' Have you the courage to speak the painful truth to others? More important still, are you willing to hear it spoken to you in turn?

Hitting home

The Lord sent the prophet Nathan to David, and he came before him saying, 'There were two men in a certain city, one rich and the other poor. The rich man owned numerous flocks and herds, whereas the poor man could afford just one young ewe lamb. He hand-reared this so that it grew up with him and his children. It ate out of his meagre resources, drank from his cup and lay in his arms, treated as though it was his own daughter. One day, however, a traveller visited the rich man and, reluctant to use one of his own animals to prepare a meal for his visitor, he took the poor man's lamb and prepared that for his guest instead.' On hearing this, David was incensed at the man's behaviour. He said to Nathan, 'As the Lord lives, the man who did this deserves to die; in recompense for his deed and in punishment for his lack of pity, he shall pay for that lamb four times over!' Then Nathan said to David, 'You are the man!' (2 Samuel 12:1-7)

Have you ever been asked to confront someone with an awkward truth? If so, then you will appreciate just how hard that is. Over the years, the lot seems to have disproportionately fallen to me more often than I would have wished, the reason being, according to others, that

I am more diplomatic than most. It's a kind thought, but entirely misplaced. The reality is that I skirt gingerly around the subject, treading on eggshells rather than cause offence, vainly hoping that the penny might drop. Occasionally, a softly-softly approach such as that may succeed but, more often than not, it will fall on deaf ears. It's far better sometimes to speak the truth candidly. Yes, it may hurt, raise people's hackles, even make an enemy for life, but, if it helps someone grow as an individual, it is ultimately a kindness.

Nathan had that sort of courage. The message God gave him to speak was not an easy one, almost bound to meet with a hostile reception, yet the words needed saying if David was to recognise the error of his ways and find forgiveness. There are times when we need to confront individuals or society as a whole with unpalatable truths. Have we the courage of Nathan to meet that challenge?

Judging others

Beyond the obvious

The Lord does not see as people see, for they look at appearances, but the Lord sees into the heart. (1 Samuel 16:7b)

Have you come across the book *Timpson's England*? If you haven't, then you've missed a treat. Written by John Timpson, the radio broadcaster, it is subtitled 'A look beyond the obvious', and that captures the book's essence perfectly. Through words and pictures, the author highlights some of the things that most people tend to pass by without even noticing them; objects and items small in themselves – a corbel here, an inscription there, a plaque, signpost, house or monument – yet which add immeasurably to an appreciation of our rich heritage.

Such an ability to look beyond the obvious is not only important in relation to objects and places but also when it comes to people, for invariably there is more to those we meet than appearances may suggest. All too easily we make snap judgements based on appearances rather than first getting to know the person underneath. Once you take the time to do that, the majority of people prove to be full of surprises, revealing unexpected gifts and qualities. Thankfully, although we tend to see what is only superficial, God looks deeper. Let our prayer be to see with his eyes, and so to glimpse the hidden riches in one another that all too often we never begin to recognise.

Digging deeper

The Lord said to Samuel, 'I want you to go to Jesse in Bethlehem, for I have chosen one of his sons to be king.' Samuel followed the Lord's instructions, and went to Bethlehem. The moment he spotted Eliab he thought, 'This must be the one God has chosen to be anointed.' But the Lord said to Samuel, 'Don't be taken in by good looks or physique, because I have rejected him. The Lord does not see as people see, for they look at appearances, but the Lord sees into the heart.' Then Jesse called Abinadab, and made him pass before Samuel, but he said, 'No, this isn't the Lord's chosen one.' Then Jesse presented Shammah, but again Samuel said, 'No, he's not the chosen one either.' Jesse made seven of his sons pass before Samuel, but Samuel said, 'The Lord has not chosen any of these.' Finally, Samuel asked Jesse, 'Are all your sons here?' He answered, 'There is one more, the youngest, but he is out looking after the sheep.' Samuel said to Jesse, 'Send for him; we will not sit down until he's here.' Jesse sent for him to be fetched in. He was handsome; his cheeks glowing and eyes shining. The Lord said, 'Get up, and anoint him; for this is the one.' So Samuel took the horn of oil, and anointed him in the presence of his brothers. (1 Samuel 16:1b, 4a, 6-13a)

Some years ago, a newspaper ran an advertising campaign based on the slogan 'One million . . . readers can't be wrong'. The implication was that if enough people subscribe to something, it must be right. It is human nature to want to follow the crowd. Those who question the established norms of society are branded as heretics, eccentrics or even revolutionaries, their challenge conveniently side-stepped through the use of such dismissive labels. Sometimes, questions may be misplaced, but equally there are times when they need asking, faith having to take a critical look at the values the world takes for granted if it is to be true to itself.

So it was for Samuel, sent by God to the house of Jesse to anoint a new ruler over Israel. He went there, imagining he was a shrewd judge of character, well able to discern God's will. He came away recognising he had much still to learn about the ways of God, who sees far deeper than most of us even begin to see. His experience counsels us never to judge by appearances and never to imagine we have understood all there is to understand.

Finding fault

Seeing that he ate with tax collectors and sinners, the scribes and Pharisees challenged his disciples, saying, 'How is it that he eats with such people?' And it happened that he was passing through some cornfields on the Sabbath, and as they made their way through these, his disciples began plucking some ears of corn. The Pharisees said to him, 'Look at what they are doing! Why do you allow them to do what is unlawful on the Sabbath?' And he entered a synagogue, and there was a man there with a shrivelled hand. And they watched him carefully, to see if he would heal on the Sabbath, looking for an opportunity to accuse him. (Mark 2:16, 23-24; 3:1-2)

It is easy when reading verses like these about the scribes and Pharisees to shake our heads and tut in disapproval at their misguided attitudes, yet to do that is to make the same mistake they did: to find fault. How often are we guilty of just that – swift to see the worst, slow to see the best; eager to criticise, reluctant to praise? We ignore a thousand good things and focus instead on one bad point, we destroy and undermine rather than build up and encourage, yet so often the faults we dwell on are trivial compared to our own.

Perhaps more disturbing still is that this response came from the overtly religious, those who believed themselves to be right with God. In similar fashion, the Church across the years has frequently been associated with narrow and nit-picking attitudes rather than a joyful celebration of all that is good. Don't let such a carping and negative spirit find a place in your life, for not only does it cause pain to others; ultimately it makes *us* the biggest losers, blinding us not only to one another but, above all, to God himself.

Judge not

Why do you judge your brother or sister? How is it you presume to look down on them? We will all stand before the judgement seat of God. For it is written, 'As I live, says the Lord, every knee shall bend to me, and every tongue shall confess God's name.' Each of us, therefore, will have to account for our actions before God. So then, let us no longer pass judgement on one another, but let us instead make up our minds never to put an obstacle or impediment in anyone's way. (Romans 14:10-13)

How well do you know those you mix with – your family or friends, your colleagues at work or fellow church members? You may think you know them, but do you? It's surprising how often when talking to someone – even someone we've known for long time – we suddenly discover a wholly unexpected facet to his or her character, which throws a completely new light on that person. Actions that previously made no sense suddenly fit into place; traits we found puzzling find a simple explanation. The experience can be profoundly humbling, bringing home all too sharply how easily and often we make judgements about people based on the flimsiest of facts. Perhaps more disturbing still is the realisation that others form conclusions about us in much the same way. No wonder, then, that the scriptures repeatedly warn us against judging others.

Pride

Recognising our limitations

Elisha sent out a messenger to Naaman, saying, 'If you wash yourself in the Jordan seven times, your skin will be made whole and you will be clean.' But Naaman was incensed and stormed away, saying, 'At the very least I expected him to come out to me, stand and call on the name of the Lord his God, and then brandish his hand over the spot, and so cure me of my leprosy! Surely the rivers of Damascus, Abana and Pharpar are infinitely superior to all the waters of Israel? Why can't I wash in them, and be clean?' He stomped off in a rage, but his servants approached him and said to him, 'My Lord, if the prophet had told you to do something complicated, would you not have done it? How much more then, when all he asks you to do is "Wash, and be clean"?' (2 Kings 5:10-13)

The higher we rise, the harder we fall – so conventional wisdom tells us. But there is another side to that observation, for we could equally say we must be brought low before we can rise high. In the story of Naaman both of these truths are well demonstrated. Asked to bathe in the muddy waters of the Jordan, Naaman storms off in a fit of pique; the idea of so demeaning himself was complete anathema. It takes the gentle coaxing of his entourage to make him see reason. What does a dent to his pride matter if it leads finally to personal wholeness? To his credit, Naaman succeeds in swallowing his pride and taking their advice.

We can hardly miss the absurdity of Naaman's initial reaction, yet do we recognise with equal clarity the same foolishness in ourselves? How often do we allow a misplaced sense of our own importance to blind us to the right way forward? How many times have we rejected sorely required help rather than admit our need of others? It is a natural human tendency to believe we can go it alone – the story of Naaman reminds us that we can't.

Seeking God's glory

Let your attitude be the same as that which distinguished Christ Jesus, who, though he was in the form of God, did not regard equality with God as something to be exploited. Instead, he emptied himself, taking the form of a servant and sharing our humanity, and, having taken on human form, he humbled himself to total obedience, even to the point of death – death on a cross. For that reason, God highly exalted him, giving him the name that is above every name, so that at the name of Jesus every being in heaven, on earth and under the earth should kneel, and every tongue should acknowledge that Jesus Christ is Lord, to the glory of God the Father. (Philippians 2:5-11)

During my ministry in Cheltenham, I had the opportunity once of touring a local radio station, and I got into conversation with the presenter of the station's Christian and religious programmes. It gave me a fascinating insight not only into the world of a radio presenter, but also into an aspect of human nature. The station, it turned out, operated on a tight budget, so much so that there was no way it could pay most of the people who appeared on its programmes. Presenters relied instead on individuals wanting to hear their voice on radio, eager to enjoy their few minutes of fame, and the system was eminently effective – there was never any shortage of applicants! Personally, the thought of being interviewed in any public forum fills me with cold dread, but I can understand the line of reasoning well enough. We all like to feel important, don't we? A bit of praise, appreciation, even admiration warms the cockles of one's heart, and there's nothing necessarily wrong with that – praise where praise is due has its place.

Yet, as Christians, we need to beware, for we are not in the business of drawing attention to ourselves. We can slip into that more easily than we might think; self-righteousness and self-congratulation being beguiling traps for the unwary. Paul points us instead to Jesus, the one who more than any other had reason to point to himself, but always his concern was to point to the Father and bring glory to him. Is that our concern too, the goal to which all our efforts are directed? Or is our faith, for all its outward piety, ultimately more about our own self-image; about what others may think of us rather than him? 'To God be the glory', says the old hymn. How far do our lives echo those words?

Relationships within the Church

Celebrating our diversity

Now there are various gifts but the same Spirit; various ministries but the same Lord; different types of service but the same God working through all of them. Just as the body is a unit having many members, with all the members, though many, being part of the one body, so it is with the body of Christ. If the foot were to say, because I am not a hand I am not part of the body, would it be any less a part of the body? If the ear were to say, because I am not an eye, I am not part of the body, would it not be part of it? If the whole body were an eye, how would we hear? If all were given over to hearing, how would we smell? God, however, has arranged every part of the body exactly as he wants it to be. If there were only one part, how could we talk of a body? The fact is that there are many members, but only one body. (1 Corinthians 12:4-6, 12, 15-20)

My wife and I did some decorating a while back. The room we were working on was gloomy, in need of a lift, so we decided to go for a creamy yellow. Decision made? Don't you believe it! The range of creamy yellows is unbelievable – 'Porcelain Bowl', 'Sunrise', 'Narcissus', 'Laughter', 'Buttermilk', 'Wicker', 'Ivory', 'Straw', to name but a few. These were all shades of yellow, yet they were all different, each with its own subtle nuance.

It doesn't take much to see where I'm going next, does it? Unity in diversity – what the Church is all about, or at least what it should be. We're all Christians – Anglican, Roman Catholic, Baptist, Methodist, Salvation Army, house church, and countless others – but we each have our own distinguishing characteristics. Within each denomination and individual fellowship, the same applies: an enormous variety of gifts, temperaments and experiences represented in every one of them. Is that a weakness? It can be, if we let it divide us, but it should be quite the opposite: a source of strength as we celebrate our unity in diversity. Imagine if there were just one shade of yellow – what an infinitely poorer place the world would be. So with the Church: we all profess Christ as Lord and all seek to follow him, but I doubt any two of us are the same. Thank God for that wonderful, astonishing and enriching diversity!

Meaningful membership *see also* Commitment

Now you are the body of Christ, each having your own place as members within it. (1 Corinthians 12:27)

Several years ago I joined the Society of Authors. It seemed a good idea at the time, if only because here was a body concerned with defending and promoting authors' rights. Every year since then, though, I have wondered whether it is worth renewing my subscription, not because of any fault on the society's part but because I have made no use whatsoever of my membership. I have been to none of its seminars or any of the regional get-togethers. I haven't met a single fellow-member, and due to the constant pressure of work I haven't even had time to read the society's quarterly magazine. In fact, all I do is stump up my yearly membership fee. Effectively, I am a nominal member, no more than a name on a bit of paper.

Such membership, of course, is meaningless, for belonging to any organisation should mean being involved and playing a part, all of which is worth bearing in mind when it comes to being part of the Church. We may carry the label 'Christian' but that by itself means nothing. We need to meet together, worship together and work together, united in the common cause of Christ. We need to offer not just our money but our time and effort, looking for ways in which our gifts can be used for the good of all. Above all, we need to make time for one another, so that we are not simply members on paper but a family in practice. To be a Christian means to be part of the body of Christ. Are we fulfilling our role within that?

A mixed bag

The names of the twelve Apostles were as follows: first, Simon, known as Peter, and his brother Andrew; then James son of Zebedee, and his brother John; Philip and Bartholomew; Thomas and Matthew, the tax collector; James son of Alphaeus, and Thaddaeus; Simon the Cananaean, and Judas Iscariot, the one who was later to betray him. (Matthew 10:1-4)

I shall always be grateful for my time at college and university. I studied there with people of different characters, backgrounds and ideas, with contrasting ideas and attitudes, representing a variety of denominations and faiths or no faith at all. We were in many ways a mixed bag, yet we were united by a common cause, a shared goal. The same could be said of the Apostles, a motley crew if ever there was one. They included a tax collector and a freedom fighter; an impulsive firebrand who wore his heart on his sleeve and a man who was to sneak off into the darkness to betray Jesus; some who were models of faith yet one who is remembered as an example of doubt – hardly those you would expect to hit it off. Yet these were those Jesus called to share in his ministry and, with the exception of Judas, those who carried it on afterwards. They didn't always see eye to eye – in fact, at times they were clearly at loggerheads – yet God was able to use them.

There is a parallel in all this with the Church today. Despite the pious twaddle we sometimes come out with, myself included, we are not always a happy family, everything sweetness and light between us. We are a curious mixture of people with different temperaments and convictions, hopes and fears, joys and sorrows, likes and dislikes. Whether these divide us or draw us closer together depends on how far we recognise that God loves us as we are, faults and all.

Shoulder to shoulder

Then I will cleanse the lips of the nations, that all people may call on the name of the Lord and serve him shoulder to shoulder. (Zephaniah 3:9)

Just a few years after the death of Jesus, Roman legions under the leadership of the emperor Claudius sailed across to Britain from Gaul and, before long, added the bulk of these shores to their already vast empire – another addition to a long list of successful conquests. So, what lay behind their astonishing success? Numerous factors were involved but few were more important than the simple yet highly effective tactic they followed in battle: the tactic of standing shoulder to shoulder and fighting as a co-ordinated unit. Not for them the wild undisciplined attacks of the Britons; instead, their success was built on teamwork, on working together come what may.

There is something of that idea in the wonderful words of the prophet Zephaniah as he looked towards a new era in which God's people would stand shoulder to shoulder in God's service; a time when instead of looking to their own interests, each would strive first for the kingdom of God. We can apply that picture to discipleship today. However great our resolve, there is little way we can grow as Christians without the stimulus and support of others. However great our faith, there is still less we can achieve in God's service on our own. If we are to make any impact on society, any significant difference to the world we live in, then we need to work together, both with those in our own fellowship and within the wider Church. Solitary discipleship may have its attractions, but ultimately it sells both God and self short. We are part of a new people, a holy nation, that God has called into being to serve him shoulder to shoulder in one faith and in the common cause of Christ.

An unbreakable bond

I appeal to you, brothers and sisters, in the name of our Lord Jesus Christ, agree among yourselves and avoid any division, so that you may be perfectly joined, of the same mind and united in a common purpose. (1 Corinthians 1:10)

Have you ever tried sticking metal with wood glue, or plastic with wallpaper paste? If you have, then you'll know you were wasting your time, for you were using the wrong tool for the job. Different glues are designed for different tasks, and what works for one may not work for another. Get it right, however, and you will create a bond to last.

Such should be the effect of the love we are called to share as Christians. The reality, sadly, is very different. For all the moves in recent years towards Church unity, there are as many if not more divisions today than ever, splinter groups breaking away over questions of doctrine, worship and church practice. Individual fellowships are equally marred by gossip, cliques, personality clashes, backbiting and so on. All too often, instead of testifying to the love of Christ, our relationships with other Christians speaks instead of our human fallibility, turning people away from the Church instead of drawing them towards it. There will always, of course, be differences of opinion and outlook among us, for we are all individuals with unique experiences of Christ. Similarly, there will be those we are more naturally drawn towards than others; that is a simple fact of life. If, though, we are truly 'in Christ', then the faith we share should transcend such differences, the love that unites us more powerful than anything that may divide.

Sensitivity towards others

Closed minds

He came to his native village and taught in the synagogue there in a manner that left all who heard him amazed, asking, 'From where did this man acquire such wisdom and the ability to perform such deeds of power? Surely, this is the carpenter's son? Isn't Mary his mother, and aren't James, Joseph, Simon and Judas his brothers? And don't his sisters live here among us? Where then did this man get these abilities?' And they took exception to him. But Jesus responded, 'A prophet is not without esteem, except among those of his own country or household.' And, due to their unbelief, his powerful deeds were few there. (Matthew 13:54-58)

Open-mindedness isn't always the quality it's cracked up to be. The way we use the term today, it is synonymous with an attitude of anything goes; anyone who dares to suggest that there are moral and ethical frontiers beyond which we should not venture being dismissed as bigoted, blinkered and out of touch with reality. The truth is, of course, that those who reason like this are themselves as narrow-minded as anyone, their minds steadfastly closed to the possibility that there could be limits to human freedom.

Open-mindedness doesn't necessarily mean that we accept everything; simply that we are ready to give a fair hearing to another's point of view, amenable to the possibility that we may need to reconsider our opinions in the light of their experience. If we are to grow in faith and mature as individuals, we all need to cultivate that quality. Those who think they have been given all they need to know and who refuse to have their horizons stretched may well find themselves in the position of the people of Nazareth, turning their backs on the truth when it was there before them.

Ears to hear

Even the sweetest of songs is as vinegar poured on a wound to one who is heavy in heart. (Proverbs 25:20)

How many times have you said the wrong thing at the wrong time and felt yourself curl up with embarrassment as you realise you've gone and put your foot in it again? Occasionally this happens through no fault of our own, the delicateness of a situation being unknown to us. At other times, though, there is no such excuse: our gaffe is due to the fact that we opened our mouths before we stopped to think. How often are we so full of our own news in conversation that we scarcely listen to what is being said to us in turn? How often are we busily framing our response before someone has barely started to speak? Little wonder, then, that we end up saying the wrong thing. Sensitivity is not some magical gift possessed by the select few; it comes from being slow to speak and ready to listen.

Watch your tongue

We all make mistakes. Anyone who can open their mouth without putting their foot in it must be perfect, able to rein in their whole body. We do that with horses, putting bits into their mouths to make them obey us and so guiding their whole bodies. Similarly, with ships – despite being so large that it takes a mighty wind to drive them, a tiny rudder steers them and the pilot directs them as he wills. So also the tongue, though a little member, can do great things. No one is able to tame the tongue – it is uncontrollably evil, full of deadly venom. Out of the same mouth we both praise God and curse one another. (James 3:2-5, 8-9)

I have always been fascinated by the power of words. A simple proverb can express the profoundest of truths; a piece of poetry can inspire us or move us to tears; a good book can capture our imagination, making us feel part of another world; a well-chosen word of thanks or appreciation can lift the spirit. However, there is a negative side to this truth. Words can too easily be used to hurt and destroy, cheat and deceive, ridicule or revile. We will all be able to recall times when we opened our mouths without stopping to think, or when we spoke cruelly, intent on wounding. We will all have encountered those who never stop talking, wearing us out with their incessant empty chatter. We will all equally be aware of the way words have been used to incite hatred and intolerance, violence and war.

Words are God's gift, but they are a gift that needs to be handled with care, for they have a tendency to run away with us, and an astonishing capacity for both good and evil. Unless we learn to watch our tongues, we may well find that words become our master instead of us theirs.

Worth of all

Behind the labels

Now tax collectors and sinners were all drawing near to him. And the scribes and Pharisees were scandalised, muttering among themselves, 'This man welcomes sinners and eats with them.' (Luke 15:1-2)

It was a conundrum: a tin without a label found in the murky depths of the kitchen cupboard. What was inside, I wondered? Beans? Peaches? Fish? Meat? There was only one way to find out and that, of course, was to open it and look inside. It brought home to me how important labels can be, for without them we may not know what's hidden underneath. On the other hand, labels can be misleading. Just because there's a brand name on the tin doesn't necessarily mean it contains a superior product; the supermarket cheap-label alternative may be just as good if not better.

When it comes to people, using labels is a dangerous thing for none of us fits easily into neat categories, each a complex mixture of good and bad, strong and weak, wise and foolish. Yet, as Jesus found throughout his ministry, it is human nature to pigeon-hole people, despite the misery and division this causes. Can anything good come out of Nazareth? Has a tax collector the right to see Jesus? Should a prostitute be forgiven? Is it possible to love a Samaritan? Could a home-grown boy possibly turn out to be the Messiah? Today it is no different; such prejudice all too easily finds a place in us. The barriers that keep us apart are as real as they have ever been. We need to look, as Jesus did, behind the label to the person beneath. Only then will we discover each individual's true worth and, as well as theirs, discover our own.

Me! Prejudiced?

If someone wearing gold rings and fine clothing enters your synagogue, followed by a shabbily dressed person, and you pay attention to the one in fine clothing, saying, 'Sit here in the best place', while you tell the poor person, 'Stand over there or sit beneath my feet', are you not showing discrimination and presuming to judge unfairly? (James 2:2-4)

A while back I watched the TV highlights of England playing a World Cup qualifying match in Eastern Europe. The result went in England's favour, but overshadowing the game were fears of a repeat of the racial harassment that had marred the Under-21 game the night before. According to the authorities in the country concerned, it was the first time many in their country had seen black people playing football – a feeble excuse, though, of course, it is not so long ago that black players in England faced similar abuse, week in, week out. The fact is that prejudice runs deep, and although sport in this country has largely succeeded in rooting out racism, all kinds of prejudice continue to scar the face of society. All kinds of measures have been adopted in an attempt to correct this, at times leading to a political correctness that borders on the ridiculous, but the fact is that legislation is sometimes the only way to protect the interests of those discriminated against.

In the Church there should be no place for prejudice but let us not fool ourselves that it has no foothold in our lives. It may not be overt discrimination on the grounds of race, gender, religion or sexuality – though sadly that is still sometimes seen – but there are other more subtle prejudices we find it hard to escape from, scarcely aware even of their hold upon us. We need to recognise their presence and to ask for God's help in seeing beyond colour, culture, creed, or anything else, to the person underneath – a person he loved enough to die for them.

Only human?

God is greater than any human being. (Job 33:12)

'Oh well, we're only human.' I expect we have all heard words similar to those more often than we can begin to remember. The fact that we are 'only human' is taken to explain, and indeed even justify, all kinds of foolish actions and errors of judgement. Few of us would argue with the assertion that human nature, despite all its potential for good, is fundamentally flawed. Yet, are we right to talk about being *only* human? Some passages in scripture seem to suggest so, none more than the bald statement above from the book of Job. In fact, throughout the Old Testament, and also in the New, there is a strand of tradition asserting the total sovereignty of God – the fact that he is unlike any other, beyond human comprehension, so holy that no one can see God and live.

Surely, then, there can be no argument. Well, not quite, for there are also passages like Genesis 1 speaking of God creating humankind in his own image; or Luke 12:7 in which Jesus speaks so eloquently of the value God places on each one of us; or Psalm 8 where human beings are said to be just a little lower than God himself. God, in other words, doesn't see us as *only* human but as wonderfully so, lovingly fashioned by his hands and infinitely important. Yes, we all know what we mean by the expression 'we're only human', but don't let's push it too far and, above all, don't let's allow it to colour our understanding of what being human means. We all have our faults, but we all also have our worth, our strengths and our God-given potential. Though we may sometimes overlook these, God never will.

A place for all

Are not five sparrows sold for a couple of pence? Yet God does not overlook a single one of them. Believe me, the very hairs of your head are numbered. Never fear, then, for you mean even more to him than many sparrows. (Luke 12:6-7)

We live today, as never before, in an impersonal society – a world in which increasingly we are treated as numbers rather than individuals. Instead of being people, we are a reference number on a tax form, a policy number with an insurance company, a national health service number on a waiting list, a telephone number to a double-glazing firm. Answer-phones, automated messages, e-mails, the Internet – these have become the order of the day, personal contact reduced to the barest minimum. Disturbingly, many young people relate more easily to a computer screen than to real-life flesh and blood.

In such a world it is reassuring to know that, in God's eyes at least, we are still real people, each one of us unique and precious to him. He values us for what we are, inviting us to share in a meaningful personal relationship with him. More than that, he calls us to recognise the value of others and, in so doing, to resist the depersonalising forces that threaten to undermine society today. Whatever you do, never forget that each person you have dealings with is not a number or an object, but precisely that – a person!

A proper perspective

I say to everyone among you, by the grace given to me, not to have a misplaced sense of your own importance, but to appraise yourselves judiciously, each according to the degree of faith that God has granted to you. (Romans 12:3)

One of the things my children most enjoyed on a recent holiday was a visit to a hall of distorting mirrors. They ran from one to the other with peals of laughter and squeals of delight, repeatedly calling us to come and see what they looked like. It is truly remarkable what a profound effect a few kinks in a mirror can have on your reflection, rendering you short and squat one moment and with the legs of a gazelle and neck of a giraffe the next!

Such distortions, though, are as nothing compared to those we can create in our own minds. Sometimes we belittle ourselves to the point of feeling we are of no stature at all, yet, conversely, we can develop such an inflated picture of ourselves that our ego is in danger of bursting. What compounds the problem is that we are usually unaware of our mistake, tending to confuse illusion with reality. Pride is a danger that numerous passages of scripture rightly warn us against, for there are few human traits less desirable yet more common. Equally, we should beware of devaluing who and what we are. God wants each of us to have a proper sense of our intrinsic worth and, similarly, an appreciation of the worth of others. We are all flawed, yet all special, none of us perfect but none irredeemable. Don't build yourself up, don't do yourself down – it's advice we would all do well to heed.

Discipleship

Cost of discipleship (*see also* Self-denial and sacrifice)

Against the grain

Enter through the narrow gate. For wide is the gate and broad the way leading to destruction, and many are those who take that route, but the path leading to the gate of life is straight and narrow, and only a few find it. (Matthew 7:13-14)

Are you a DIY expert? I wish I was but, sadly, such skills have always eluded me. Take the time at school many years ago, when I was furiously planing a piece of wood that stubbornly insisted on splintering and snagging at every thrust of the blade. One look from my woodwork teacher told me I had gaffed again. 'Plane *with* the grain,' he told me, with a weary groan of despair, 'not *against* it!' There was a simple lesson in that, not just for woodwork but also for life. Attempt to go against the grain and you will have problems – guaranteed.

Yet, as the words of Jesus make clear, on occasions we must be willing to do just that; to go against the grain of self-interest and received wisdom, of force of habit and expected behaviour, of family loyalties and personal inclination. It is not that we rebel for the sake of it, but there will be times when faith brings us into conflict with accepted norms and when the call of Christ means renouncing the way of the world. Such a path is never easy and we will always face the temptation to take a less-demanding option, a course of less resistance, but though that way may seem attractive, its lure is ultimately deceptive, for in running from the challenge we run from life itself; the life God wants us to know in all its fullness.

Carrying our cross

He said to all, 'If any want to come after me, let them deny themselves and take up their cross daily, and then follow me. For those wishing to save their life will lose it, but those who lose their life for my sake will save it. (Luke 9:23-24)

'I'm delighted to tell you that you've won a free holiday in our prize draw competition.' Have you had a phone call like that recently? It's sales talk, of course; just one of the many marketing ploys used to convince us that we're getting something for nothing, whereas, in fact, the opposite is more likely true. Another tack is the one sometimes employed by book and music clubs: 'Buy any four for 99 pence each', only we then have to buy another four at full price during the next year. It's easy to be swept along by wonderful-sounding promises, without stopping to consider the commitment entailed.

In terms of the Christian faith, though, there should be no such danger, for Jesus never attempted to conceal the real cost of discipleship. If you want the reward, he tells us, there's a price to pay. To get something out of faith we must also put something in. There is no sales hype, no dressing things up with fantastic offers, yet the irony is that in this case the price is more than worth paying!

Speaking out

'What have you done to me?' Balak demanded of Balaam. 'I summoned you here to pronounce a curse on my enemies but instead you've blessed them from the moment you arrived.' Balaam answered, 'Do I have any choice but to utter the words that the Lord puts into my mouth?' (Numbers 23:11-12)

The writer, Alexander Solzhenitsyn, spent eight years of his life, between 1945 and 1953, in prison. His 'crime' was to speak out against the way Stalin had acted during the Second World War. Twenty-one years later he was arrested again and sent into exile for having dared in his book *The Gulag Archipelago* to document the era of Stalinist terror. More dramatic still is the story of Nelson Mandela, who in 1961 was imprisoned for his campaign against apartheid, spending the next twenty-nine years in prison until his eventual release in 1990.

For me, the example of Balaam calls to mind the courage of those two men. Summoned by Balak, king of the Moabites, to pronounce a curse on the Israelites, he did the very opposite and pronounced a blessing. That must have taken some doing, for he was well aware of the reaction this would provoke, but he spoke the words that he believed God wanted him to say. We may not be put on the spot quite like any of these individuals, but there will be times when we know it is right to make a stand, either in support of good or against evil. What will we do then? Will we say what people want us to say, for the sake of a quiet life, or will we, instead, have the courage to speak out?

Journey of discipleship (*see also* Commitment; Epiphany: Wise men still seek him)

A childlike faith

People brought their children to him so that he might touch them, but the disciples spoke harshly to them. When Jesus saw this, however, he was angry and said to them, 'Let the little children come to me; do not stop them; for the kingdom of God belongs to such as these. I tell you this, whoever does not receive the kingdom of God like a little child will never enter it.' And he embraced them, laid his hands on them, and blessed them. (Mark 10:13-16)

To spend quality time with a young child is a profoundly moving experience. Yes, children can drive you to distraction sometimes, yet in the honesty, openness, innocence and simple trust of the very young, coupled with their unquenchable zest for life, there is something uniquely precious. Every parent will know the feeling of wanting to preserve those qualities for ever, safeguarding them against the ravages of time. We can't do that, of course – each of us has to become streetwise in order to survive in the harsher realities of daily life.

Yet while much that is childish is by necessity outgrown, there are certain childlike qualities we lose at our peril. However old we are, we still need to look at the world with wonder, glimpsing God within it, if our souls are not to be starved of nourishment. We need to trust God even when we do not understand what is happening to us. We need to approach life with that same sense of openness and that same hunger to learn, seeking God's help and guidance in our unfolding journey. It is one thing to be childish, quite another to be childlike. Have we lost sight of the difference?

Following my leader

Walking beside the Sea of Galilee, he saw two brothers, Simon, known as Peter, and Andrew his brother, casting a net into the lake – for they were fishermen. And he said to them, 'Come and follow me, and I will make you fishers of people.' Straightaway they left their nets and followed him. (Matthew 4:18-20)

I was reminded recently that Jesus only talked once during his ministry of being born again but spoke of the need to follow him on innumerable occasions. There is an important point behind that observation, for there is a danger sometimes of making the moment of conversion all-important and forgetting that discipleship is, or should be, an unfolding journey. Peter and Andrew, together with the rest of the Apostles, followed Jesus not knowing what he was calling them to or where their response might lead. They responded in faith, trusting that he would guide them and, apart from Judas, they kept on following even when it led to sacrifice, hostility, rejection and the death of their Master on a cross. How many of us would have followed through all of that? Would we still have been there by his side after the first altercation with the Pharisees? Would we have had second thoughts when Jesus spelt out the cost of discipleship?

Even the Apostles' faith had its limits, of course, on the night of Gethsemane each briefly failing to follow. It needed the risen Christ to greet them once more, speaking his word of peace and reaffirming his call, before they felt able to resume their journey. We too may encounter moments when commitment is tested and we no longer follow as we should, but Jesus will always be there, summoning us forward along the road of discipleship. Committing ourselves to Christ is a necessary step for all of us, whether that involves a dramatic experience of conversion or a gradual coming to faith, but it is only a first step. Don't mistake it for more.

Following through

As you therefore have received Christ Jesus the Lord, continue to live your lives in him, rooted and built up in him and established in the faith, just as you were taught, abounding in thanksgiving. (Colossians 2:6-7)

There was a time when I had delusions of mastering the game of golf. I hacked my way eagerly round a variety of municipal courses, dreaming one day perhaps of attaining a reasonable standard but, sadly, my skill never matched my enthusiasm. To put it bluntly, I was hopeless. Instead of soaring majestically down the fairway, my ball would dribble a few yards into a divot, veer wildly into the rough or dip disconsolately into the nearest water hazard. What was the problem? There were all too many, but one was an inability to follow through. Where I should have continued after the ball in a graceful arc, I instead chopped down on it with a vicious stab, burying my club in the turf and all but breaking my wrists in the process.

It's not just in sport that following through is important but also in so much of life and faith. It's easy enough to start something; a different matter to finish it. So often we start off full of enthusiasm, only then to lose interest. Many likewise commit themselves to Christ, impulsively responding to the message of the gospel, but soon realise that they have taken on more than they first anticipated. Is that true of us? We may have professed our faith in Christ and started on the journey of discipleship but that finally is not what counts. What matters is whether we complete the course; whether having put our hands to something we are ready to follow it through.

The God who travels with us

The Lord went ahead of them the whole time, a pillar of cloud to guide them by day and a pillar of fire to lighten their way by night, so that they could travel by day or night. Neither the pillar of cloud by day nor the pillar of fire by night moved from its place in front of the people. (Exodus 13:21-22)

Imagine what it must have been like to be one of the people of Israel during the forty years of wandering in the wilderness. Many, no doubt, must have thought their flight from Egypt would be short, leading swiftly on to an exciting if somewhat uncertain future. The reality, however, was that a lifetime's journey lay ahead, living as nomads in search of the Promised Land. Precisely where that was and when they'd get there seemed hidden even from Moses. Yet, though the final destination was unclear, the route they had to take was not a matter of guesswork, for God was there to guide them. Just as he led Abraham, so now, through a pillar of cloud and fire, he directed their footsteps. They did not travel alone; God was travelling with them.

Few are privileged to receive such a clear sign of God's presence with them, but the principle is one that applies to each of us. As we journey through life, God is always there to share our pilgrimage – leading, encouraging, equipping, providing. We have no more idea of where our path may take us than Abram or Moses had, but we have the assurance that wherever we are asked to travel, he will travel with us.

Into the unknown

The Lord said to Abram, 'Leave your country, your kinfolk and your father's house and head for a land that I will show you. I will make a great nation of you. I will bless you, and make your name celebrated, so that you will be a blessing. I will bless those who bless you, and curse whoever curses you; and through you all the families of the earth shall be blessed in turn.' So Abram set off, as the Lord had told him. (Genesis 12:1-5)

What are you most scared of? Spiders? Snakes? The dark? Possibly even all of these? According to those who claim to know, there is one thing probably all of us are scared of still more, and that, quite simply, is the unknown. Familiarity may breed contempt, but it also brings a sense of security, and the thought of venturing out into uncharted waters can be a daunting challenge that most of us prefer to avoid. It can be traumatic enough moving to a new house or starting a new job – any change more radical than these can be bewildering indeed.

This, though, was the challenge faced by Abram, later to be called Abraham. Comfortably settled in the town of Haran, he suddenly felt a call to move on. The destination was unclear, as were any details as to what he might find when he reached it. This was to be a step into the unknown, a journey of faith. Few of us today will be asked to make a bold decision, yet there are times when we need to let go of the tried and trusted nonetheless. We may be called to a new venture, new responsibilities or a new lifestyle, not knowing where these might lead or what will be demanded of us. We may be asked to make new friends, embrace new ideas or explore new horizons that, once again, we have no way of quantifying. Will we be ready to respond if we believe God is speaking – not putting off a decision to weigh up all the implications or brushing aside what we would rather not hear, but following in faith? We may not know what the future holds, but we do know who holds it – let that be sufficient inspiration for us.

Letting go

As he prayed, his face was transformed and his clothes became a dazzling white. Then two men appeared, Moses and Elijah, talking with him. Peter and those who were with him, having fallen asleep, were startled into wakefulness and they saw his glory and the two men alongside him. As these two departed Peter said to Jesus, not really knowing what he was saying, 'Master, it is good for us to be here. Let us make three tents: one for you, one for Moses and one for Elijah.' (Luke 9:29-30, 32-33)

Some moments mean so much to us that we wish we could pop them into a bottle and preserve them unchanged so that the happiness they bring never fades. I feel like that as I write, having spent a wonderful weekend with my family, away from it all – no work, no telephone, no pressures – an opportunity to unwind, spend some quality time with the children and rejoice in the indescribable beauty of this world God has given us. The memories of that weekend are still fresh in my mind as I sit now in my garden, the last rays of the sun dipping below the trees and a blackbird singing its heart out nearby. If I could put time on hold, I couldn't choose a better moment than this. Yet, could the moment be stored, how long would it continue to satisfy? Unpalatable though it is to admit it, familiarity would soon dull its lustre. In this world, life must move on if it is to keep its sparkle.

That was a truth Peter was to learn at that mysterious event we call the Transfiguration. He recognised the moment as special and wanted to keep hold of it, to the point of suggesting that he and his colleagues build tents so that Jesus, Moses and Elijah could remain there a little longer. It wasn't to be, of course. Life had to move on. Jesus had to walk the way of the cross for which he had been born; Peter and his fellow Apostles had more to learn, more to experience and more to understand.

The lesson holds true for us today. One day we will savour a joy that will never fade or end but, until then, we must treasure every God-given moment for what it is and then move on. We cannot preserve any moment, no matter how special. Attempt to do so and far from holding on to it, we will destroy it instead.

Perseverance

So then, since we are surrounded by so great a crowd of witnesses, let us discard everything that encumbers us and the sin that clings so closely, and let us run with perseverance the race set before us, looking to Jesus, the beginning and end of our faith, who, focusing on the joy set before him, endured the cross, disregarding its shame, and has taken his seat at the right hand of the throne of God. (Hebrews 12:1-2)

When I was a student at Bristol Baptist College, the students of the local Methodist College challenged us to a cross-country run. The day dawned grey and drizzly but I was young, fit and raring to go. As I jogged comfortably along, I held secret hopes of dashing triumphantly over the finishing line in first place. Then we reached it: a steep climb fully half a mile long. I swear to this day that it was the Methodists' secret weapon, carefully chosen as part of the route. It may even be that they had prayed for rain! Whatever the case, the slope was so slippery that, after a couple of steps, my feet gave way and I slid wretchedly back down the hill to where I had started. Before long I was joined by a succession of fellow-Baptists in similar plight. Strangely, the Methodists had no such problem; they sailed up that bank as though they had sprouted wings. Did I ever complete the course? Eventually, yes, but only after some of my colleagues had inspired me through their heroic efforts to persevere for the sake of those following.

The Christian life can be equally demanding sometimes. We start off thinking it's plain sailing but suddenly unexpected obstacles appear in our path. At times we can feel like giving up, but we have the example of those who have gone before us to inspire us onwards, and a responsibility to future generations to lead the way in turn. Whether the race is easy or hard, we need to persevere, looking to Jesus and the joy set before us. For me, that day, the incentive finally was very simple – a hot shower and a cup of tea! The joy we look to through Jesus is something far more wonderful – too wonderful for words.

Evil, triumph over

see also Easter

Confronting evil

As we were on our way to a place of prayer, we were met by a young girl possessed by some strange spirit, who brought a wealthy living to her masters through her claims to foretell the future. She followed us, crying out, 'These men are servants of the most high God, and have come to announce to you the way of salvation', and she did this for many days. Paul, greatly troubled at what was going on, spun round and said to the spirit, 'I command you in the name of Jesus Christ to come out of her'; and immediately it came out. Her masters, seeing their comfortable livelihood disappearing, seized Paul and Silas and dragged them to the marketplace before the rulers and magistrates who, having heard the charges, had them thrown into prison, their feet securely fettered in the stocks. (Acts 16:16-20a, 24)

When a mass protest took place at the meeting of the World Trade Organisation in Seattle in December 1999, what was intended as a peaceful demonstration was taken over by a small group of anarchists, and violence erupted. The majority of protestors, however, had come for one purpose – to voice their concern over what they saw as exploitation and oppression resulting from unimpeded free trade. Whether they were right or wrong in that assessment is open to debate, but I have to admire their willingness to stand up for their convictions. It is all too easy apathetically to turn a blind eye to injustice; to believe something is wrong yet leave it to others to do something about it.

The Apostle Paul could have done much the same with regard to the young girl who was being unscrupulously exploited for her supposed gifts of fortune-telling, but he recognised that the way she was being treated was unequivocally evil and he refused to walk by on the other side. Confronting evil may well prove costly, just as it did for Paul and his companions, but there are times when it is a necessary part of discipleship.

The light of life

In him was life, and that life was the light of all. The light shines in the darkness, and the darkness could not overcome it. (John 1:4-5)

During my time with Toc H, a charity dedicated to breaking down barriers of prejudice and intolerance in society, I was privileged to visit the place where the movement started: Talbot House, in Belgium. It was here that the Revd Philip Clayton, known affectionately as 'Tubby' to friends and colleagues, started a club for soldiers serving in the front line, a club open to all – irrespective of colour, culture, creed or rank – which was to shine as a beacon of light in a world that seemed to have been plunged into darkness.

Walking today among the seemingly endless rows of gravestones that dominate the landscape in what was once the Western Front, it is astonishing that anyone managed to keep hope and faith alive amid scenes of such dreadful carnage, yet somehow the light could not be extinguished. As Tubby Clayton put it, 'All the darkness in the world cannot extinguish the light of one candle' – another way of expressing those wonderful words from the beginning of John's Gospel.

There is much in life that seems to suggest sometimes that darkness has gained the upper hand and that evil has defeated good, but faith reminds us that from the darkness of Calvary dawned the day of resurrection – light that can never be extinguished. However dark life may seem, God has promised that his light will ultimately break through.

Faith

see also Commitment; Discipleship: Journey of discipleship

Asking in faith (*see also* Prayer: Asking in faith)

The faith to ask

He entered a house, intending to keep his presence there hidden, but he could not escape notice. A woman whose little daughter had an unclean spirit immediately heard about him, and she came and prostrated herself at his feet. The woman was a Gentile, by birth a Syrophoenician. She implored Jesus to rid her daughter of the demon, but he said to her, 'Let the children be fed first, for it would not be right to take the children's bread and throw it to the dogs.' 'Ah yes, sir,' she retorted, 'but even the dogs under the table eat the children's crumbs.' Jesus answered her, 'For an answer like that, you may go – the demon has left your daughter.' The woman went home, and found the child lying on the bed, the demon having gone. (Mark 7:24-30)

There's no denying it – scripture can be hard to understand sometimes. Take this encounter of Jesus with the woman of Syrophoenicia. To put it kindly, his response comes across as abrupt and aloof; to be more blunt, it appears downright rude; a dismissive, heartless rejection of an earnest plea for help. So what was Jesus thinking of? Why react like he did? One possibility is that Mark exaggerated the severity of Jesus' reply; another, that Jesus wanted to test the woman's faith to ensure she was genuinely seeking help rather than just inventing a story to get near him. I don't seriously believe either.

In my view, he recognised this woman's sincerity straightaway, and saw in her an opportunity to illustrate a fundamental truth at the heart of faith. According to Jewish teaching, the woman, as a foreigner, had no claim on his help; he knew it, she knew it. Yet she came, nonetheless, not because she deserved anything from him but because she understood both what he had to give and that he would be ready to give it. That's the point here: Jesus is saying to the crowds, 'Look at this woman. She understands who I am even if you don't. She knows that I will respond, not because of any worth on your part, but because of who and what I am.' It's a message we need to learn in turn. None of us has any claim on Christ's goodness or any right to demand his love, but he is ready to hear our prayer and to meet our innermost needs. All we have to do is ask, and mean it!

Coming to faith

Getting in deep

A woman of Samaria came to draw water, so Jesus asked her, 'Give me a drink.' The Samaritan woman responded, 'How can you, a Jew, ask me, a woman of Samaria, to give you a drink?' (Jews have no dealings with Samaritans.) Jesus answered her, 'If you knew the gift of God, and who has asked you, "Give me a drink", you would have made the request to him, and he would have given you living water.' The woman replied, 'Sir, the well is deep and you have no bucket, so where will you get this living water?' Jesus said to her, 'Anyone drinking the water here will thirst again, but whoever drinks the water I will give will never be thirsty.' The woman said to him, 'Sir, give me this water, so that I need never thirst or come here again to draw water.' (John 4:7, 9-11, 13-15)

When I first started college at Oxford, I decided to join a local student orchestra. I'd played the flute regularly during my schooldays, and also occasionally during my time at Bristol, but I wanted now to take things a little more seriously. The day of the first practice arrived, and I eagerly picked up a copy of the music, only to freeze in disbelief. There was no way I could even begin to play such a complex piece, yet my fellow-flautists launched into the work without a moment's hesitation. Clearly, I had bitten off more than I could chew – and that, I'm afraid, was the end of my musical ambitions.

The woman at the well was to find that she also had taken on more than she'd bargained on, though in a rather different sense. Approached by a stranger asking for a drink, the next thing she knew he seemed to be offering her an inexhaustible source of water of her very own. No wonder she was excited, for it must have been hard work toiling to and from that well each day. She wanted to take things further, to gain access to this personal spring, and only slowly did the truth dawn that Jesus was talking about something very different to what she had in mind. She suddenly found herself drawn into a searching examination of her life, facing facts that she had never questioned before. Meeting Christ is like that, or at least it should be. It involves a penetrating and ongoing challenge that draws us into ever-deeper waters. Unlike my ill-fated musical aspirations, however, we need never be out of our depth, for our ability to meet the challenge depends not on us but on him. Through meeting Jesus, the Samaritan woman came face to face with her true self as never before. Are we prepared to do the same in turn?

A living testimony

Since many undertook to compile a record of the events fulfilled among us, just as they were passed on to us by those servants of the word who, from the start, were eyewitnesses to them, it seemed right for me, after carefully checking all my sources, to write an accurate account for you, most excellent Theophilus, so that you might know the truth concerning everything you have been taught. (Luke 1:1-4)

To believe in something we haven't seen for ourselves isn't easy, especially when that something stretches credulity to the limit. If I were to tell you, for example, that I just looked out of the window and saw a Martian spaceship alighting on my lawn, you wouldn't believe me, would you? So why should we believe the gospel records concerning Jesus, with their startling claims of God made flesh, nailed to a cross and rising from the tomb? To my mind, the best reason of all is encapsulated in those words at the beginning of Luke. Unlike Matthew and John, Luke wasn't one of the original Apostles; indeed, so far as we know he didn't meet with Jesus at all during his earthly ministry.

So how did Luke know so much about Jesus? Quite simply, through the testimony of others. Luke found himself in much the same situation as we are in today, dependent upon other people's words of witness for everything he knew about Jesus. Would he just have accepted this unthinkingly? I don't think so. On the contrary, both in his gospel and his sequel to it, the book of Acts, he clearly took pains to check his facts before setting them down on paper. That's one reason to accept his testimony, but there's another, more important still. Eyewitness accounts alone wouldn't have been sufficient to win Luke to faith; they needed to be backed up through experience. Luke doesn't write simply as a historian but as someone who has experienced the reality of the risen Christ in his own life and who enjoyed an ongoing relationship with him. Though he never met with Jesus in the flesh, he clearly met with him in the Spirit, enough to change his life for ever. That's why he wrote his gospel: to let others know what Jesus meant to him. And that's why we can believe his words and the testimony of others to the life-changing power of Christ – because we too can know and experience his presence for ourselves.

Seeing is believing

Philip found Nathaniel and told him, 'We have found the one written about in the law of Moses and the prophets: Jesus of Nazareth, the son of Joseph.' Nathaniel responded, 'Can anything good come out of Nazareth?' Philip answered, 'Come and see.' (John 1:45-46)

If I were to tell you that I can tear a telephone directory in half with my bare hands, or that I can run a three-minute mile, or that I've just been voted the best-dressed man in Britain, would you believe me? Of course not! You'd either think I'm the most big-headed or misguided person in the country, or the worst liar you've ever come across. If you could see those things actually taking place, on the other hand, it would be different: there would be no question then – after all, seeing is believing. Sadly I can lay no such claims to fame, but let me paint another scenario. If someone arrived claiming to be the Messiah, able to heal the sick, forgive sins and raise the dead, would you believe them? I doubt it. And neither did Nathaniel when his friend Philip told him that he had found the deliverer they had long waited for. After countless barren years of expectation, could it be true, and, if so, could the Christ have come from Nazareth of all places?

Philip's reply was the best he could possibly have given: 'Come and see.' His words remind us that the gospel is not about speculation or philosophy but is a testimony to the experience of innumerable people whose lives were directly touched by the ministry of Christ. It includes eyewitness accounts of concrete events and a flesh-and-blood person. Most important of all, it invites us to put our faith in Jesus, to respond to his promises, and so to see for ourselves the truth of who he is and all he means.

Essentials of faith

What God requires

He has made clear, everyone, what is right; quite simply, what the Lord wants from you is just dealings, loving kindness, and unassuming service. (Micah 6:8)

Some time ago, the government of the day embarked on a programme that it called 'Back to Basics'. As with so much concerned with politics, the public treated it with a healthy dose of scepticism, which was just as well given that the initiative was to backfire in truly spectacular fashion. Nonetheless, in theory, at least, the idea was a good one, for there are times when we become so absorbed in details that we lose sight of the simple principles that underlie our convictions. As Christians we are not exempt from that danger – in fact, many would say we are most vulnerable to it, since there are so many things that people within the Church feel strongly about, to the point of making them articles of faith. All too easily, we make the gospel more complicated than it really is. Some insist on assent to certain creeds, others on a particular style of worship, others again on church structures and organisation, and so it goes on. Nor are these the only distractions, for we can just as easily become bogged down in questions of doctrine or over-concerned with the minutiae of faith.

At such times, we need reminding of what serving God is all about, just as the people in Micah's day needed reminding. Of course, doctrine is important, but don't let it obscure the basics. Of course, worship, fellowship and theology matter, but not if they hinder rather than further the work of God's kingdom. I'm reminded of the celebrated words of the theologian Herbert Butterfield: 'Hold fast to Christ, and for the rest be uncommitted.' Or, as Micah puts it, 'do justice, love kindness and walk humbly with your God'. Get that right, and the rest can take care of itself.

Faith in action (*see also* Serving others)

Coming and going

Coming together, they asked him, 'Lord, is this the time when you will restore the kingdom of Israel?' He replied, 'It is not for you to know the time or seasons that the Father has laid down by his own authority, but you will receive power when the Holy Spirit comes upon you and you will be my witnesses both in Jerusalem, and all Judea and Samaria, and to the ends of the earth. (Acts 1:6-8)

It's a law of nature that what goes up must come down; we cannot have one without the other. In similar fashion, we talk of give and take, and of getting out what we put in. Certain concepts belong together. There are two words, however, that – in the Christian life at least – we don't perhaps associate as much as we should do: 'coming' and 'going'. We have no trouble with the first, so much of the gospel about coming to Christ, receiving his love, enjoying his presence. How often, though, does coming to him result in going for him? Too easily what we call discipleship becomes a personal and private affair between him and us, faith turned inwards instead of outwards.

Such an understanding bears little relationship to the call given by Jesus throughout his ministry and beyond; a call that involves following him in sacrificial service, going out to proclaim the gospel and bringing light to others. We need to come to him first – of that there is no question – for only then can we find the resources we need to follow his way, but if our relationship ends there, then we need to look at it very carefully, or we may find it concludes in more ways than one.

Good intentions

'What do you make of this? A man had two children. Approaching the first, he said, "My child, go and work in the vineyard today." He answered, "I'll go", but he didn't. The father went to the second and asked the same thing; and he answered, "Sir, I won't go", but he had second thoughts and went. Which of the two did the father's will?' They said, 'The latter.' (Matthew 21:28-31)

How many times have you intended to do something and failed to do it? I expect it's been more often than you care to remember. It's easy to make a promise, much harder to honour it. The reasons, of course, are many. Sometimes we just forget or are too busy. At other times, we find we've taken on more than we bargained for, swept along on a tide of enthusiasm, only to find that, in the cold light of day, the task we've committed ourselves to appears less attractive than we thought. On other occasions still, we can be guilty of sheer old-fashioned laziness.

With luck, our failure to honour our intentions may not matter all that much. On the other hand, it may matter a good deal, having consequences far greater than we might envisage. It may even be that the opportunity we have missed may never come our way again, so if God is calling you to do something and if the job needs doing, don't put it off. Act now before it's too late!

In Christ, in . . . ?

From Paul, by God's will an apostle of Jesus Christ, and Timothy our brother, to the holy and faithful brothers and sisters in Christ in Colossae: grace and peace to you from God our Father. Whenever we pray for you, we always thank God, the Father of our Lord Jesus Christ, because we have heard of your faith and love for all the saints, springing from the hope stored up for you in heaven that you heard about in the word of truth, the gospel that has come to you. So then, having received Christ as Lord, continue to live in him, rooted and growing in him, established in the faith taught to you, and overflowing with thanksgiving. (Colossians 1:1-6a; 2:6-7)

For today's reading I could just as easily have chosen the opening words of any of Paul's letters, for they all have one thing in common –

they each relate to a specific group in a specific place called to a specific task. One or two letters were intended as circulars, to be passed on to other groups in a similar situation, but the underlying intention was always the same – Paul wrote to encourage Christians in a variety of locations to work out their faith where God had put them.

It may seem a small point but it's a vital one, for it earths faith in reality, underlining the need for commitment to be visible in the routine business of daily life. We can all be Christians in church on a Sunday. We can all make the right noises in our personal devotions, locked comfortably away in the privacy of our own homes. We can all seem suitably devout in our concern for the needs of the world or the ills of society in general. Yes, such things are important but they are second to what really counts: to putting our faith into practice here and now, wherever we find ourselves. This is the acid test of commitment and the yardstick whereby we will be judged by others: whether the faith we profess is reflected in the things we do; whether the person we *are* corresponds to the person we claim to be; whether the love we talk about is seen in action. We may profess the name of Christ as often as we wish, but what Paul would want to ask us is this: is our commitment evident to others?

Living the good news

I therefore, a prisoner of the Lord, urge you to lead a life commensurate with the calling to which you have been called, patiently dealing with one another with humility and kindness in love, striving always to maintain the unity of the Spirit in the bond of peace. (Ephesians 4:1-3)

What would you make of it if the former US President, Bill Clinton, were to produce a book called *My Life as a Monk*, or if the Archbishop of Canterbury were to come out with a title *The A to Z of Safe-breaking?* You would, I think, rightly surmise that you were being taken for a ride. If, however, they were to produce the respective titles *The Lewinsky Affair: My Side of the Story* and *Joys and Sorrows of an Archbishop*, then you'd take the books seriously, for you'd know that each author was writing from experience. It's all a question of credibility, and the same is true when it comes to living and witnessing to the Christian life.

We are told by Christ himself to share our faith, to witness to the truth of the gospel, and that is an important part of discipleship, but the effectiveness of our outreach will always depend on the transparency of our lives: how far what we say measures up to what we do. If our words say one thing but our lives another, then our testimony will always be taken with a pinch of salt, however much we urge people to judge the message rather than the messenger. We cannot hope, of course, to present anything like a perfect picture but we cannot afford to put across an image radically different from the one we purport to represent. Do that, and no matter what we say or how often we say it, there will be few people willing to listen.

Making a difference

On some have compassion, making a difference. (Jude verse 22)

It was only the smallest of mistakes, a single letter inadvertently inserted in place of another, but it made all the difference. Instead of reading 'The bishop much enjoyed the singing' it read – you've guessed it – 'The bishop much enjoyed the sinning'! One apparently minor change can make all the difference to the way something is seen and understood! Indeed, the verse above is a case in point. The *New Revised Standard Version* translates it 'have mercy on some who are wavering', while the *New English Bible* goes for 'there are some doubting souls who need your pity'. My own rendering leans heavily on the King James translation of the Bible and is probably the least accurate of any, yet the message could hardly be more important, for if there is one thing that should characterise our lives as Christians it should surely be making a difference. It doesn't take much: a word here, a deed there, and the effects can be remarkable. Few of us will make an indelible impact through our discipleship, let alone change the world, but all of us, if our faith is what it ought to be, should make a difference somewhere. If it doesn't, something is badly wrong.

Shedding light

You are the light of the world. Just as a city situated on a mountaintop cannot be hidden, so nobody lights a lamp and places it under a bushel basket, putting it instead on a lampstand in order that it might shed light throughout the house. Similarly, let your light shine before others, so that they may see the good deeds you do and give glory to your Father in heaven. (Matthew 5:14-16)

There is something reassuring about light, isn't there? I remember as a child how I always wanted a light left on when I went to bed and how scared I was of the dark; and my own children, in turn, like to have a night-light left on throughout the hours of darkness. No wonder, then, that light is a symbol shared by almost every religion and by many movements and organisations that profess no faith at all. Within the Christian faith, there are few more enduring or better-loved images than that of Jesus coming as the Light of the World.

The picture Jesus paints here, however, is rather different, and one that comes as something of a shock, for it stands the image on its head. 'You are the light of the world', he tells us, and suddenly, as well as receiving light we are those called to illuminate the lives of others. It reminds us that faith involves give as well as take, responsibility as well as privilege, service as well as reward. It's not all down to us, of course – it is ultimately the light of Christ that must shine through us – but if we think we can have one without the other, then it's time to ask some searching questions of our faith, for we may just find that we've taken a step back into the darkness.

Showing off?

Conduct yourselves wisely in your dealings with those outside the faith, making the most of every opportunity. May your speech always be gracious, seasoned with salt, in such a way that you know how to respond appropriately to everyone. (Colossians 4:5-6)

How would you feel if you'd spent a fortune on a wonderful new hairstyle, only for no one to notice? Or how about if you rolled up to work one day in a spanking new Rolls-Royce and no one batted an eyelid? You'd be disappointed, wouldn't you? How about if you were dining in a top-notch restaurant and you spilled soup down your front, or if you were about to meet someone on a first date and suddenly your mother turned up with a scrapbook of you as a baby – how would you feel then? Pretty embarrassed, to say the least! There are some things in life we like to show off and others we definitely don't!

Which brings us to the words of Paul to the Colossians, for what he was effectively telling them to do was to show off. Not in the sense we usually use that expression – blowing our own trumpet, being puffed up with our own importance – but instead, showing the love of Christ and his renewing transforming power. Don't be shy about your faith, said Paul. Let people see what you're made of, what you have to offer in Christ, what a difference he has made to your life. Let your honesty, sincerity, compassion and genuine concern for others set you apart, serving as a beacon to others. Is that showing off? Not in the way the world understands it, no – it's more a matter of letting it show; and that brings us to the crunch question that we all do well to ask ourselves. We may make time for devotions, we may attend church on a

Sunday, we may commit ourselves day after day to the service of Christ, but when we get out into the world, into the routine business of life, how far will any of this show itself in action?

Theory and practice

Put the trumpet to your lips! A vulture soars over the sanctuary of the Lord, because they have broken my covenant and defied my law. They appeal to me for help, crying, 'We know you, Lord God of Israel.' But Israel has rejected what is right, and in consequence will be pursued by the enemy. They established kings against my wishes; they set up leaders without my knowledge; they have created idols of silver and gold for themselves. (Hosea 8:1-4)

Take an exam today and the chances are that you will find a much greater emphasis upon practical work than was once the case. Increasingly, it is recognised that while theory is important, it is equally important to know how to use it; to be able to apply knowledge to daily life. On paper, we may know everything there is to know about a subject, yet we barely have a clue how to act upon it. On the other hand, in some tests the emphasis upon theory has been stepped up. Enrol now for a driving test and as well as showing the examiner that you know how to drive you must also display a sound knowledge of the Highway Code. The fact is that both theory and practice are important, each complementing the other.

Sadly, when it comes to serving God, this is all too often forgotten. So it was with the people of Israel in the days of the prophet Hosea. They believed that they knew God inside out but they were mistaken. They knew *about* him – what he had done and what he promised to do – but they no longer acted upon it. Faith had become divorced from life, with disastrous consequences. The danger is just as real today. We can all too easily become nominal Christians, professing faith in Christ and yet showing no evidence of commitment in terms of the way we live. Equally, we can turn commitment into a matter of doing good works, loving others and working for a better society, forgetting the underlying message of the gospel. We need to make room for both if faith is to be authentic, spending time in prayer, study and reflection in order to know God better, but also acting upon what we learn of him and his will for our lives. Theory and practice – don't let either one get the better of the other.

What's in a name?

Those who had been scattered following the persecution that developed in response to the martyrdom of Stephen travelled as far as Phoenicia, Cyprus and Antioch, though preaching the word only to the Jews. Some among them, however, were Cypriots and Cyrenians, and when these came to Antioch they preached about Christ to Greeks as well. And God's hand was upon them in such a way that a great number of them believed and turned to the Lord. It was there in Antioch that disciples were first called 'Christians'. (Acts 11:19-21, 26b)

Do you know what your name means? Mine, apparently, means 'carried away in triumph' or 'borne away in victory'. A nice thought, but I'm still waiting, and there's no sign of much happening yet! The fact is, of course, that our names don't signify very much, chosen because our parents liked the sound of them rather than because they say anything about us. A nickname, by contrast, is different. Typically, it says something about a person; the name designed to encapsulate some distinguishing feature.

So it was for believers in Jesus who had fled to Antioch following persecution for their faith. There they proclaimed and lived out the gospel with such resounding success that they earned a nickname that has stuck ever since: 'Christians'. It wasn't just an empty label; it said something about them, highlighting the fact that these people followed the way of Christ. Would anyone today, I wonder, looking at our lives, think to label us 'Christians'? Would it stick out a mile that we are followers of Jesus? Many still call themselves 'Christians' but they don't see that as having any bearing on the way they live. It's up to us to show them differently.

A working faith

Some may argue, 'You have faith and I have works.' Show me your faith without works, and I will show you my faith by my works. You have sufficient faith to believe there is one God. Well done! Even demons believe that and tremble at the thought. Can't you get it into your head, you nitpicker, that faith divorced from works yields nothing? (James 2:18-20)

'Do as I say, not as I do.' It's easy to empathise with the sentiment behind those words, for probably most of us are all too aware of the gulf between the principles we claim to follow and those we actually live by. 'Don't be put off,' we want to tell people; 'look at the theory rather than the practice.' Only, of course, they don't – actions invariably speak louder than words. We can talk about faith all we like.

We can speak of God's love and his care for all until we are blue in the face. It will count for nothing if the way we live puts across a different message.

Our faith needs to show itself in the things we do and the people we are; only then will people stop and take notice. To use another old saying: 'Precepts may lead, but examples draw'.

Growth in faith (*see also* Grace: Growth in grace)

About turn

You will have heard of my former conduct within Judaism – how I vigorously persecuted and laid waste the Church of God and how I progressed in Judaism beyond most of my contemporaries, defending the tradition of my fathers with a fanatical zeal. When, though, the one who elected me from my mother's womb chose by his grace to reveal his Son through me, so that I might preach him among the nations, I did not discuss it with anyone, or go to Jerusalem to meet with those who were Apostles before me, but went away to Arabia before returning to Damascus. I was unknown then except by name to the churches of Judea, they having heard only that their former persecutor was now preaching the faith, and they praised God because of me. (Galatians 1:13-17, 22-24)

Early in her term as prime minister, Margaret Thatcher made a proud boast that was to become a trademark catchphrase: 'The lady is not for turning.' Was that a quality or a flaw, a sign of strength or a weakness? The answer, I suspect, is a bit of both. It takes courage to hold on to our convictions, not least in politics. On the other hand, there may be times when we need to listen to other opinions, explore other avenues and even change direction altogether.

We see the last of those options graphically illustrated in the life of the Apostle Paul. Imagine the courage it must have taken for him, the archetypal Pharisee and destroyer of the Church, publicly to declare he had got things wrong. You might have expected him to keep his conversion quiet, adopt a low profile, but not Paul. Instead, he pursued his new faith with the same vigour with which he had pursued his old. Conversion for us may be a far less dramatic experience, yet nonetheless there is a change for us all – turning our backs on the old self and embracing the new. As with Paul, it is a two-fold response, involving not just a moving away from our former life but a moving towards Christ. It takes courage to accept that all is not as it should be and to commit oneself to a lifetime of discipleship. It takes more courage still, having made that initial step, to recognise that the job, far from being finished is only just begun. Conversion is not a one-off experience but an ongoing process – a turning and turning again to Christ.

Body-building

You, my friends, building yourselves up on your most holy faith and praying in the Holy Spirit, keep yourselves in the love of God, and look forward to that day when, in his mercy, our Lord Jesus Christ will give us eternal life. (Jude verses 20-21)

In the paper a while back, I spotted a truly grotesque picture. It related to an article concerning the possible inclusion of body-building as an official Olympic sport, and featured two muscular body-builders, biceps bulging, sinews stretching and veins popping. All right, so I wouldn't have minded a few of those muscles myself, but not to the point of becoming an Arnold Schwarzenegger look-alike!

There is, though, a sense in which we all need to build ourselves up, and that is in terms of our relationship with Christ. Faith is not something that grows automatically, like some seed that we can plant and then forget about until the fruits start to appear. It needs to be nourished and nurtured, so that it will develop in the way it should, strong and healthy. That means more than the occasional prayer or quick dip into our favourite Bible verses. It requires a diet that will both sustain and help us to grow further, until we reach something of the measure of the stature of Christ. That, though, is only half of it, for faith also needs to be exercised if it is to stay in shape, put through its paces in the daily treadmill of life. We may not aspire to become Christian heavyweights but what is our goal in discipleship? Are we content to be spiritual weaklings, or do we hunger to grow strong in the Lord?

An evolving faith

He said to them, 'What about you – who do you say that I am?' Peter answered, 'You are the Christ.' Then he warned them to tell no one about him. And he began to teach them that it was necessary for the Son of Man to suffer many things, to be rejected by the chief priests, the elders and the scribes, to be killed and on the third day to rise again. He made no secret of it. Then Peter, taking him aside, began to reproach him. But he spun round, and seeing the disciples there, he took Peter to task, saying, 'Get behind me, Satan: for you are preoccupied not with the things of God, but the things of man.' (Mark 8:29-33)

The moment when Peter confessed his faith in Christ tends to be portrayed as one of the most momentous events in the gospel narratives – a supreme moment of understanding and a corresponding expression of commitment. To me, though, it is also an enigmatic moment; as much a day Peter would have wanted to forget as remember. Certainly, he declared Jesus to be the Messiah, but was he alone in this perception or simply voicing the opinion held by his fellow Apostles. The idea that *he* understood who Jesus was more clearly than *they* did is given the lie in what follows, when far from being the rock of the Church, as he is described in other accounts of this incident, he is labelled 'Satan'. Strong stuff indeed!

Perhaps the greatest lesson we can draw from this story is that coming to faith is not the one-off event we sometimes imagine but an ongoing process that never ends. Peter thought he had understood the nature of Christ, yet, of course, he was later to deny his faith three times. Even after that he was still learning, coming to recognise that the age-old distinction between Jew and Gentile, clean and unclean, had no place in the Christian message. Faith was never a finished article but always on the production line, being shaped, added to, refined, polished. Beware those who think they've arrived and who believe they have fathomed the depths of the gospel. Avoid such an error yourself. We may know part of the truth but, in this life at least, we will never know the whole truth.

Eyes to see

As he and his disciples were leaving Jericho, followed by a large crowd, a blind beggar, Bartimaeus, the son of Timaeus, was sitting by the roadside. When he heard that it was Jesus of Nazareth passing by, he started to cry out, saying, 'Jesus, Son of David, have mercy on me!' Many in the crowd rebuked him, telling him to be quiet, but he called out yet more loudly, 'Son of David, have mercy on me!' Jesus stopped in his tracks and said, 'Call him here.' They called the blind man, saying to him, 'Take heart and get up, for he is calling you.' So, throwing off his cloak, he leapt up and came to Jesus. Then Jesus said to him, 'What do you want me to do for you?' The blind man answered, 'Teacher, grant that I may see again.' Jesus said to him, 'Go; your faith has healed you.' Immediately, he regained his sight and followed him on the way. (Mark 10:46-52)

There is a supreme irony in the story of Bartimaeus, just as there is in the account in John's Gospel of the man by the Pool of Siloam. Both stories concern a blind man seeking help from Jesus and in both cases there is, initially at least, hostility from the crowd. In Mark's story, this is directed against Bartimaeus for presuming to bother Jesus; in John's, it is directed against Jesus for presuming to heal and forgive sins. What unites each account is the contrast between this misguided response and that of the one Jesus heals: Bartimaeus believes that Jesus has time for everyone, and he is not disappointed. The result is that he ends up following the way of Jesus. The blind man in John's Gospel falls on his knees in worship and declares his faith in Jesus as the Son of God (John 9:38).

The blindness that both evangelists want us to think about is not so much the absence of physical but spiritual sight. The crowds think they see but they don't. The two men know they cannot see, but in recognising their need of Jesus they see more than anyone else, not just with their eyes but with their souls. For us, too, there is more to life than our eyes tell us. The problem is that many of us do not or will not see it. We need to follow the example of Bartimaeus and to ask Jesus, 'Grant that I may see'.

Pot-bound Christians?

He gave some to be Apostles, some prophets, some evangelists, and some pastors and teachers, to prepare God's people for practical service and to build up the body of Christ until we are united in faith and the knowledge of the Son of God, attaining maturity corresponding to the full measure we see in Christ. Then we will no longer be like children. Instead, speaking the truth in love, we will in every respect grow into the one who is the Head; that is, Christ. (Ephesians 4:11-14a, 15)

I couldn't work it out at all. It had been doing well until then – a beautiful healthy plant growing with seemingly inexhaustible vigour – but now something was wrong; the once glossy leaves a listless yellow, new growth sparse and the stems spindly. I tried feeding, watering, pruning it, but to no avail – the malaise continued to worsen. Then, suddenly, I realised the problem, a tangle of roots protruding from the base of the container providing the vital clue. The plant was pot-bound, crying out for space in which to spread its feet. A few weeks later, repotted with a liberal supply of fresh compost, it was romping away with all its former exuberance.

The analogy with faith is clear enough. When we start out in discipleship, growth is rapid, everything new and exciting, so much to learn and discover – our commitment seeming to blossom with every passing day. Imperceptibly, however, the process stutters, slows, stops, until, instead of growing in faith, our devotion starts to shrivel and our enthusiasm to fade. We become comfortably ensconced in the same old soil, resenting any disturbance, unaware that our faith is being starved and suffocated, inexorably sucked dry. If it is not ultimately to die, we need to be open to new horizons, receptive to ideas other than our own, and ready to explore new avenues of service. You may have grown once, you may think you are growing still, but the reality may be that you've become a pot-bound Christian. The more vehemently you reject that possibility, the more likely it is to be true.

Wrestling in faith

Grappling with God

Jacob was left alone; and a man wrestled with him there until dawn. When the man saw that he had not defeated Jacob, he struck him on his thigh as they wrestled, such that he dislocated Jacob's hip. He said, 'Let go of me, for dawn is breaking', but Jacob responded, 'I will not let you go, unless you bless me'. 'What is your name?' he asked. 'Jacob,' came the reply. Then the man said, 'You will no longer be called Jacob, but Israel, for you have contended both with God and with humans, and prevailed.' Then Jacob asked him, 'Please tell me your name.' 'Why do you ask my name?' he said, but then he gave him his blessing. So Jacob called the place Peniel, saying, 'I have seen God face to face, and yet my life has been spared.' The sun rose upon him as he passed Peniel, limping because of his hip. (Genesis 32:24-31)

Grappling with God – it's a strange idea, isn't it? Very different from the more traditional picture of humbly and obediently accepting God's will. Yet that is what we find in one of the most dramatic if enigmatic incidents in the Bible. The imagery is crude, if not shocking – a mysterious stranger who accosts Jacob by the ford at Jabbok turning out to be none other than God himself. More puzzling still, so tenaciously does Jacob hold fast during the ensuing test of strength that God is unable to extricate himself without first granting a blessing. As Alice might have said, 'It all gets curiouser and curiouser'.

Yet it is precisely the primitiveness of this encounter that, for me, makes it so compelling. There is no false piety here, no alabaster saint as far removed from our human condition as it is possible to be. Here is an individual like you or me, coming warts and all before God and struggling to come to terms with the complex realities of life and faith. Who knows quite what Jacob wrestled with in the darkness of that night – doubt, fear, pride, guilt – you name it and it was probably there! Symbolic the whole story may be, but its power remains undiminished, giving hope and encouragement to all those who grapple with God in turn.

Faithfulness of God

see also Will and purpose of God

Bearing our burdens

Humble yourselves under the mighty hand of God so that, in due course, he may exalt you. Cast all your burdens upon him, for it matters to him what happens to you. So then, let us come boldly before his throne of grace, so that we may obtain mercy and find grace to help in time of need. (1 Peter 5:7; Hebrews 4:16)

It's often said that we should bear one another's burdens. That's all very well, and in an ideal world it would no doubt provide most of the support we could ever have need for. Only this isn't an ideal world, and there are problems that we either feel unable to share, or that no one can help with, or that people simply do not want to know about. I imagine we've all been in situations when we've felt utterly over-whelmed by a situation and haven't known who to turn to; hence the existence of organisations like the Samaritans.

Thankfully, we do not depend merely on human support for assis-tance – we are able to share our cares and burdens with God. Do that and, though the problems will not magically disappear, we will find a new perspective on them, an inner peace whatever our trouble, rest for our souls.

The divine seal

When you heard the word of truth, the good news of salvation, and believed in him, you likewise were marked with the seal of the Holy Spirit – the guarantee of our inheritance when God redeems his people, to the praise of his glory. (Ephesians 1:13-14)

A while back I received a letter in the morning post, the seal of which had somehow come unstuck in transit. Whether it had gone to a wrong address and been opened by mistake or whether it had not been prop-erly stuck in the first place wasn't clear, but what interested me was a sticker over the envelope bearing an apology from the Post Office. Clearly the fact that the seal had been broken was considered a serious thing, serious enough to merit some kind of formal acknowledgement. As it turned out, the contents of the letter were unimportant, just another of those innumerable circulars that turn up with such monotonous regularity, but the incident shed new light for me on the words of Paul to the Ephesians. If a seal is important today, it was ten times more so in his time, the personal seal of an important dignitary or official investing a document with that sender's authority. It guaranteed safe passage and the authenticity of what lay within.

So it is with the gift God has sent in Christ. The promise of mercy, renewal and new life in him is given by God's authority and with his guarantee. He has accomplished all that needs to be done, overcoming everything that keeps us from him. The promise is sure, the inheritance certain – signed and sealed.

Don't forget it

Hear, O Israel: The Lord is our God, the Lord alone. You shall love the Lord your God with all your heart, and with all your soul, and with all your might. Keep these words that I am commanding you today in your heart. Recite them to your children and talk about them when you are at home and when you are away, when you lie down and when you rise. Bind them as a sign on your hand, fix them as an emblem on your forehead, and write them on the door-posts of your house and on your gates. (Deuteronomy 6:4-9)

Are you the sort of person liable to forget your own head if it wasn't screwed on? I am! I've lost count of the various items I've mislaid on my travels. Last time it was a pair of trousers left in a hotel wardrobe; before that a pullover at a friend's house: and before that there was a succession of diaries, combs, wallets, utensils, books, umbrellas and countless other bits and pieces. You may not be quite so forgetful but we all have limits to what we can remember, whether trivial things or matters of greater importance.

That's why the writer of Deuteronomy laid such store on teaching God's commandments and recalling his marvellous deeds across the years. He knew that no matter what God does for us, we can all too easily forget it, singing his praises one moment and bitterly complaining the next. Don't fall into that trap. Don't lose sight of the many blessings you have received, the promises God has given, the help and strength he still longs to give, the future he has in store for you and all who love him.

An enduring kingdom

I know that whatever God does endures for ever; nothing can be added to or taken away from it. God has done this, so that all must stand in wonder before him. (Ecclesiastes 3:14)

I had the pleasure recently of copy-editing a book on archaeology. It was a fascinating read, documenting civilisations that existed centuries before Christ, some so technologically advanced that it has taken nearly seven millennia to rediscover the skills they took for granted. At the time these civilisations must have filled surrounding nations with awe, and the prospect of such mighty empires ever declining must have seemed quite unthinkable. Yet decline they did, to the point that, barely fifty years ago, we knew next to nothing about them.

There is one kingdom, and one kingdom only, which is different; and that, of course, is the kingdom of God. When everything else has passed away, when the brief existence of this planet we call Earth is long since over, his kingdom will endure – unending, unchanging, unshakeable. All this is not to disparage the wonder of this world or the joys of this life. Rather it reminds us of the need to place our ultimate trust in what is of ultimate significance – in a hope that will never let us down.

An eternal promise

We can confidently say, 'The Lord is my helper, I will not be afraid; what can anyone do to me?' (Hebrews 13:6)

Sitting there in the dentist's waiting room, contemplating yet more fillings and other equally hideous forms of legalised torture, those words suddenly rang rather hollow. 'What can anyone do to me?' Well, a great deal, actually. All right, so a visit to the dentist is not so dreadful, but you have only to read the account in Hebrews 11 of the sufferings inflicted on God's people in days gone by to realise the atrocities that can be perpetrated by our fellow human beings: 'They were stoned to death . . . sawn in two . . . killed by the sword . . . persecuted, tormented.' Nor does being a Christian in any way guarantee an exemption from physical suffering. For many it has been the opposite; their commitment to Christ bringing suffering, if not death itself. That is not to say God will not give us strength to face such times, for he has clearly done just that on countless occasions, but if we see faith as some kind of insurance policy for health and happiness, then we may be in for a bitter disappointment.

What the writer to the Hebrews had in mind when he said so confidently, 'What can anyone do to me?', was not our immediate fate but our eternal destiny. He knew well enough the trials Christians can go through, and yet he also knew what God has promised. That is precisely why he wrote as he did. None of us knows what we may face in this world, whether good or ill, but we do know that God's love is with us, not just now but for all eternity, and that nothing will ever finally be able to undermine that promise. We too, then, can confidently say, 'The Lord is my helper, I will not be afraid. What can anyone do to me?'

The everlasting arms

The everlasting God is your home, and his arms are perpetually beneath you. (Deuteronomy 33:27)

Anyone who has had children will never forget the magical moment when they first began to walk. It was probably a few stumbling steps, no more, but it marked another stage in the journey of life. For such steps to happen, however, one thing is usually needed – a mother or father close at hand with arms outstretched, waiting to catch their offspring should they start to totter and fall. The knowledge that someone is there to offer support is all important, giving children the confidence they need to take not just their first faltering steps en route to proficient walking but also their first steps in so much else – exploring new horizons, meeting new people, starting a new school, taking on new responsibilities and so on. Sometimes this will lead to success; at other times to failure; but always there will be – or at least should be – the knowledge that a mother or father is there for them, ready to pick them up, offer a comforting embrace, and urge them onwards.

So it is with God. He is always there watching over us, ready to offer a helping hand in times of need, to lift us up when we stumble, to comfort us in sorrow and reassure us in times of fear. Even in death, those arms are there, enfolding us as we meet the last enemy and leading us to life eternal. God delights in us as much as we do in our own children, and whether we see it or not, we rest secure in his everlasting arms.

The God who never forgets us

Cry out for joy, O heavens; exult, O earth; burst into song, O mountains; for the Lord has comforted his people and shown compassion to them in their time of distress. Yet Zion claims, 'The Lord has abandoned me, God has forgotten me.' Is there any way a mother could forget the baby at her breast and fail to show compassion to the child she has borne? Even if she could possibly forget, I will not forget you! Look and see, I have engraved you on the palms of my hands. (Isaiah 49:13-16a)

Elephants, they say, never forget. Whether that's true or not, I've no idea, but one thing of which I'm fully convinced is that God never forgets us. It may seem otherwise sometimes; indeed, in several places in the Bible, and in the Psalms particularly, we often encounter the anguished cry of someone who feels utterly abandoned by God. Yet, invariably, even the most heart-rending of these passages ends up with a realisation that God was present all along – a fact that leads to a spontaneous outburst of praise and thanksgiving.

At other times, we may feel God has justifiably turned his back on us, not because he doesn't care but because *we* have forgotten *him*. A sense of guilt can lead us to dismiss any idea that he is still interested in us. When it comes to people, even those we may have counted valued friends, that can sometimes happen, but with God never! No matter how often we fail, frustrate or deny him, how estranged we may feel or undeserving we may consider ourselves, we are always in his thoughts, his love reaching out to bless and his hand outstretched to lead. Even though *we* may forget *him*, *he* will not forget *us*.

Going astray

We have all gone astray like sheep; each going our own way, but the Lord has laid on him the offences of us all. (Isaiah 53:6)

One of the television programmes I used to enjoy watching was the BBC series *One Man and His Dog*. The skill of the handlers and the devoted obedience of the sheepdogs never ceased to amaze me. Equally fascinating were the actions of the sheep: at times seeming plain stupid, at other times wilfully stubborn.

It is little wonder that biblical writers so often drew an analogy between sheep and people, because we too have a penchant for displaying precisely those characteristics. We blindly follow those around us instead of thinking for ourselves. We stumble from one mistake to another. We act on impulse rather than from reason and can even on occasions resist those who try to help us. Yet, however far we go astray, ours is a God who comes looking for us; a God who has given his all to restore us to his side. Give thanks for the wonder of that love.

A never-failing spring

Again, the Lord spoke to me: Because this people have turned their backs on the gently flowing waters of Shiloah, the Lord will bring up the mighty flood-waters of the Euphrates against it, the king of Assyria and all his glory. It will rise ever higher and burst its banks, and it will sweep on as a mighty flood into Judah, spilling over until it reaches neck height. Its outstretched wings will fill every part of your land, O Immanuel. (Isaiah 8:5-8)

There was chilling news announced today: a warning from Tearfund that within the next 25 years over two-thirds of the world's population will be facing an acute shortage of water. As never before, water is becoming a precious commodity, bought and sold on international markets, and the trend is set to continue as nations compete for supplies of this life-giving resource. The 'waters of Shiloah' that the prophet Isaiah spoke of can, on one level, be understood simply in these terms. He is referring to a canal that flowed gently but irrepressibly into Jerusalem, fed by the spring of Gihon and culminating in the Pool of Siloam. It was hugely valued – understandably so, given the arid climate of Israel – for not once had it been known to dry up; indeed, the spring still supplies water for Jerusalem to this day.

For Isaiah, though, it was more than simply an unfailing source of water, it was also a symbol of the faithful, enduring and unceasing love of God; a love that never stopped flowing out to his people but which they had now turned their backs on. The result, he warned, would be an unstoppable disaster in the form of Assyrian oppression, which, in contrast to God's quiet provision, would engulf them all in turmoil. The theology may be crudely simplistic, but the underlying message is sound: if we put our faith in God, his love will sustain us, whatever we might face. If we look elsewhere for something on which to base our lives, we may find we have unleashed more than we bargained for.

A point of reference

I, the Lord, do not change. (Malachi 3:6a)

Searching through my bookshelves the other day, I came across a couple of books about my home town, Southend-on-Sea – *Southend Past* and *Edwardian Heyday*. The two comprise a fascinating collection of photographs showing the town in bygone days, and to see the difference that just over a century has made is truly astounding. Take the area of Prittlewell, where I spent most of my childhood years and where my parents still live. Today, it is a busy, featureless area with little to distinguish it from the urban sprawl that has swallowed it up, but 120 years ago it was the main habitation in the area and a truly delightful village full of timber-framed cottages and rustic charm. Were it possible to travel through time, a visitor from the past would imagine they had come to the wrong place, except for one feature: the parish church of St Mary's that still presides majestically over its centre – a welcome point of reference in a forever changing landscape. Not that you have to go back a hundred years to notice changes: almost every shop I remember as a boy has either closed down or changed its use, and once quiet roads are now busy thoroughfares.

The case of Southend, of course, is repeated in towns up and down the country, and is but one more example of the way life itself is in a constant state of flux. As the years pass, not only places change but also people, our attitudes, opinions, beliefs and convictions repeatedly challenged and shaken, if not completely undermined. Many find themselves not knowing what to believe in, life apparently without meaning or direction. Yet, as the prophet Malachi reminded the inhabitants of Judah centuries ago, there is a point of reference for us all in the one true God; the God who tells us, 'I, the Lord, do not change'. That is a promise which generations of believers across the years have found to be true, in a world where everything else seems never to stay the same.

Raise your sights

Who has gauged the waters in the palm of his hand and set the boundary between heaven and earth? Who has weighed up the raw materials for this planet, calculating the proportions of hills and mountains? Who advised the Lord's spirit, offering counsel and instruction? Who did he confer with for guidance, and who showed him the way of justice? Who educated him, and gave him wisdom? Whole countries and cultures are like a drip from a bucket, nothing more than dust when weighed in the balance. (Isaiah 40:12-15a)

How many grains of sand are there on a beach? How many stars in the universe? None of us knows the answers to such questions, but I expect any guess we might make would fall well short of the correct number, for we are dealing here with a scale that stretches human comprehension to the limit.

There is something of this idea in the wonderful picture of God given by the prophet Isaiah. His words were addressed to a people in crisis: a people who, after years of exile in Babylon, had concluded that God was either unwilling or unable to help them. They considered themselves beyond forgiveness. They feared that their God must be inferior to the gods of Babylon. They felt powerless, defeated and bereft of hope. Into their despair, Isaiah brought a simple but profound message: raise your sights! God is unwilling to forgive them, they say? Think again: he is more than ready to pardon. He is inferior to the gods of Babylon? Think again: he is the creator of the ends of the earth, ruler over space and time. The future is bleak? Think again: he will renew their strength and restore their hope. Here is a glorious reminder of the sovereignty of God; the God who is more loving, more powerful and more gracious than we can ever begin to imagine.

Rock of ages!

The Lord is my rock, fortress and deliverer. God is my rock, the one in whom I take refuge – my stronghold, refuge and saviour. He is a shield for all who take refuge in him – my shield and the horn of my salvation. Who is the rock except our God? The Lord lives! Praise be to my rock! Exalted be God, the rock, my Saviour! (adapted from 2 Samuel 22:2-3, 31b-32, 47)

Some places live on in the memory long after you last visited them. For me such a place is Lindisfarne Castle up on the Northumberland Coast. No, it wasn't just the mead brewed locally by the monks, delicious though that was; it was the sight of that castle perched majestically on its rocky outcrop as the sea lapped across the causeway that separates its island location from the mainland at high tide. It is almost as though castle and rock are one, and it is easy to imagine the castle proudly standing there for centuries to come in defiance of the wind and the waves that batter against it.

The memory of the scene breathes life for me into the repeated references in scripture to God as our rock and our fortress, giving a vivid impression of the sort of qualities each writer was seeking to convey. Ours indeed is a rock who will endure not just for centuries but for all eternity; a stronghold that nothing shall ever overcome. Though all else may change, God remains the same. Though all else may fail, he will not!

Fulfilment, true nature of

The cost of greed

A voice called out of the crowd to him, 'Teacher, tell my brother to divide the family inheritance with me.' But he replied, 'Man, who appointed me to be a judge or arbiter over you?' And he warned them, 'Beware! Guard against all types of greed; for the value of a person's life cannot be measured in terms of possessions.' (Luke 12:13-15)

I could hardly believe it, but there it was in black and white: 'Take as much as you can eat.' Well, I wasn't going to waste that chance, was I? So I set about piling up my plate, eyes wide with anticipation as I surveyed the bewildering range of delicacies before me. A bit of this, a bit of that, and a bit more just for luck. So it went on, until I was almost staggering under the mountain of food I had assembled. It seemed like a good idea at the time, but a short while later, with my belt tightening and every mouthful becoming more of an effort, I began to reconsider. For all my endeavours, the mountain had scarcely diminished and it was clear that there was no way I could eat it all. Yet I couldn't let everyone see that my eyes were bigger than my stomach – I had to do my best to clear my plate. The result was that what should have been a gourmet's delight turned out to be a gastronomic nightmare – one that I have never forgotten to this day.

I should, of course, have been content with enough but, sadly, I wasn't. We can all be guilty of something similar, wanting that little bit extra even though we probably already have too much. That extra possession we acquire, for example – does it really bring us happiness, or is it simply another insurance risk, another item to clutter up the home, another five-minute wonder soon to be discarded, another empty treasure that we will hoard away with scarcely a second glance? Not only the stomach pays the price of greed; body, mind and soul can pay also. Beware!

First things first

Consider how you have fared. You have sown much, but have harvested little. You eat, but never have as much as you would like. You drink, but never have your fill. You clothe yourselves, but are never warm. You earn wages, but it is as though you put them into a bag full of holes. You look for much, but it comes to little; and what you bring home, I blow away. Why? says the Lord of hosts. Because my house lies derelict while each of you rush off to your own houses. (Haggai 1:6, 9)

We live today, so we are told, in an age of rampant materialism, an era in which everyone is always grasping after the newest gadget, the latest fashion, the most up-to-date model.

It is difficult to argue with such an assessment of modern society, but is the phenomenon as new as we sometimes tend to make out? The book of Haggai suggests not. As we scan its pages, we could well be reading a socioeconomic analysis of Britain today, such are the similarities in tone. The technology and resources at our disposal may be far greater than those in Haggai's time, but the underlying cravings are no different. Greed, materialism – call it what you will – is an age-old, and probably universal, characteristic, yet ironically it rarely seems to bring happiness, all too often indeed the reverse. Creature comforts have their place, as Haggai would I'm sure have been the first to accept, but if we put these before our spiritual needs the result is a never-ending striving for an inner fulfilment which will forever remain tantalisingly out of reach.

Food for our souls

Pay attention, everyone who is thirsty, come and find water; and you that have no food, come, buy and eat! Come, buy wine and milk, not for money but beyond price. Why spend your money on that which is not bread, and why offer your labour for that which cannot satisfy? Listen carefully to what I say, and you will eat what is good, delighting yourselves in the richest of food. (Isaiah 55:1-2)

One of the hardest aspects of parenting must surely be getting one's children to eat. Offer them a bar of chocolate or a bag of sweets and there's no problem, but give them a healthy balanced meal and they will sit there picking at it for all the world as though you're trying to poison them! Sometimes they just don't know what's good for them!

That's not just true of children but all of us. When it comes to nourishing our souls, we all tend to be addicted to junk food rather than to what can truly satisfy. We cram so much into our lives in an effort to find fulfilment, yet still cannot fill the aching void deep inside. It's nothing new: countless generations have done the same since time immemorial. As the prophet Isaiah knew all too well, we are hopelessly addicted to instant satisfaction; to that which instinctively appeals to our senses yet cannot begin to meet our innermost needs. We need to make time for God, space for prayer and reflection, and room in our lives for spiritual sustenance. Fail to do that and, though our stomachs may be full to overflowing, our emaciated souls will slowly starve within us.

The key to contentment

Do not exhaust yourself in an effort to get rich; be sensible enough to avoid that trap, for though you see it one minute, it will be gone the next; suddenly taking wings to itself and flying off into the sky like an eagle. The miser rushes to get rich, apparently ignorant of the fact that loss is sure to come. Whoever loves money will not be content with money; nor the one who loves wealth, with gain. (Proverbs 23:4-5; 28:22; Ecclesiastes 5:10)

In 1957 the then Prime Minister, Harold Macmillan, informed the British public, 'Most of our people have never had it so good.' Nearly half a century later, we in the Western world have it better still in terms of material possessions. We live today in a country more prosperous than it has ever been; a society that enjoys a standard of living that our forebears could only have dreamt of just a few decades ago. So, are we correspondingly happier than those who lived before us, more content and fulfilled than previous generations? Paradoxically, the answer is no. If anything, the opposite is true, a deep sense of emptiness pervading the lives of many. All this is, of course, is not to deny that possessions can bring pleasure, nor that they make life easier in a variety of ways, but they can never meet our deepest needs.

It remains true that you cannot buy happiness. To discover that, we need to look deeper: we need to nurture our soul rather than our body, to unearth treasure that will last when all else has faded away. It is treasure such as this that Jesus promised to those who follow him.

A small price to pay

A certain ruler questioned him, 'Good Teacher, what do I need to do to inherit eternal life?' Jesus said to him, 'Why do you call me good? Only God is good, no one else. You know the commandments: "Do not commit adultery; do not murder; do not steal; do not bear false witness; honour your father and mother."' The man replied, 'I have kept all these since I was a boy.' Hearing this, Jesus said to him, 'There is one thing still missing. Sell everything you own and share the money among the poor, and you will have treasure in

*heaven; then come, follow me.' But, hearing this, the man became sad, for he
was exceedingly wealthy. Jesus looked at him and said, 'How hard it is for the
well-to-do to enter the kingdom of God! Truly, it is easier for a camel to pass
through the eye of a needle than for a rich person to enter the kingdom of God.'*
(Luke 18:18-25)

Does the story of the rich ruler make you uneasy? It does me. Despite
the fact that many rationalise its message, essentially suggesting that it
should be understood today as a hypothetical challenge rather than a
generally applicable principle, it is impossible to escape the feeling that
these words of Jesus represent a forcible challenge to our comfortable
twenty-first-century lifestyles. Of course money isn't everything, we
tell ourselves. Of course we'd happily give it up if asked. But would we?
I doubt it very much.

Thankfully, Jesus probably doesn't want us to give up all our possessions; the economic and social consequences, if we did, would be
alarming. Yet, it is equally probable that he wants us to give up a lot
more than we are usually prepared to sacrifice. In a world of massive
poverty and suffering, in which the divide between rich and poor grows
wider every day, can any of us really say we are doing enough? When
we think of what Jesus gave for us, how does our giving to others compare? The price asked of the rich ruler may seem large but it is small by
contrast. No wonder the story makes us uncomfortable.

Grace

Grace of God (*see also* Confession and forgiveness)

All talk?

Simon Peter said to him, 'Lord, where are you going?' Jesus replied, 'You cannot follow me where I am going now, but you will some day.' Peter said, 'Lord, why can't I follow you now? I will lay down my very life for you. Even though everyone else might fall away, I will not.' Jesus responded, 'Mark my words: today, this very night, before the cock crows twice, you will disown me three times.' Peter, though, protested forcefully, 'Even if I have to die with you, I will never disown you.' The others all said the same. (John 13:36-37; Mark 14:29-31)

'A penny off income tax, cheaper fuel, more investment in the health service and education, higher pensions, tough measures on crime . . . ' We've heard it all before, haven't we? The words trotted out by politicians every four years or so as the country braces itself for another election. It's not that the politicians set out to deceive us (well, not most of them, anyway); rather that they are swept along on the tide of the moment, only to find when it comes to it, that they simply can't deliver – their fine words exposed as all talk.

So it was for Peter in the moments leading up to the cross. 'Even though everyone else might fall away, I will not. Even if I have to die with you, I will never disown you.' Rash, impulsive words, no doubt, but he meant every word and fully believed he could honour such promises. Events, of course, were to prove him wrong. So what is the message here for us? That we, like Peter, are false and faithless? That we are often prone to empty rhetoric? Both are probably true. The key detail, however, is that Jesus knew full well that Peter would fail him, that his words were all talk, yet still he loved him – enough to continue to the cross, enough to have chosen him as the rock of his Church. That's the wonder of this incident: that far from wanting him to punish himself afterwards for his failure, Jesus wanted Peter to know that he knew his weakness, understood he would fail, and yet still loved him. Here is the awesome message of the gospel – the message that gives hope to us all.

Cancelling our debt

God forgave us all our sins, cancelling the debt written against us in the ledger with its legal requirements, irrevocably doing away with it by nailing it to the cross. (Colossians 2:13)

Have you ever been in debt? Apparently, this is the most widespread social problem of our time. It's a horrible situation to be in and one that I've always taken care to avoid since my days living on a student grant. Each term I would end up forty, fifty, even one hundred pounds overdrawn, and though that may seem a relatively small amount today, at the time it felt like a giant millstone around my neck. At Oxford, with no grant at all, and reliant upon a number of small trusts and the generosity of my home church, it was harder still. I spent many a sleepless night tossing and turning as I brooded over how far I could stretch the overdraft and how I could ever hope to repay it. It is not just financial debts, however, that can eat away at our peace of mind. To owe even an apology to someone can weigh heavily upon us and to owe recompense that we cannot possibly make is harder still.

It is such a debt that we owe to God, for we have all failed him in innumerable ways, each deserving of punishment according to the Law of Moses. No matter how hard we try, we can never pay what is due, no amount of good works able to earn our salvation. Yet, that is where we come to the heart of the gospel, the good news of God's gracious mercy in cancelling the debt. We do not need to wrestle with a burden of shame or guilt, for it has been taken from us, nailed with Christ on the cross and buried in the tomb; unlike him, never to return. There are no easy answers to owing money; somehow or other it has to be paid or, if it is written off, a black mark is put against our name. Thank God the debt we owe to him is freely and lovingly cancelled; we need only to ask.

A clean sheet

In the year King Uzziah died, I saw the Lord enthroned on high, exalted over all; and the hem of his robe filled the temple. Seraphim waited upon him, each having six wings; two of which they used to cover their faces, two to cover their feet, and two to fly. They called back and forth to one another, saying, 'Holy, holy, holy is the Lord of hosts; the whole earth is full of his glory.' At the sound of their voices the threshold shook and the house was filled with smoke. And I cried out, 'Woe am I! I am lost, for I am a man of unclean lips, living among a people of unclean lips; yet with my own eyes I have seen the King, the

Lord of hosts!' Then one of the seraphim flew to me, holding in his hand a burning coal taken from the altar with a pair of tongs. The seraph touched my mouth with it and said, 'Since this has touched your lips, your guilt is no more and your sin is done away with.' Then I heard the voice of the Lord saying, 'Whom shall I send? Who will go for me?' And I said, 'Here I am; send me!' (Isaiah 6:1-8)

One of the tragedies of the Church is that it has acquired a reputation for being smug, self-righteous, holier than thou. How this has happened I do not know, for while some in the Church are more than ready to sit in judgement, by far the majority are too aware of their own faults to point the accusing finger at others. Such, at least, has been my experience. The heart of the Christian message is one of forgiveness rather than judgement; about the God who is ready to accept us as we are, rather than as we should be. Of course this involves a desire to change, but it begins and ends with God rather than ourselves. The truth of this is most clearly demonstrated through Christ, but it was discovered centuries before by countless others.

So it was that a young man, worshipping in the temple of Jerusalem, suddenly found himself faced by the call of God. Hopelessly inadequate though he felt, burdened by a profound sense of unworthiness, Isaiah discovered that God is always ready to take the initiative in offering us a fresh start. All he needed to do was respond, and with that began one of the most remarkable prophetic ministries of all time, his words touching the hearts of generations across the centuries. All *we* need to do is respond in turn, to discover the new beginning God longs to bring us; a new beginning not of our own making but entirely of his grace.

Getting it wrong

So what are we to make of this? Should we carry on sinning so that grace may flourish all the more? Certainly not! If we've died to sin, how can we willingly persist in it? Do you not realise that in being baptised into Christ we've also been baptised into his death? In consequence, we can enjoy new life, just as the Father gloriously raised Christ from the dead. (Romans 6:1-4)

This was nice, I thought, as I lay in bed relaxing – a gentle tickle from my wife. Only then it dawned on me that she was busy reading, both hands holding her book. So if *she* wasn't tickling me, *what was*? With a mixture of trepidation and curiosity, I pulled back the duvet . . . and there it was – the biggest, hairiest spider I've ever seen, scampering up my armpit and on to my chest! Rarely have I moved so fast as at that moment. Rarely had the spider moved so fast either! Things were not as they had seemed; I had misread the situation completely.

So it was, in a very different sense, for the Church in Rome. Some there were suggesting that, since justification comes by faith in Christ, it doesn't matter how we live; that we can go out and do what we like, confident that God will forgive us. Some, indeed, pushed the idea even further, suggesting that we should purposely sin so that he might display his mercy yet more fully. I doubt any of us would consciously entertain thoughts like those for a moment, but we can nonetheless stray inadvertently down that road. It won't matter if I bend the rules just this once, we tell ourselves; God will understand. I needn't worry about the odd thing being wrong; God will forgive. No doubt he will, but we should never use that as an excuse for complacency. We are justified by God's grace, and for that let us daily give thanks, but we are also called to newness of life, and towards that let us daily strive – not in order to earn God's love but to thank him for it.

The God who believes in us!

God loved the world so deeply that he offered his only Son, so that all who believe in him need not die but can enjoy eternal life. (John 3:16)

'I believe in God, the Father almighty, maker of heaven and earth.' So say the opening words of the Apostle's Creed, a statement of faith designed to encapsulate the essential convictions of Christian belief; to summarise what we believe, or, at least, what we are meant to believe. Yet, all such creeds leave one thing out; a statement that, for me, is more important than any other, and that is the affirmation that *God* believes in *us*! We are talking, of course, about a different kind of belief, though it is not as different as you might at first think. What we see in the birth of Jesus is God firmly and resoundingly declaring: 'I believe in humankind!'

To understand the full wonder behind that statement we need to remind ourselves what, in the biblical sense, it means to say, 'I believe'. It doesn't mean accepting the existence of something, in the sense that we might believe in ghosts or flying saucers. It means belief in the sense of trust, putting our faith in something, and being ready, if necessary, to stake our name and reputation on the object of our belief. Seen in that light, how many people do we truly believe in? Yet, that is the belief God has in us. He doesn't see us through rose-coloured spectacles. He is not blind for a moment to our fallibility and sinfulness.

Yet, despite all that is wrong in our lives, he sees something precious in us, special and worth saving – even worth dying for! In the stable in Bethlehem, the child in a manger, and the life, death and resurrection that followed, we see God's emphatic 'yes' to humankind, his affirmation of our worth! The creeds are important, don't get me wrong, but they don't quite say everything, for it seems to me that if we haven't understood that God believes in us, we haven't really understood what it means to say, 'I believe in God'.

The God who is ready to welcome

He started back towards his father's house, but as he made his way his father spotted him in the distance and, overcome with emotion, rushed to embrace and kiss him. 'Father,' said the son, 'I've failed both you and God, so I don't deserve to be called your son.' The father, however, ordered his servants, 'Hurry, fetch a robe – the best one – and put it on him; place a ring on his finger and shoes on his feet. Kill the fatted calf and let's have a feast to rejoice; for my son was dead and has been brought back to life; I lost him, but now he's found!' (Luke 15:20-24)

Have you ever sat in a waiting room, wondering when you will be seen to? It's all too common, isn't it, as anyone who has sat in a hospital casualty department or DSS office will know only too well. How much longer will we have to wait? Is there some problem? Will we be seen at all? Such questions inevitably cross one's mind. Even worse, though, is sitting as a child outside the headteacher's office, waiting to be summoned after committing some misdemeanour – not that I would know, of course! What sort of reception will we get? What kind of punishment is in store for us?

Some people approach God like that, wondering whether he will receive them and afraid of the consequences if he does. 'Can he truly have time for someone like me?' we ask ourselves. 'Surely not! Can he possibly forgive my many mistakes? It beggars belief.' If that's how you feel, then look again at the parable of the lost son, for there we see one of the most memorable pictures of God in the whole Bible; a God who waits to greet us while we are still far off, reaching out to embrace us in love. With him, there is no question of being kept outside, left to stew and finally made to suffer. On the contrary, we need only make the first tentative steps of approach and he is there waiting to receive us, longing to welcome us home.

The God who seeks us out

He told them this parable: 'If a man had a hundred sheep and lost one of them, wouldn't he leave the ninety-nine in the desert and go in search of the one that is lost until he finds it? And, when it is found, he places it over his shoulders rejoicing. And then, coming home, he calls together his friends and neighbours, saying, "Rejoice with me, for I have found my sheep that was lost." In exactly the same way, I assure you that there will be more joy in heaven over one sinner coming to repentance than over ninety-nine righteous people who have no need to repent.' (Luke 15:3-7)

Why is it that when you we drop something it always falls into the most awkward and inaccessible of places? Instead of falling into the middle of the room, somehow it invariably ends up in some obscure nook or cranny, never to be found again. How long we are willing to keep on looking for it depends on the item in question. If it's a penny piece, we'll soon shrug and abandon the search; a gold ring, on the other hand, and we'll keep on looking for many weeks, probably always hoping that it will finally turn up. Few if any of us, however, will keep on looking for ever.

Yet this is the wonderful picture that Jesus paints of God in the parable of the Lost Sheep. God, we are told, is like the shepherd who goes on looking for his missing sheep 'until he has found it'! What a wonderful picture that is – a truly astonishing testimony to God's amazing grace! Here is the 'love that will not let me go' of which the hymn-writer George Matheson speaks; a love that goes on looking for us whenever we go astray; never resting and never giving up until we have been restored to the Father's side. It is a love unlike anything else we can ever know.

The graciousness of God

The people of Nineveh believed God's message. They announced a public fast and clothed themselves in sackcloth, from the least to the greatest. When God saw their response, how they renounced their wicked ways, he decided against bringing the punishment on them he had intended and he did not do it. Jonah, however, was piqued, and flew into a rage. He prayed to the Lord and said, 'O Lord! Is this not what I feared would happen back in my own country? This is the reason I took flight to Tarshish when you first called; for I knew you to be a gracious God, merciful, slow to anger, and overflowing in the constancy of your love, and all too ready to surrender thoughts of punishment. Now Lord, I implore you, take my life from me, for I'm better off dead than alive.' (Jonah 3:5, 10-4:3)

Many of the characters in the Old Testament seem almost too good to be true. We can feel daunted by the depth of their piety, devotion and commitment. When it comes to Jonah, however, it's a different story. One of the great appeals of this short book is the raw humanity of this reluctant prophet. Irascible, cold-hearted and petulant, he is just about the last person you would expect God to call into his service; his faults, if only he could see, equally as great as of those he was called to preach to. That is the beauty of this tale, for it vividly portrays God's amazing grace in action. No one in the narrative remotely deserves his blessing, yet all end up receiving it.

The same holds true for us. We may pray 'Forgive us our trespasses as we forgive those who trespass against us', but thankfully God is willing to go a good deal further than that. The consequences, if he wasn't, don't bear thinking about!

More than we deserve

There is no distinction, since all have sinned and fall short of the glory of God; they are now justified by his grace as a gift, through the redemption that is in Christ Jesus. (Romans 3:23-24)

My son, Samuel, has a clear sense of right and wrong, to the point sometimes that, having been naughty, he will deny himself a subsequent treat. 'No,' he says, 'I don't deserve it.' No amount of argument can persuade him to believe otherwise. Even when he has said sorry and we tell him whatever he did wrong is over and done with, his resolution remains undiminished.

There is something of that attitude in all of us when it comes to receiving the grace and forgiveness of God. We want to believe in it, but we are so ashamed of our mistakes and so conscious of our unworthiness that we find it hard to accept his pardon. We feel that we must suffer some further penance; that we need to punish ourselves before we can even begin to earn forgiveness. That may be our way but it is not God's. Forgiveness is not earned; it is given. None of us deserve it, yet all can receive it. We need only to acknowledge our mistakes and confess to being truly sorry. He asks no more!

Ready to receive

Sin pays a wage, and the wage is death, but God gives freely, and his gift is eternal life in union with Christ Jesus our Lord. (Romans 6:23)

It is more blessed, we are told, to give than to receive. We can interpret that in two ways. Most of all, of course, it is an encouragement to generosity, reminding us of the joy that comes through giving to others, but if we turn that around, there is another truth beneath the surface, for it can actually be surprisingly hard to receive. When someone presents us with an unexpected gift, or perhaps helps us out of financial difficulties, we can feel embarrassed and indebted. 'You shouldn't have done that!' we say, or, 'I can't possibly accept that.' We want to do something in return. Some go further, actually feeling angry, refusing to accept what they see as charity. Most of us have an innate feeling that we need to earn something rather than have it given.

Such a way of thinking easily spills over into our relationship with God. Although we talk of being justified by faith, deep down we feel that we must do something to show we deserve his mercy. That, though, is to forget the key message of the gospel: that God's love is not earned but is freely given through Christ. We do not have to prove our worth or pay God back. He asks us simply to receive.

An unexpected encounter

Jacob left Beersheba and set off towards Haran. He reached a certain spot and stopped off there for the night, because the sun had gone down. Taking a stone he came across, he tucked it under his head and lay down in that place. And in his dreams he saw a ladder rising up from the ground, its top reaching into heaven, the angels of God climbing up and down it. And the Lord appeared, standing beside him, and said, 'I am the Lord, the God of your father Abraham and the God of Isaac . . .' Jacob woke and said, 'Surely the Lord is in this place, and I didn't know it!' And he was afraid, and said, 'How awe-inspiring is this place! It is nothing less than the house of God, the very gate of heaven.' (Genesis 28:10-13a, 16-17)

Of all the great figures of the Old Testament, few showed less initial promise than Jacob. He comes across as an opportunist and a cheat, callously tricking his brother Esau out of his birthright, and then compounding this with the shameful deception of his father. As he made his way towards Haran, it was, no doubt, with a smug sense of self-satisfaction at having secured the prospect of a highly prosperous future. The last thing on his mind would have been God.

God, though, had other ideas, confronting him during the night in a vivid and unforgettable dream. It was the beginning of a gradual change in Jacob's life. No, he didn't change overnight – far from it. He continued in many ways to be the wily schemer of old. Yet the seeds had been sown; God had met with him and opened up a new perspective on life and the beginning of a new relationship. It was one, ultimately, that would see Jacob revered as one of the founding fathers of the Jewish faith and a celebrated 'man of God'.

Unlikely choices (1)

Here is an account of the genealogy of Jesus the Messiah, the son of David, the son of Abraham. Abraham fathered Isaac, who fathered Jacob, who fathered Judah and his brothers, who fathered Perez and Zerah by Tamar. Perez fathered Hezron, who fathered Aram, who fathered Aminadab, who fathered Nahshon, who fathered Salmon, who fathered Boaz by Rahab. Boaz fathered Obed by Ruth, and Obed fathered Jesse who was the father of King David. David was the father of Solomon by the wife of Uriah. (Matthew 1:1-6)

The opening chapter of Matthew's Gospel is surely one of the least inspiring in the Bible – or is it? At first sight, it looks like nothing more than a list of names, but appearances can be deceptive. Look deeper, and a different story emerges – for four of the names are anything but dull: Tamar, who conceived twins by her father-in-law Judah after deceiving him about her identity; Rahab, the prostitute in Canaan who sheltered Joshua and his colleagues when they were spying out the Promised Land; Ruth, the Gentile from Moab who married Boaz and settled in Israel; and 'the wife of Uriah' – Bathsheba– who had an illicit affair with King David that led indirectly to the death of her husband. It was unusual in Jewish circles to mention women in a genealogy; more unusual still to mention Gentiles, and as for those like Rahab, Tamar and Bathsheba who had been caught up in tawdry sordid affairs – frankly, they'd have been seen as an embarrassment.

So what's going on here? The answer is simple and wonderful. Here is a graphic demonstration of God's grace in Christ, even before he was born. He came, not through the morally perfect or ritually clean, nor through the accepted and expected routes, but through those deemed imperfect, unsuitable and unworthy. The pattern was wonderfully continued in the choice of Mary, an insignificant girl in Nazareth; in the selection of rough-and-ready shepherds as the first to hear the good news; in the call of fishermen, a tax collector and a zealot to be his disciples; and in the willingness Jesus showed to mix with 'tax collectors and sinners' throughout his ministry. Here is the God who has time for anyone, whoever that person may be; who has time for everyone, whatever they may have done. Here is the God who has time for you!

Unlikely choices (2)

You did not choose me; I chose you. (John 15:16)

Imagine that you had just been handed a freshly opened box of choco-lates. Which would you choose? It would be a tough decision, wouldn't it? If you're anything like me, though, you'd reject some options immedi-ately. You know the sort – the coffee creams, toffee cracknel or nougat that always end up left over at the end of every box. When you have a choice, you can afford to be choosy. All of which makes the words of Jesus in John's Gospel the more remarkable, for he is telling his disci-ples here that of all the thousands of people he could have chosen to be his Apostles, he chose them! Not that he was wrong to do so – history has more than vindicated his judgement – but, to put it kindly, they were not the obvious choice; hardly those you would expect anyone to choose if they planned to start a world-changing movement.

Yet Jesus had selected these above all others, recognising qualities in them that he could take and use towards the fulfilment of his purpose. So it continues today. We do not *choose* to follow Jesus; we *respond* to his call. He is the one who takes the initiative in establishing a relation-ship, not us. Why does he do that? Because, once again, he sees in us something special, something that he infinitely values. The greatest wonder of all is that he leaves no one out when choosing, no discards at the end of the pile. Though many will reject him, he has a place for everyone who is ready to receive him. Do you sometimes question whether you have any place in his kingdom, any right to call yourself a Christian? Then remember this: before you even knew there was a choice to make, Jesus chose you.

Use for the 'useless'

Consider the nature of your calling. Not many of you were wise in human terms; not many were important; not many were well born. God, however, chose the foolish of this world in order to shame the wise, the weak to shame the strong, the lowest and the despised – those considered as nothing – to quash those who consider themselves something, so that nobody may boast before him. (1 Corinthians 1:26-29)

It looked to me like a pile of old junk – a curious assortment of bric-a-brac and cast-offs barely worth a second glance. Clearly, however, some people saw things differently, for there was a queue outside waiting for the doors to open and the mad scramble to begin. I never felt altogether comfortable at those jumble sales, for I was keenly aware that for some people the goods on sale represented all they could afford, yet in my first church they were a fact of life – the only way to keep the doors open and keep me in a job. I learned something useful, however, from the experience; namely, that what might seem useless to one person can be anything but to another; a lesson that is equally applicable when it comes to assessing people. All too easily, we write people off, judging them by our own set of values and concluding that they fail to pass muster.

Strangely, we can do the same of ourselves, convinced that there is no way God can possibly use us. God, however, invariably has other ideas, able to use people in the most unexpected and surprising of ways. Never consider that you or anyone else is useless, for as far as God is concerned, 'useless' is a word that doesn't exist.

Growth in grace (*see also* Faith: Growth in faith)

Bearing fruit

He told this parable: 'A man, having planted a fig tree in his vineyard, came looking for fruit on it but found none. So he said to the vinedresser, "Look here! I've been coming here looking for fruit on this fig tree for the last three years, but I've found nothing. Chop it down! Why carry on letting it be a waste of space?" He replied, "Sir, leave it for this year, until I've had the chance to dig in some manure around it, and then let's see if it bears fruit next season. If not, you can chop it down."' (Luke 13:6-9)

What sort of comments did you get on your school reports? For me there was one remark that seemed to reappear with depressing regularity: 'Shows promise, but could do better.' Does that ring a bell? I thought it might! But, more important, was it true? How many of us, I wonder, wish we had worked just that little bit harder while we had the chance? How much more could we have achieved? How different might life have been? If only, if only, if only!

Sadly, we don't often get the chance to make up for past mistakes, not in terms of academic qualifications anyway, but when it comes to what matters most of all, thankfully it's another story. In the parable above, the vinedresser asks for one year's reprieve, in which the fig tree might bear fruit. Jesus goes further still, asking the Father to give us not just one more chance but as many as it takes for us finally to fulfil our potential in his service. Though we repeatedly grieve him through our failure to grow and bear fruit, he never gives up believing that the harvest may yet come.

The bitter end

Get rid of all bitterness, rage, temper, backbiting and insults, together with all malice, and be kind to one another, compassionate, forgiving one another as God in Christ has forgiven you. Be vigilant, in case anyone should fail to grasp the grace of God, ensuring that no root of bitterness springs up to spread unrest among you, through which many may be brought to ruin. (Ephesians 4:31-32; Hebrews 12:15)

Few of us in our lifetime will be fortunate enough to escape being badly let down or hurt by someone. A close relationship may end in acrimony, a trusted friend betray a confidence, a broken promise deny us a long-dreamed-of opportunity, or a moment's carelessness wreck our lives.

How do we cope with such experiences? There are two options: either we face them for what they are, working through the pain until we finally come to terms with it, or we can dwell on the injustice of life, licking our wounds and wallowing in self-pity. The latter reaction is perfectly understandable but ultimately tragic, for it succeeds only in adding insult to injury, robbing life of its joy and beauty. Few people are lonelier than those who are bitter in spirit. Get rid of your bitterness, then, through bringing it openly and honestly to God, before bitterness has the chance, metaphorically speaking, to get rid of you.

Christ in you!

I have been crucified with Christ, so that it is no longer I who live but Christ who lives within me. The life that I now live in the flesh is lived by faith in the Son of God, who loved me and gave himself up for me. (Galatians 2:19b-20)

'What's got into you?' When did someone last ask you that? It may be that you woke up like a bear with a sore head, snapping and snarling at everyone you met. Equally, you may have been on top of the world, full of the joys of spring, to the point that you seemed positively to radiate sunshine.

I suspect that many in the days of the early Church must have been asked something very similar. Take the day of Pentecost, for example, when the Apostles were filled with the Holy Spirit and began powerfully to preach the gospel; a number of the crowd looked on incredulously, suggesting they were drunk or out of their minds. Or consider Paul, changed overnight from being a persecutor of the Church to one of its most ardent proponents. Again, people must have reacted with disbelief, wondering what could have brought about such a change. So it must have been for countless others – one moment devout Jews, followers of the gods of Greece and Rome, or having no faith at all, and the next declaring a personal relationship with Christ; a relationship that had made an unmistakable difference to their lives. To anyone who asked what had got into them, the answer was very simple: it was Jesus. As Paul was to put it in his letter to the Colossians, 'Christ in you, the hope of glory.'

Remember those words, for they remind us that the gospel at its heart is not about us striving to be like Jesus, but about Jesus working within us. Yes, he wants us to become more like him so that our lives speak to others, but that all comes down not to our own efforts but to his presence within us, and to the renewing work of his Holy Spirit. Open our heart and soul to his grace and people may indeed look at us and say, 'What's got into you!'

Christian clothing

As God's chosen ones, therefore, holy and greatly loved, clothe yourselves with compassion, kindness, humility, meekness and patience, being merciful to one another and forgiving any quarrel you may have; in other words, forgive as the Lord forgave you. Above all, clothe yourselves with love, which binds everything together in perfect harmony. (Colossians 3:12-14)

What sort of clothes do you wear? Are you the daring flamboyant type or one who prefers a little more restraint – the kind of person who likes to dress casually or one who only feels comfortable when more formally attired? Clothes, we are told, say something about those wearing them, giving an insight into their character and disposition.

All of which takes us to the heart of what Paul was saying in his letter to the Colossians. Having just discussed various undesirable characteristics that we should strive to put off, he moves on to the qualities we need to put on, and the language he uses is carefully chosen. He doesn't just say be compassionate, kind, humble and so on, but urges the Colossians to *clothe* themselves with such things, or, to put it another way, to make those attributes so much a part of themselves that they are self-evident to all they meet, the first thing people will see; unmistakable, eye-catching. Compassion, kindness, humility, meekness, patience, mercy and love – these are the essential items in every Christian's wardrobe. This is not, of course, an exhaustive list, but it gives us a clear idea of what God wants and expects to see in our lives. Are these the 'clothes' we wear, the qualities that mark us out, or are we still more often than not turned out in the uniform of pride, greed, envy, bitterness and other such garments of the old self? If the latter, then isn't it time we heeded those wonderful words of Paul, and started measuring up?

Like little children

They brought little children to him so that he might touch them, but the disciples scolded them. Seeing this, Jesus was angry and said to them, 'Let the little children come to me; do not impede them; for the kingdom of God belongs to such as these. I tell you this, whoever does not receive the kingdom of God like a little child has no hope of entering it.' Then he enfolded them in his arms, laid his hands on them, and blessed them. (Mark 10:13-16)

Few parents will be at risk of sentimentalising the teaching of Jesus concerning children and our need to become like them. Children are by no means all sweetness and light – not even little ones. They can be mischievous, bad-tempered, spiteful, temperamental and much else besides. Yet, at the same time, few people who have raised a family will be at risk of missing the innate truth in what Jesus said, because there is something in children that is very special. It is hard to put that something into words, but it has to do with innocence and enthusiasm for life, total trust and unreserved love, and that amazing ability to be brawling one moment and to forgive and forget the next – just some of the qualities that make being a parent such a joyful and rewarding responsibility. One look, one word or one gesture after an exhausting day that has driven you to your wits' end suddenly makes it all seem worth it a thousand times over. No child is perfect, but all have precious gifts and characteristics thus far untarnished by the world. We need to recapture those qualities in terms of our relationship with God if we are truly to become his children.

Following suit

If then there is any encouragement in Christ, any reassurance in love, any belonging together in the Spirit, any compassion and empathy, make my joy whole: be of the same mind, having the same love, being in complete harmony and of a common mind. Let the same mind be in you that was in Christ Jesus. (Philippians 2:1-2, 5)

Lovers of card games like bridge, whist, solo or piquet will know that there is one rule that must always be observed: following suit. If a heart is laid, you must lay a heart; if a spade, then a spade; the only exception being when you have no cards of that suit left in your hand. Ignore this rule and it is impossible to play the game: it is a recipe for chaos.

When it comes to Christian commitment, we must again follow suit, though in a rather different way. We are called, so far as possible, to follow the lead of Christ in all our actions, showing the same love, compassion, dedication and devotion as he did. We may sometimes struggle to do so – indeed, without his help, we will often find it impossible – but this nonetheless should be our goal, for it is not a game we are talking about here but how far our lives point others to Jesus. Are you following suit as carefully as you should be?

The mind of Christ

Who has known the mind of the Lord and who can presume to instruct him? Yet we have the mind of Christ. (1 Corinthians 2:16)

How far do you think it's possible to read someone's mind? Personally, I've always been sceptical about the idea, but there can be no denying that sometimes a person can have a special bond with another; a general sensitivity that borders on telepathy. When we are truly close to someone and have grown to know them inside out, there are times when we can be pretty sure what they are thinking and how they will react in a given situation.

For me, that is the key to Paul's extraordinary statement to the Corinthians; a claim that, at first glance, seems to border on the blasphemous. The last thing Paul is suggesting is that we can know what Jesus is thinking – that would be tantamount to making ourselves God. The idea, rather, is of becoming so close to him and making him so much a part of our life, that his will becomes our will and his way our way. It speaks of a personal relationship, of knowing Christ in such a manner that it influences our whole way of thinking. In the final analysis, the picture becomes not us reading his mind but him being able to shape ours.

Reflecting Christ

Because the veil has been taken from our faces, we all reflect the Lord's glory like a mirror, and we are being transfigured to be ever more like him, from glory to glory, through the Lord who is Spirit. (2 Corinthians 3:18)

What do you get when you look in the mirror each morning? More likely than not, an unwelcome shock! Yet, where would we be without mirrors? Try shaving, combing your hair or cleaning your teeth without one and you'll soon realise how important they are to us. It's not, however, only glass that can reflect things; there's water, metal and plastic – and people too. We talk about actions reflecting well or badly on somebody, and we also recognise that the things we say and do may be taken as a reflection on others, whether parents, family, friends or associates.

It was very much this latter idea that Paul had in mind in his second letter to the Corinthians in what were, at once, both simple yet truly astounding words. We, he said, reflect Christ's glory! Is that true of us? Do people glimpse anything of Christ in our lives, let alone see his glory reflected in us? The trouble is, of course, that mirrors don't always do their job. They mist over, crack, even distort an image, so that what we see in them is a travesty of our true reflection. Too easily, the same is true in our lives – the picture of Jesus we present to the world unrecognisable from the Lord we are meant to be serving. So, next time you look in the mirror, as well as considering your own reflection, think also about how far your life is reflecting something of Jesus to those around you.

The spitting image

He is the image of the invisible God, the firstborn of all creation, because through him all things in heaven and on earth were created, both visible and invisible, whether thrones, dominions, rulers or powers – each has been created through him and for him. He is before all, and everything holds together through him. In him, God was pleased fully to dwell, and through him to reconcile all things to himself, whether on earth or in heaven, by making peace through the blood of his cross. (Colossians 1:15-17, 19-20)

'Isn't he like his dad!' we often say, or 'Isn't she like her mum!' 'Look at those eyes, that nose – the spitting image of his father! Look at her chin, her mouth – a dead ringer for her mother!' The similarities between parent and child can indeed be remarkable, and that usually extends further than mere physical resemblance. Like it or not, our gestures, mannerisms, temperaments and attitudes all betray our origins, far more than we might realise. Not that two people are ever the same, but there can be remarkable likenesses between them. However great these may be, though, they are nothing compared with the likeness Paul speaks of in his letter to the Colossians: that between Jesus and

God. Here is a parallel unlike any other, closer and more striking even than perfectly identical twins, for the Son does not just resemble his Father; he is one with him, fully and completely making him known. To know Jesus is to know God, to look at his life is to see God at work, to experience his love is to be touched by God's love in turn, and so it goes on.

This is a startling claim at any level, but altogether astonishing when we recall that the God we are talking about here is the same God who, according to the Old Testament, is enthroned in righteousness, mighty in power, greater than the human mind can comprehend and so holy that nothing impure can stand before him. A yawning gulf had separated him from humankind, any knowledge of him partial and once removed, but suddenly it is different – God made flesh, sharing our humanity and inviting us to share his life. That is the truth at the heart of the gospel, the message we celebrate today and every day. We are not limited simply to knowing *about* God; we are invited to know him *for ourselves* in a daily relationship with Christ – the spitting image of the Father!

Take aim

Our prayer is that you may achieve perfection. (2 Corinthians 13:9)

Achieving perfection – the very idea's ridiculous, isn't it, for which of us can possibly hope to reach anywhere approaching such a goal? Put in those terms, there's no denying it – the target is utterly and hopelessly beyond us – but look again and we will see that Paul isn't suggesting we will be perfect; simply, that we should make this our aim. It is a small but vital difference, well illustrated by my misspent days at college. When I wasn't playing table tennis, space invaders or snooker, I used to enjoy the odd game of darts. Unfortunately, I wasn't all that good, so I developed a strategy of aiming at the lower-left quadrant of the board where a number of average point-scoring segments are clustered together. The strategy didn't work all that well – largely because I tended to miss the board altogether! – but it was doomed to failure anyway, since I was purposely aiming low and so had little hope of getting anywhere near a maximum score, except by a sheer fluke.

How often in Christian discipleship do we do something similar, settling for second best instead of striving to become more like Christ? We are afraid of committing ourselves fully in case we cannot measure up to the challenge. We are reluctant to respond with body, heart and soul, in case God asks more of us than we feel able to give. We tell ourselves that there is no way we can serve him properly but that he would rather have partial, half-hearted service than nothing at all. The reality, of course, is that if we aim low, we will probably end up hitting a mark even lower. We have set ourselves up for failure before we have even begun. I don't think for a moment we will ever be perfect in this life, but that doesn't excuse us from trying. It isn't reaching the goal that counts but striving towards it. Can we settle for less?

Guidance

see also Will and purpose of God

The God who opens doors!

I will remain at Ephesus until Pentecost, because a great door for valuable work has opened to me, and there are many who oppose me. (1 Corinthians 16:8-9)

'It's not what you know but who you know.' How often have we heard that expression? Times may have changed, but in some areas of life it's still probably the case that a friend in high places or a mention of the old school tie can mean more than all one's qualifications and credentials. Put simply, knowing the right people opens doors. When that involves graft, corruption and nepotism, we rightly deplore it, yet there is a sense in which this saying accurately describes the essence of being a Christian, for at its heart faith is not about *what* you know but *who* you know. We do not become a Christian from learning dogma or memorising scripture but through a personal encounter with the living Christ.

The analogy, though, can be pushed further, as Paul's words to the Corinthians make clear. Commitment to Christ does not open doors to fame and fortune but it opens doors nonetheless. It brings opportunities for service and gateways into new experiences of his grace and power. It offers fresh avenues and new possibilities to explore, opening up directions that we may never before have thought possible. What we may consider beyond us, Christ can equip us to meet. What we deem impossible he renders feasible. Where we see no means of entry he shows the way through. Christian discipleship is not about arriving at a safe destination but about discovering doors into uncharted territory. We cannot open such doors on our own, but thankfully, we don't have to because for us, more than anyone, it's not what we know but who we know. Thank God for that!

The God who takes hold of us

I am the Lord your God, who takes hold of your right hand and says to you: Never fear: I will help you. I, the Lord, have called you in my goodness; I will take hold of your hand. (Isaiah 41:13; 42:6)

A while back I taught my son Samuel to ride a bicycle without stabilisers. It took him some time, but eventually, with much cajoling and encouragement, he cracked it. If it was hard for him, it was hard for me too, for the only way I could persuade him to have a go at first was to promise to be there alongside him, always there to support him should he lose his balance or start to wobble. I learned then that even a young child can go surprisingly fast, especially for one the wrong side of forty!

We all need a little support sometimes, don't we; someone to hold on to us when the going gets tough, when we're unsure of our ground, when our confidence fails and we feel ourselves slipping? The message of scripture is that we have such a one in God. Across the ages he has reiterated his promise to support us along the journey of life; to stay close by our side so that, in times of crisis, we can rely upon him to keep us safe. There were moments when Samuel felt like giving up; there will be moments when we feel like that too. But just as my being there gave the reassurance needed for Samuel finally to succeed, so the knowledge of God's constant presence will give us the confidence we need, when we need it.

One step beyond

They were on the road leading to Jerusalem. Jesus was walking ahead of them, and they were amazed for, as they followed, they were afraid. He took the twelve aside once again, and began to tell them what was going to happen to him. (Mark 10:32)

What would you do if someone told you to lie on a bed of nails, walk across hot coals, bungee jump off the Severn Bridge or parachute off the Empire State Building? If you've any sense, you wouldn't do it – I know I wouldn't! But how about if the person who posed such challenges promised to do each of them first, so that you could watch and learn from their experience, assured that each could be done before you followed suit? I personally would still be unconvinced; a few bolder souls might perhaps be tempted to give it a go. When someone is willing to lead the way it makes a big difference, giving some people at least the courage they might not otherwise have had.

That willingness to take the lead characterised the life and ministry of Christ. It's there in our reading, Jesus knowing that his journey to Jerusalem was going to lead to his death, yet, far from holding back, dragging his feet or making an excuse to go no further, we see him leading the way, one step ahead of his disciples. We see it again follow-ing his resurrection, women going to the tomb to anoint his body, only to be told, 'He is not here. He has been raised from the dead and has gone ahead of you to Galilee. There you will see him' (Matthew 28:6a,

7b). The message holds for whatever we may face. Whether it be a time of testing or blessing, darkness or light, tears or laughter, we can be sure that Jesus is with us; not simply by our side but leading the way, one step beyond.

Remembering what was

Remember what the Lord your God did. Remember the way the Lord your God has led you. (Deuteronomy 7:18; 8:2)

Certain times of the year seem to be given over to remembering. I think especially of November. First, there comes All Saints' Day followed by All Souls' – occasions that remind us of those who have gone before us in the faith. Then, there is Guy Fawkes' Night; not, of course, a Christian festival but part of British folklore, reminding us of a long-distant plot against Parliament that reflected the religious tensions of that time. Next, there comes Remembrance Day, as we recall the sacrifice of so many in two World Wars and other conflicts. So much to remember, so much to learn from, so much that calls us to build for the future in the light of the past.

For the people of Israel, remembering was an integral part of their faith; the story of how God had delivered them from Egypt and led them safely through the wilderness to the Promised Land repeated by parents year after year, to their children and children's children. The memory of God's goodness and guidance across the years sustained, enriched and encouraged their faith. For the Christian, too, remembering has a special place. 'Do this in memory of me,' said Jesus (1 Corinthians 11:24). Such words remind us that our faith is not based on wishful thinking or idle speculation, nor on some clever deception or well-intentioned philosophy, but is rather rooted in history, in what God has done. Make time, then, to remember – not just today or on those days given over to remembering, but every day.

When one door closes

Having been prevented by the Holy Spirit from speaking the word in Asia, they travelled through the districts of Phrygia and Galatia. Coming towards Mysia, they attempted to go into Bithynia, but again the Spirit of Jesus did not allow them; so, passing by Mysia, they journeyed on to Troas. That night, Paul had a vision, in which a man from Macedonia stood begging him for assistance, saying, 'Come across to Macedonia and help us.' In the light of that vision, we immediately tried to cross over to Macedonia, being persuaded that God had called us to preach the good news there. (Acts 16:6-10)

When I first felt the call to Christian ministry there was one problem standing in my way: for some years, I had suffered from a speech impediment; a stammer that, at one point, reached such a peak that I could barely put two words together. Hardly the ideal qualification for a would-be public speaker, you might say! I was encouraged, however, to carry on and, though the problem never completely left me through-out my fifteen years' of pastoral ministry, few would have guessed I had any difficulties. Towards the end of that time, however, I began to struggle rather more than previously, enough to make public events an ordeal rather than a pleasure. Eventually I felt I could not continue as things were. Yet, as one ministry ended, another began with the publi-cation of my first book. Since then the written rather than spoken word has been the vehicle for communicating my faith.

That experience brought home to me what the Apostle Paul had discovered centuries earlier as he tried first to enter Asia, and then Bithynia, before finally recognising a call to Macedonia: the simple fact that when one door closes God invariably opens another. Life rarely goes as smoothly as any of us would like – our hopes sometimes dashed, our plans often thwarted – but through it all God is able to provide fresh avenues of service and new possibilities to explore.

It's your choice

Look, I present you today with a straight choice between life and death, good and evil. If you obey the commandments of the Lord your God that I am giving you today – loving the Lord God, following his ways and keeping his commandments, instructions and laws – then you will live and prosper, and the Lord God will bless you in the land you are about to take possession of. If, though, you turn your hearts away and refuse to listen, misguidedly paying homage to other gods and offering them service, I tell you straight that you will perish; you will not live long in the land you are crossing the Jordan to occupy and possess. I invoke heaven and earth to witness against you today that I have presented you with a choice between life and death, blessings and curses. Choose life, so that you and your descendants may live. Love the Lord your God, obey him and hold fast to him. (Deuteronomy 30:15-20a)

You will probably have noticed the plethora of television programmes recently featuring robots. There's *Techno Games*, *BattleBots*, and the queen of them all, *Robot Wars*. It all makes for good viewing, particularly the sight of various high-tech creations smashing the living daylights out of each other. I'm tempted to say that it can't be much fun for the robots but, of course, the robots simply don't care either way. The day of the thinking, feeling robot is, we're told, on the way, but for the time being robots simply do what they're programmed to do, with no feeling, no emotions, no will and no purpose of their own.

I suppose God, if he'd wished, could have made us like that – mindless automatons at his beck and call. There would have been no disobedience then, no sin to spoil the world, but then again there wouldn't have been any pleasure or fulfilment either. For that, you need free will, with all its associated dangers and problems. We can abuse that gift, as we often do, or we can use it wisely, seeking God's help and guidance in the decisions we make. He invites us to respond, but he will not take decisions from our hands or seek to control us – it's our choice.

Hope

see also Sorrow and despair

The assurance of things hoped for

Some will say, 'How can the dead be raised and what sort of body will they have?' (1 Corinthians 15:35)

Faith, we are told, is one of the great qualities of the Christian life, an essential ingredient of genuine discipleship. But living with faith is far from easy, for most of us prefer cast-iron certainties to promises we must accept on trust. Nowhere is this more so than when it comes to the fact of death and our hope of eternal life. We believe in the resurrection and the kingdom of heaven, but we can't help wishing we knew a bit more about it. Where will it be? How will we get there? When will it come? What will it be like? These and a host of other questions all too easily play on our minds, insidiously undermining our confidence. 'If only we knew,' we tell ourselves. 'If only we could see, then it would all be so much easier.' But the fact is we do not need to see anything more than God has already revealed, for true faith should be based on what we experience today as much as what we're promised tomorrow. When God is an ever-present reality in our life, we need no proof as to the future.

Daring to hope

Look, the day of the Lord is coming when everything looted from you will be returned and redistributed. That time will see an end to frost and ice. Instead, day will never end (as it is already with the Lord), there being no night and thus no such thing as day for it will be light always. On that day irrepressible streams of waters will gush from Jerusalem, half of them flowing to the sea in the east and the other half to that in the west. Similarly, winter will be like summer. The Lord will be enthroned over the earth, and he will be all in all, one Lord and one God. (Zechariah 14:1, 6-9)

To have our hopes raised only to see them dashed again is a cruel experience. The result can be to plunge us into a deeper sense of despair than anything we faced previously. So it was for the people of Israel after they returned to Judah following their time of exile in Babylon. An initial mood of jubilation soon gave way to an overwhelming feeling of anticlimax, as the Utopia that people had expected to dawn failed to materialise. It wasn't just hope that took a battering in consequence; for many it was their faith. Where was the glorious new kingdom God had promised his people?

Today the kingdom we expect may be different, but the question can seem equally valid. We look forward to the day when God's purpose will be fulfilled, when his will shall be done and his kingdom come on earth, but when will that be? Do we have the courage to keep on hoping, even when everything around us seems to undermine belief?

The gift of hope

My soul waits quietly for God; my confidence comes from him. He, and he alone, is my rock, my deliverance and my stronghold; nothing will shake me. (Psalm 62:5-6)

Of the three great Christian gifts spoken of by the Apostle Paul, the most neglected is surely 'hope'. We hear much in the Church about faith and love, but hope seems to be the poor relation, seldom getting much of a mention. Yet what would life be without it? I don't mean hope in the sense of wishful thinking – that is simply an illusion – nor in the sense of hoping against hope – that would be plain foolishness. No, the hope God gives us is a confidence in the future based upon our present experience of his love. We do not know the precise details of what that future holds, nor do we need to know. We have the assurance that God is at work in our lives, and that one day his purpose will be fulfilled. What more could we want?

An unfading hope

When the principal shepherd appears, you will attain an unfading crown of glory that will never tarnish. (1 Peter 5:4)

It was a fascinating display – a wonderful collection of tools and machinery from years gone by. Steam engines, ploughs, tractors, threshing machines, wagons and horse-drawn carriages, and much more – a wonderful reminder of yesteryear. It struck me, though, looking at the dates of the various items, that yesteryear was not so long ago. The earliest vehicle was barely a century old; in other words, dating back just a couple of generations. What today are obsolete museum pieces would have been state-of-the-art technology in my great-grandparents' time, the treasured possession of some proud new owner. It was a stark reminder of the transience of life and the pace of change.

Contrast this with the hope of the gospel as summed up in those words above. New life in Christ is not here today and gone tomorrow but is a gift for all eternity. Though everything else may change, it will not. Though generations come and go, it remains the same. The promises of God will not tarnish, and our hope will never fade, for the kingdom of God, unlike this world, is built to last; to endure not simply for our brief lifespan but for all eternity.

Joyful response

see also Praise

An affair of the heart

During his time at Bethany, while he was dining at the house of Simon the leper, a woman came in carrying an alabaster jar of expensive ointment of nard, and, breaking open the jar, she poured the ointment on his head. Some there muttered angrily to each other, 'Why has she wasted the ointment like that? Such ointment could have been sold for over three hundred denarii, and the proceeds given to the poor.' And they reprimanded her. But Jesus said, 'Leave her be; why are you criticising her? She has done a wonderful thing for me.' (Mark 14:3-6)

How far should we allow our hearts to rule our heads? Not at all, you might well say, and, generally, you'd be right. Yet are there not occasions when we need to act on impulse? While it pays to look before we leap, it would be a sad business indeed if we felt it necessary to analyse the pros and cons of every action before ever doing anything. The impulsive gesture can be our undoing, but equally it can be the road to happiness, bringing joy to others and fulfilment to ourselves.

When it comes to relationships, this is all the more so. When we love someone, we want to show it. So it was for the woman who anointed Jesus' feet. She loved Jesus, not in the sense of being physically attracted to him but because of who he was and what he meant. She recognised he was someone special, offering a new dimension to life, and instinctively she responded. Do we still have that urge within us to show how much Jesus means to us? Do we find ourselves spontaneously offering our love, our lives, our money, our service? Is our faith still an affair of the heart?

Because we may

Let everyone give as their heart leads them to do, not reluctantly or because it is expected of them – for God loves a cheerful giver. (2 Corinthians 9:7)

There are few things we like less than having something done for us out of duty. What might otherwise have been a valued act of service brings instead a sense of humiliation; what appeared to be an act of friendship becomes a cause of rancour; what seemed a hugely generous gift feels suddenly like a tarnished trinket, all but worthless. We want people to respond to us not because they feel they should but because they want to. We want their dealings with us to be transparent rather than hiding some ulterior motive. What we don't want, above all, is to be patronised.

We do well to bear that in mind when it comes to our dealings with God, for all too easily the service we offer him becomes a matter of duty rather than privilege. We don't intend it to happen, nor are we always conscious of it doing so, but little by little the sparkle in our faith fades and the spontaneity that once characterised our relationship with God gives way to routine; an empty going through the motions. We bring our offering because it is expected of us; we read the Bible because we feel guilty if we don't; we say our prayers because we feel we ought to – and we hope God won't notice. Is that what he wants from us? Of course not. He wants us to love him, serve him and worship him not because we must but because we may. He wants us to offer our discipleship not because we should but because we can. If we bring it for any other reason, it is time to stop and think, for it might be that God feels just as we would in his place – that he'd rather we didn't bring it at all.

Counting our blessings

The blessings your father gives are greater than those of the everlasting hills, greater than their eternal riches. (Genesis 49:26)

Occasionally in life we pause to remember how much we have to celebrate – the many blessings and gifts that God so freely showers upon us. Sadly, such moments are all too rare. More often than not, we lurch from one demand, one crisis, one responsibility to another, scarcely finding time to draw breath and reflect on the reasons we have to give thanks. If we are not careful, we end up brooding on the things we haven't got, sucked into a vicious circle of self-pity, the more sorry we feel for ourselves the more grounds there seem to be for such feelings.

We need to stop sometimes and, in the words of the old hymn, make time to 'count our blessings', for when we do that, life seems very different. There is so much that is not only good but indescribably wonderful, beautiful beyond words. The words of Genesis, above, were concerned not with God's blessing but with Jacob's blessing to his sons, but they could speak more appropriately of all God has done for us. Pause to consider such things and, far from feeling sorry for yourself, you will realise how much reason you have to give thanks.

The gift of laughter

A merry heart makes for a cheerful countenance, but a morose disposition crushes the spirit. Every day in life is wretched for the downtrodden, yet those with a cheerful heart feast continually. (Proverbs 15:13, 15)

Towards the end of my ministry in Cheltenham I organised a special if rather unusual service – a celebration of laughter. We had held music services and songs-of-praise services, so why not a laughter service? The idea caught on and, through a series of such events, we thanked God for the ability to laugh. Not everybody, however, thought it was a good idea. Shortly after advertising the first service, I spotted a letter in the local paper roundly condemning my heretical idea and suggesting it would undermine the solemnity and reverence of worship. Others were intrigued, so much so that the service earned a mention in a national newspaper and led to a live telephone interview on Radio Newcastle. Is the idea of God enjoying a good joke so shocking? I hope not, for heaven will be a dull place if it is! To my mind, laughter is one of God's most precious gifts: one that can be abused, it's true, but one that can also bring happiness and enrichment beyond measure.

Learning to say thank you

It is good to give thanks to the Lord, to sing praises to your name, O Most High; to declare your steadfast love in the morning, and your faithfulness by night. For you, O Lord, have made me glad by your work; at the works of your hands I sing for joy. (Psalm 92:1-2, 4)

What is one of the first words we learn to say as a baby? After 'mama' and 'dada', I suspect it's probably 'thank you' or, more precisely, 'ta'. So now another question: What's one of the first words we forget to say as Christians? The answer, I suspect, is once again 'thank you'. Of course, *you* may be the exception that proves the rule, but, if you are anything like me, your prayers are long on 'please' and short on 'thank you'. We ask God for this, that and everything else, bombarding him day after day with a string of requests, but when he answers our prayers and provides for our needs, how many times, I wonder, do we make a point of showing our appreciation? When it comes to people, few of us would dream of not saying thank you for a kindness, if only out of politeness. Why should it be any different when it comes to God? As the psalm reminds us, 'It is good to give thanks to the Lord.'

A meaningful offering

Looking up, he saw well-to-do people putting their gifts into the treasury, and also a poor widow offering two small copper coins. He said, 'Mark my words, this poor widow has put in more than all of the others; for they have contributed out of their plenty, but she, despite her poverty, has put in everything she had to live on.' (Luke 21:1-4)

'And now the collection will be received.' It's surprising how often you hear announcements like that in church. Even more common is to hear members of the congregation use the same terminology. It may be innocent enough, but, personally, it makes me wince, for it can subconsciously encourage a fundamental misunderstanding of what Christian giving is all about. The implication is that we give out of duty: not because we may but because we must, because it is expected of us. What a contrast between that and the widow at the treasury. Humanly-speaking her gift was pathetic, barely worth the bother of counting it, but as far as God was concerned it was a priceless treasure, because it was given not as a collection but as an offering. She gave it because she wanted to, because she was eager to respond, and she gave sacrificially because she wanted to tell God how much he meant to her.

We can apply her example not only to the giving of our money but also of our time, our prayers, our love and our service. Do we truly *offer* those to God, or do we give them mechanically, half-heartedly, grudgingly? Do we bring them out of routine or habit, or as a spontaneous expression of love and thanksgiving? 'It's the thought that counts', we are often told. In terms of our response to God, those are words well worth pondering.

Singing his praises

Praise the Lord! Let my soul praise the Lord! I will extol the Lord all my days; I will honour him lifelong with songs of worship. What a joy it is and how appropriate to sing praises to our God. (Psalm 146:1-2; 147:1b)

How do you feel when someone offers you praise? Do you nod in eager agreement and ask them to continue? I doubt it, unless perhaps you are trying to hide your embarrassment. While a little praise every now and again is undeniably welcome, too much is hard to handle, especially if we're in the company of others at the time.

What about God? Is he any different? Does he positively revel in praise, lapping it up and asking for more? Does he not only enjoy but also expect it? The words of scripture, and indeed of public worship, can give that impression sometimes, but I think it's misleading, for, like so much else in prayer, the opportunity to praise God is given as much for our benefit as his. It gives us the opportunity to put our feelings into words, to express the sense of thankfulness and joy that bubbles up within us, and in so doing it reminds us of what God has done and who he is. It is a way of responding; of telling him we haven't just taken his goodness for granted but that it is special to us. I've no doubt God takes pleasure in such words but I don't for a moment think that he demands them. We offer him praise not because we ought to but because we can; because, truth be told, we cannot help ourselves.

You shall!

You shall know the truth, and the truth shall set you free. I have come so that you shall have life, and have it to the full. Ask and it shall be given to you; seek and you shall find; knock and the door shall be opened to you. (John 8:32; 10:10; Matthew 7:7)

'Don't do that!' 'Stop it!' 'Leave it alone!' There are times when being a parent feels like constantly nagging, forever saying no. The same, sadly, is the impression some people have of the Church; a view reinforced by those old Wayside Pulpit posters you still sometimes see, starkly proclaiming 'The wages of sin is death' or some other equally cheery message! Undeniably, there is a negative element in the Bible, epitomised by the majority of the Ten Commandments with their stern preface: 'Thou shalt not . . .'

This, however, is by no means the whole story, for in the teaching of Jesus the message is reversed. Instead of 'You shall not' it becomes 'You shall', all the negative commandments being summed up in one positive: 'A new commandment I give you: Love one another' (John 13:14). Repeatedly it is the same story: you *shall* have, you *shall* know, you *shall* find – the blind shall see, the lame walk, the imprisoned be set free, the pure in heart see God, the hungry and thirsty be satisfied, and so on and so on. Never think that being a Christian is about what you *can't* do, still less give that impression to others. Above all, it is about what you *can* do; about the possibilities the love of Christ opens up; about the sheer potential of life!

Judgement of God

see also Will and purpose of God

Called to account

At that time I will search Jerusalem with a lantern, and I will punish those who sit smugly over the last of their wine, assuring themselves, 'The Lord won't do anything to us, either good or bad.' Their wealth shall be plundered, and their homes laid waste. Though they build houses, they will never live in them; though they plant vineyards, they will drink no wine from them. The great day of the Lord draws near, rushing ever closer upon us; the sound of that day will be bitter, and the warrior will cry aloud there. It will be a day of wrath, of misery and hardship, ruin and desolation – a day of clouds and thick darkness, of trumpet blast and battle cry against the fortified cities and lofty battlements. (Zephaniah 1:12-16)

The older one gets, the more one comes to recognise that life isn't fair. The heady idealism of youth gives way to the hardheaded realism of middle age, as the truth slowly dawns that, in this life at least, people don't always get what they deserve. Honesty may be the best policy when it comes to peace of mind, but it is not necessarily the most lucrative; the unpleasant truth is that all too often cheats *do* prosper.

Coming to terms with facts like this is a painful business and one that can test faith to the limit, just as it did in the time of Zephaniah. There were many in his day who, faced by the apparent injustices of life, concluded that God was either disinterested in human affairs or powerless to intervene. It was an understandable mistake, but one that the prophet had no time for. In God's time, he warns, justice will be done and seen to be done by all. We lose sight of that at our peril.

Reaping what we sow

Do not be taken in: God will not be made a fool of. Whatever someone sows, that person will also reap; the one who sows what the body wants will reap corruption, but the one who sows what the Spirit desires will reap eternal life through that same Spirit. So, then, let us never grow weary of doing what is right, for, provided we do not give up, we will reap at harvest-time. (Galatians 6:7-9)

Several years back, my wife took a fancy to the Welsh poppy, deciding that it was something we ought to grow, so every time we visited a garden centre, we looked for a specimen. Eventually, we found one and with eager anticipation we planted it in the border. We were not disappointed; the plant flowered its heart out for month after month. The following year, though, we were in for a shock, for suddenly we didn't have one Welsh poppy, we had hundreds – yet another sprouting, so it seemed, wherever we cared to look! Here was a classic case of reaping what you sow, even if it was the birds and wind rather than ourselves that actually scattered the seeds. A little more research and we would have known exactly what we were letting ourselves in for.

How far, though, can we apply this principle to life? Hard work is not always rewarded, honesty doesn't always pay, effort doesn't guarantee success, and love doesn't guarantee love in return. Yet, having said that, there is another level at which we do reap what we sow, both in this life and beyond. The rewards associated with Christian discipleship may not be tangible, but they are there nonetheless. The rewards for loving others, offering our service and pursuing good may not be quantifiable in human terms, but they are no less real. Similarly, wrongdoing and injustice, though they may seem to go unpunished, carry their own cost. We can sow with no thought of tomorrow if we wish – God will not stop us – but he tells us repeatedly throughout the scriptures that the time will come, whether in this life or the next, when we will reap the harvest. What, then, will we sow? It's our choice.

An unwelcome surprise

You have exhausted the Lord with all your talk, yet you ask, 'In what way have we wearied him?' By claiming that those who do evil are good in the sight of the Lord, and that he takes pleasure in them, and by asking, 'Where is the God of justice?' 'Look,' says the Lord of hosts, 'I am sending my messenger to prepare the way for me, so that the Lord whom you seek will suddenly come to his temple. The messenger of the covenant whom you so eagerly anticipate is coming, but who can endure the day of his coming or stand when he appears? For he is like a refiner's fire and fullers' soap; he will preside as a refiner and purifier of silver, and he will purify the descendants of Levi. I will approach you in judgement, and be swift to bear witness against the sorcerers, the adulterers and those who bear false witness; against those who exploit their hired workers, the widow and the orphan, who thrust aside the alien, and who do not fear me,' says the Lord of hosts. (Malachi 2:17-3:3a, 5)

Anyone who has ever listened to Handel's *Messiah* will be familiar with those words of the prophet Malachi. They make sobering reading, not least because those to whom they were first addressed were convinced they were more than ready to welcome God's promised deliverer, and assured of his approval when he came. From Malachi came the call to think again – a warning that the day of the Lord would be anything but welcome. Why? Because their lives were a pale shadow of what the Messiah would expect from them. Their expectation of God's blessing had become divorced from their daily lives, and the result, warned the prophet, would be an unpleasant shock.

There is a danger that we today can make the same mistake. We may believe that we are ready to face God's judgement, whenever and however that may come, but before we sit back complacently we would do well to examine our consciences, assess our lifestyles and ask whether everything in our life is quite as it should be. Fail to do that, and we may find the day of the Lord not quite the occasion we like to imagine.

Kingdom of God

Glimpsing the kingdom (1)

The disciples approached him and asked, 'Why do you speak to them in parables?'
He answered, 'Because though it has been given to you to know the secrets of
the kingdom of heaven, it has not been given to them, yet those who have will
have much more given to them, whereas those who have next to nothing will
lose even that. In other words, I speak in parables, because though they look
they see nothing, and though they hear they neither listen nor understand. In
them is fulfilled the prophecy of Isaiah saying: "You will hear but not under-
stand, and see yet not perceive. For this people's heart has grown complacent,
their ears hard of hearing, and their eyes closed; they see nothing, hear nothing
and understand nothing that might make them turn to me so that I might heal
them." Blessed, are your eyes, however, for they see, and your ears, for they
hear. I tell you this, many prophets and righteous people longed to see what
you see, but did not see it, and to hear what you hear, but did not hear it.'
(Matthew 13:10-17)

'Much of what we see depends on what we are looking for.' In other
words, we often miss something that is staring us in the face, either
because we are closed to the possibility of seeing it or because we are
preoccupied with something else. Jesus was aware of that problem, his
use of parables designed to break through people's preconceptions so
that they might see the world in a new light.

That need is as real today as ever, especially when it comes to
understanding the kingdom of God. All too easily, we relegate that
kingdom to some far-off place and time. Certainly, the final consum-
mation of God's purpose must come later, but, as Jesus proclaimed at
the very start of his ministry, 'The time is fulfilled, and the kingdom of
God has come near' (Mark 1:15). The fact is that the kingdom has
already dawned, if only we have eyes to see it. Like yeast or a mustard
seed, it is slowly growing, its presence evidenced in countless lives
being changed every day, in numerous expressions of love and service,
in the work and worship of the Church, and in so much more. As well,
then, as looking to the future and praying 'Come, Lord, come', we
need to nurture the seeds that Jesus has already sown, ensuring we do
all in our power, through his grace, to see them grow.

Glimpsing the kingdom (2)

The kingdom of God is comparable to having scattered seed on the ground. Those who sow it sleep and wake night and day, and the seed sprouts and grows, though they have no idea how. The earth brings forth a crop by itself, first a shoot, then the head, then the full ear of grain. When, though, the grain is ripe, they set to work at once with their sickles, because the time for harvest has come. (Mark 4:26-29)

In 1516 Sir Thomas More wrote *Utopia* in which he set out his vision of a society marked by peace, justice and harmony. Here was a picture of the way life could and ought to be. In 1949 George Orwell wrote *Nineteen Eighty-four*, a novel about the nightmare scenario of a totalitarian state in which every thought and action is regulated, encapsulated in the stark warning 'Big Brother is watching you'. Here was a picture of the way life could but mustn't be. What vision, I wonder, do we have of the future? Do we look forward with hope or fear, with anticipation or dread? What of the future beyond this life? Do we believe there is meaning to our existence even beyond death, or do we regard the grave as the end of all our striving?

Most of us would like to think the world can be a better place and we probably all want to believe in an afterlife but, as the years pass, our confidence can take a battering. The harsh realities of life seem to contradict the idealistic dreams of youth. The first flush of faith fades to a mere shadow of what it used to be. Yet, as so many of the parables of Jesus remind us, if we only have eyes to see, the signs of the kingdom are all around us. Not only is it coming but, in a real sense, it is here already, the miracle of changed lives taking place every day and every moment. To know Christ is to be given a foretaste of all that is yet to come; not simply a vision of what might be but a promise of what will be. If we cannot see signs of his coming kingdom, perhaps we are looking in the wrong place or for the wrong things!

Vision for the future

The wolf will live with the lamb, the leopard lie down with the kid and the calf, lion and fatling together, led by a little child. Cattle and bears will graze together, and their young slumber together; and the lion will eat straw like the ox. Babies will play over the nest of a cobra, and the weaned child will put its hand in the adder's den. Nothing will not hurt or destroy anywhere on my holy mountain; for, just as water fills the sea so will the earth be filled with the knowledge of the Lord. (Isaiah 11:6-9)

A vision of the future or sentimental nonsense – what do you make of those words of Isaiah? Are they poetic imagery or prophetic foresight? In terms of this life, at least, both those appraisals contain an element of truth. In recent years we have seen startling moves towards peace in some quarters of the world, yet there have also been unspeakable atrocities and mind-boggling inhumanity. Sadly, for every reason to hope there seems to be still more cause to despair, and, eventually, dis-illusionment sets in. We'd like to believe in a world such as the prophet paints – a new age of peace and harmony when violence, discord and hatred will be a thing of the past – but most of us take such claims with a strong pinch of salt. Life, we tell ourselves, is just not like that.

Such an attitude is understandable given the lamentable record of human history and the continuing divisions in our world today, yet it cannot finally be acceptable. *We* may abandon the world to its fate – God never will. He will not rest until his will is done and his kingdom established, on earth as it is in heaven. It may seem light years away from the world as we know it today, but we must never lose that vision of what life can become, nor stop working towards it.

Love

God's love for us

The God of love

Dear friends, let us love one another, because love comes from God; all those who love are born of God and know God. Whoever does not love knows nothing of God, for God is love. God demonstrated his love like this – he sent his only Son into the world in order that we might live through him. In this is love, not that we loved God but that he loved us and sent his Son to be the expiation for our sins. God is love, and all who dwell in love dwell in God, and God dwells in them. (1 John 4:7-10, 16b)

On my shelves at home I have a variety of dictionaries and thesauri which I have cause to consult on innumerable occasions, and one of the things that invariably surprises me is the sheer complexity of words. A single term can have a wide range of nuances, and many have several completely different meanings. Even everyday terms can prove surprisingly difficult to define. You would have thought, then, that one word in particular would be harder to define than any – the word 'God' – and in a sense that is true, for you could probably find as many interpretations as there are people. Some would stress his holiness, others his power, others, again, his ineffability – so many aspects of God that could justifiably be highlighted.

Yet, in our reading today, we see another approach that, in the light of all of the above, is truly remarkable, for according to John, one word says it all: God is *love*! For some, such a definition is far too loose; so vague and insipid that it ends up saying nothing. Yet, the fact is that, when it comes to God, no other word will do, for God *is* love! It's as simple and straightforward as that – the one description that says it all, and if we lose that one simple truth, we lose everything. He longs to bless, not punish; to give, rather than take away; his nature always to have mercy, show kindness and fill our lives with good things. No, we don't deserve such goodness, for we continue to fail him, day after day, but that's what makes God's love so special, for, despite the feebleness of our response, it goes on cleansing, renewing, restoring, forgiving – refusing to let go, come what may. One word to describe the one true God, but what a word and what a God!

The God who has time for us

As he walked by, Jesus spotted a man named Matthew sitting at the custom house, and he said to him, 'Follow me.' And, springing up, the man followed him. (Matthew 9:9)

Few events can have elicited such a massive public display of grief as the death of Diana, Princess of Wales. Theories abound as to what it was about her that captured the public imagination, but the quality most often cited is the fact that she had time for people. Whether it was the victim of a landmine or an AIDS sufferer, she showed that she cared, and she did it in such a way that people believed they really mattered to her.

There was something very akin to this in the experience of Matthew. As a tax collector, and thus a collaborator with the Romans, he was used to rejection and hatred, to people passing him by with a gesture of contempt or simply ignoring him altogether. Suddenly, though, here was Jesus, not just stopping to talk with him, not simply looking him in the eye, not even merely treating him as a person, but asking him to follow, to become his disciple. It must have been an astounding moment, and we can well imagine Matthew pinching himself to make sure he wasn't dreaming! Yet it was true, and not just for him but for us. God has time for every one of us. For all his splendour and sovereignty, he values us as individuals and wants us to be a part of his kingdom. That, too, is a mind-boggling fact, a truly astonishing invitation: have we begun to grasp it?

A love that will not let us go

When Israel was a child, I loved him, calling my son out of Egypt. I was the one who taught my people Ephraim to walk, who cradled them in my arms; but they did not know it was me who nurtured them. I restrained them with love and led them with cords of kindness. I was like a parent lifting an infant to their cheek, kneeling down to feed them. How can I let you go, Ephraim, and Israel, how can I relinquish you? How can I make you like Admah or treat you like Zeboiim? My heart flinches within me; my devotion burns tenderly within me. I will not give vent to my fury; I will not again destroy Ephraim; for I am God, not human, the Holy One among you, and I will not come in anger. (Hosea 11:1, 3-4, 8-9)

We talk a lot about the love of God but I wonder how many of us have even begun to grasp it. I suspect we think of God in terms of judgement as much as grace; as a somewhat stern and forbidding Father ready to reach out and punish the moment we step out of line.

Certainly there are times when discipline is necessary but, as the wonderful words of Hosea make clear, this is never something he delights in doing. Taking his own broken marriage as a model, the prophet paints a graphic and moving picture of the anguish God feels at the repeated rejection and betrayal of his people, and the resolve he has to restore a relationship with them, come what may. Here is an unforgettable glimpse of a love that finally will not let us go, however much we may throw against it. Few passages can more beautifully portray the true nature of the God we serve.

Love yourself

There was a man named Zacchaeus – a chief tax collector and wealthy – who was trying to see who Jesus was, but because he was short in stature he could not see through the crowd. He ran ahead, therefore, and climbed a sycamore tree to get a better view, knowing Jesus was going to pass by that way. When Jesus reached the spot, he looked up and said to him, 'Zacchaeus, come down quickly, for I feel it right to stay at your house today.' Zacchaeus hurried down and joyfully welcomed him. (Luke 19:2-6)

Love yourself? Surely our problem is that we love ourselves overmuch already, too full of our own importance, own interests and own ideas. Perhaps so, but are such things the same as loving oneself? On the contrary, selfishness is often not so much a sign of self-love as of self-loathing. A shopping, eating or drinking binge can represent a desperate attempt to disguise a sense of inner emptiness. Apparent know-it-alls may be trying to deny, even to themselves, their deep-seated insecurity. The reality is that few people, for all the material blessings they may enjoy, feel at one with themselves, many wrestling permanently with a debilitating negative self-image.

I suspect Zacchaeus felt much the same. For all his wealth, he was clearly looking for something else in life, evidenced by the lengths he went to in order to see Jesus. No doubt he went more in hope than expectation, but hope was vindicated, for instead of the usual rejection he was subjected to, he was treated as a person, an individual in his own right. For the first time in many years he was able to face himself and, in consequence, to let go of the prop of money he had clung to for support. He felt guilt and shame, certainly, but he also recognised that God valued him and was ready to accept him as he was. Yes, there are things about ourselves that we would all like to change and some things we need to change, but we should never forget how much we mean to God, warts and all. Until we learn to love ourselves, we can never truly love others.

A passionate God

We see love not in our love of God but in his for us; in his willingness to send his Son as an offering for our sins in order to put us right with him. (1 John 4:10)

What things are you truly passionate about? The question was put in a sermon I heard recently, and it opened up a dimension of faith that I'd never really considered before – the idea of a God who is passionate about us! The word is from the Greek παθημα meaning 'emotion', 'passion' or 'sacrifice', which, in turn, derives from the word πασχω, meaning 'to suffer' or 'to endure evil'. Emotion, suffering and sacrifice – all three are deeply interwoven, for to care passionately about someone means you are ready to suffer for them, to make personal sacrifices to secure their happiness.

Such is the love God has for us. It is not just a vague feeling of benevolence or a general concern and affection; it is a passionate and consuming love that gave all, even his own Son, to restore our broken relationship with him; to draw us closer to himself. It is the 'love divine, all loves excelling' spoken of by the hymn writer; the 'love that will not let us go'. We're not used to thinking of God in terms of high emotion – or, at least, *I'm* not – but we should be, for the wonder of the gospel is not simply that God loves us but that he loves us passionately!

Shepherd of the sheep

The Lord is my shepherd, I want for nothing. He makes me lie down in fertile pastures; he leads me beside tranquil waters; he restores my soul. He leads me in right paths for his name's sake. Even though I walk through the darkest of valleys, I fear no evil; for you are with me, your rod and staff a constant source of comfort. You prepare a table before me in the presence of my foes; you anoint my head with oil; my cup brims over. Surely goodness and mercy will accompany me all my days, and I shall dwell in the house of the Lord my whole life long. (Psalm 23)

Few words have brought greater comfort and inspiration across the centuries than Psalm 23, this being one of the few passages of scripture that most people have at least some knowledge of. The words somehow seem to strike a chord in people, resonating within them at some deep unconscious level. Perhaps one of the secrets of its enduring popularity is that David himself, in his youth, was a shepherd. In other words, when he wrote 'The Lord is my shepherd' he knew what he was talking about, the words rich with personal associations. Here was no sentimental comparison. It was rather the testimony of someone who understood the commitment and devotion that shepherding requires and who, in an outpouring of wonder, realised that here was an illustration of God's astonishing love for all his people.

For us, that love has been revealed all the more wonderfully through Jesus Christ and his willingness to offer his own life for our sakes. He is the one who walked through that darkest of valleys, the valley of the shadow of death, so that truly we need fear no evil. Nothing now, in life or death, can ever finally separate us from the love of God expressed through him.

Totally devoted to you!

Then they reached Jerusalem. (Mark 1:15)

Some years ago, there was a song in the charts from the hit musical *Grease* with the title 'Hopelessly devoted to you'. It was a song about love – a love sufficiently strong to overcome hurt and rejection in order to establish a lasting relationship. There is a sense, though on a far deeper level, in which that title perfectly sums up the attitude of Jesus towards the whole of humankind, nowhere exhibited more clearly than in the week leading up to the cross.

We see it, believe it or not, in those four simple words of our reading. They look simple enough, don't they? – but beneath the surface they bear eloquent testimony to the awesome love of Christ, for, humanly speaking, Jerusalem was the last place Jesus should have been heading for. The knives were out for him, his enemies determined finally to silence him, and Jesus knew it as well as anyone. Yet he carried on, setting his face towards Jerusalem, refusing to be deflected from his path. He went willingly to his death, despite all it cost him – despite the emotional, physical and spiritual trauma he endured, just like any other human being. Why? Quite simply, because he loves us, his devotion to us greater than any we might show to him. That song title could have been written about Jesus, except for one thing; his love wasn't hopeless – anything but – it brought hope, joy and life to all. What we see in Christ is something more wonderful still: the one who is *totally* devoted to you!

Loving others

Learning to love

Dear friends, since God has loved us in this way, we should similarly love each other. Nobody has ever seen God but he lives in all who love each other, his love being completed in them. (1 John 4:11-12)

There's a hymn I used to sing as a boy, with the chorus: 'They'll know we are Christians by our love, by our love; yes, they'll know we are Christians by our love.' What a beautiful picture that paints, and how special life would be were it true. Sadly, most of the time it's not. Although we warm to everything Jesus said about loving others – even our enemies – and although we want to love more than anything, most of the time we are not very good at it. The truth is that we find it hard to *like* some people, let alone *love* them.

We can't change that by ourselves, of course; no amount of effort on our part can make us feel something we don't, but when we open our lives to God's grace we catch a glimpse of what love is really all about. None of us deserves that love, and yet God glimpses in each one of us something that is special – precious enough to die for. If *he* can see that in *us*, surely *we* can see it in *others*.

Love your enemies!

You have heard that it was said, 'You shall love your neighbour and hate your enemy.' But I tell you, love your enemies and pray for those who persecute you, so that you may become children of your Father in heaven; for he causes his sun to rise on the evil and the good, and the rain to fall on the just and the unjust. (Matthew 5:43-45)

There was a young man during my time at senior school who made my life a misery. At any and every opportunity he would hit, punch, or kick anyone unfortunate enough to cross his path. Like many others, I lived in fear of his approach. So one day, when I saw him making a beeline towards me, you can imagine how I felt – petrified. Even when he greeted me with a beatific smile, clasped hold of my hand and started to pour out apologies for all his past behaviour, I was convinced this sudden friendliness was just a front concealing some devious plan. But it wasn't. The change was real and remarkable, the remorse genuine, and from that day to the time he left school to go out into the mission field as an evangelist, I received only kindness and consideration from his hands. Yet, for all that, I still automatically flinched whenever I saw him, and still found myself waiting for the bubble to burst.

Love your enemies? It's hard enough, even when they stop being that and extend the hand of friendship. To love those who continue to hurt us – it's asking a lot, isn't it? Yet, that is the way of Christ. It doesn't mean liking them, or even feeling affection; that, surely, is expecting too much. It means being ready to forgive, to meet rejection with acceptance, to wish good rather than evil, to recognise our common humanity and the needs that tie us together. Can you do that? I'm still not sure I can but I am sure I should. One look at the world, with all its tensions and conflicts, violence and division, prejudice and intolerance gives us a bleak picture of the alternative.

Love your neighbour

A lawyer questioned Jesus, hoping to catch him out. 'Teacher,' he asked, 'which of the law's commandments ranks first?' Jesus answered him, 'You shall love the Lord your God with all your heart, and with all your soul, and with all your mind. This is the first and greatest commandment. The second is similar: You shall love your neighbour as yourself.' On these commandments hang all of the law and the prophets. (Matthew 22:35-40)

The whole law encapsulated in two commandments revolving around one word: love – it all sounds so easy, doesn't it, so wonderfully straightforward. Or at least it does until we realise that the neighbours Jesus refers to are not just those who live next door or nearby, but everyone, everywhere; and then, suddenly, we feel overwhelmed by the scale of the challenge and the enormity of our responsibility.

Far from reducing the demands God places upon us, this suddenly intensifies them, for instead of giving us a list of things to avoid, it challenges us to explore what we are able to do. The list is endless, for there is virtually no limit to the human need within our world. In our own society and beyond there is a multitude crying out for support and help, desperately in need of a little kindness and compassion. We cannot, of course, respond to them all, and I don't for a moment expect that Jesus intends us to, but how far do we respond to any? Our response to others must always be the acid test of our commitment; indeed, it is cited in the first letter of John as the truest yardstick of our love for God. Faith begins with God's love for us and our love for him in response, but it cannot end there, for wherever our neighbour is in need God is in need too, asking us to tend his wounds.

The missing ingredient

If I speak in the tongues of people or angels, but do not have love, I become nothing more than a blasting trumpet or a clashing cymbal. If I have the gift of prophecy and understand all mysteries and all knowledge, and if I have faith such as to remove mountains, yet do not have love, then I am nothing. If I dispense all my goods and surrender my body to be burned yet do not have love, it profits me nothing. (1 Corinthians 13:1-3)

It looked good, it smelled good and, as I set the meal on the table, I was confident that it would taste good as well. But it didn't. Instead of setting the taste buds tingling as I'd anticipated, it was bland, lifeless, unappetising; a culinary flop rather than a cordon bleu masterpiece! Why? Because instead of adding chilli powder I'd mistakenly put in paprika – the vital ingredient was missing.

The analogy may be different, but the Apostle Paul was talking along much the same lines in his celebrated words on love to the Corinthians. He sets out what looks to be the perfect recipe for Christian discipleship: faith to move mountains, spiritual and human gifts, generosity and commitment to the point of unreserved self-sacrifice – what more could you possibly want? Yet, says Paul, without that one vital ingredient of love, it counts for nothing. We may have heard that message innumerable times, but we still need to hear it again, for it is impossible to overestimate its importance. We turn faith so easily into a matter of outward observance: of thinking or believing this, of doing or supporting that – the deed more important than the motive behind it. Don't let that happen. Whatever you do, whatever you count important, never confuse the incidentals of Christian discipleship with the one ingredient that really matters: loving others as God has loved us.

New beginnings

see also Easter

Celebrating the new morning

Satisfy us each morning with your unswerving love, so that we may rejoice and celebrate all our days. (Psalm 90:14)

Mornings are not my favourite time, and I suspect many would say the same. We may occasionally greet the new day with a song in our hearts, but probably more often it is with a groan of dismay, the pressures and responsibilities of daily life weighing so heavily upon us that we wake with a sense of foreboding rather than anticipation. Yet every morning is God's gift, full of immeasurable potential and untold possibilities, if only we have eyes to see and ears to hear. Make time, when you wake, to acknowledge God's goodness and to commit the day ahead to him. Make time to recognise that it symbolises the wonderful truth at the heart of faith: that God is looking each moment to offer us new beginnings.

Changing course

In those days John the Baptist appeared in the wilderness of Judea, proclaiming, 'Repent, for the kingdom of heaven has come near.' Then the people of Jerusalem and all Judea went out to him, and all the region along the Jordan, and they were baptised by him in the River Jordan, confessing their sins. (Matthew 3:1-2)

Repent. It's not a word we use much nowadays, but there are few words that better express the message at the heart of the gospel. To become a Christian is not just about accepting a truth or confessing our faith in Christ. Nor is it simply an acknowledgement of wrongdoing and seeking of forgiveness. It is about a change of direction, a reorientation of life, pursuing a different course. The essence of the gospel is that we need to turn from our old way to the way of Christ. For some that change, initially at least, may be more marked than others, their past lifestyle standing in stark contrast to their new-found faith, whereas those who have been brought up within the circle of the Church may find the outward change needed so negligible as to be almost imperceptible.

Repentance, though, is not a one-off thing – if only it were! We go on making mistakes every day of our life, inadvertently going astray with monotonous regularity. Before we know it, we are on the wrong road again; in all likelihood heading back the way we have come, such that we need to repent yet once more. The word may be archaic but the meaning is not. Whoever we are, whatever we have done, however many times we may have done so before, it is never too late to change course.

Done and undone

There is, then, no condemnation now for those in Christ Jesus, because the law of the Spirit of life has set us free from the law of sin and death. I am convinced that nothing can separate us from Christ's love. Neither death nor life, nor angels nor demons, nor the present nor the future, nor any powers, nor height nor depth nor anything else in all creation, will ever be able to separate us from the love of God that is ours in Christ Jesus our Lord. (Romans 8:1-2, 38-39)

Why is it that a piece of string, no matter how carefully you put it away in a drawer, always ties itself into knots? Even more perplexing, how is it that children's shoelaces, however painstakingly you may tie them, manage to come undone within a few paces? Whoever succeeds in answering such mysteries will be a rich person indeed! It's not just string and shoelaces, however, that become tangled into knots or come undone; we find the same in so much in life. Tackle a pile of washing up or ironing, mow the lawn or weed the garden, clean the car or paint the house, and before you know it the job needs doing again, but make one simple mistake and, however hard we try, we can't undo it. Or can we?

At the heart of our faith lies a triumphant message of something both done and undone. On the one hand, nothing can undo what God has done in Christ. Through his death and resurrection, he has destroyed the power of evil and opened the way to life for all. What needed doing has been done, and nothing can ever change that! Yet, on the other hand, through that decisive act, everything else done can be undone, for God is always ready to put the past behind us and to help us start again. To assume that we are bound by what has gone before is to deny the glorious resurrection message. Whatever we are, or have been, we can always be a new creation! The past is done with, the future is open – thanks be to God!

A new beginning

When eight days had passed, the time came to circumcise the child; and they called him Jesus, the name the angel had given even before conception. When the time came for him to be purified according to the law of Moses, they brought him to Jerusalem to present him to the Lord (as it is written in the law of the Lord, 'Every firstborn male shall be designated as holy to the Lord'). They offered a sacrifice as prescribed in the law of the Lord, 'a pair of turtledoves or two young pigeons'. When they had done everything the law of the Lord required, they returned to their hometown of Nazareth in Galilee. The child grew in strength and wisdom; and God's favour rested on him. (Luke 2:21-24, 39-40)

'And it's from the old I travel to the new' – so runs the popular hymn of Sydney Carter – and those words perfectly capture a truth at the heart of the gospel: that in Christ we see a new beginning. Yet, read the account of Jesus' presentation at the temple and you could be excused for thinking that nothing was going to change after all. Jesus was brought according to the law of Moses; presented at the temple as it is written in the law of the Lord, and a sacrifice offered as prescribed in the law of the Lord. It was only when they had done everything the law required that Mary and Joseph felt able to return home.

Do not be fooled, however, for once Jesus began his ministry it became clear that he brought a decisive break with the old. 'You have heard it said', he told the crowd, concerning various points of the law, 'but I say to you', after which he set out a new and revolutionary interpretation of established wisdom. This was a break with the past, a parting of the ways between old and new, but it was not a complete parting, for he was also able to say, 'Do not think I have come to abolish the law or the prophets; I have come not to abolish but to fulfil.' From the old had come something new. Turn from the birth to the death of Jesus, for thirty-three years later he was presented to God in Jerusalem once again, only this time there were to be no sacrifices offered on his behalf – he *was* the sacrifice! Here, supremely, is the Christ who brings new life out of old, transforming what *has* been into what *shall* be. He continues to do the same in our lives today, taking what we are and reshaping our lives day by day into a new creation.

A new creation

Anyone united with Christ is a new creation; the old self has passed away in its entirety; everything is made new. (2 Corinthians 5:17)

Do you still make New Year resolutions? If you're anything like me, you used to once but you've long since come to realise that the chances of living up to them are remote if not non-existent. Is this a healthy realism or the counsel of despair, practical common sense or weary resignation? The answer is a bit of both. By ourselves, we can change to a point, but to change our spots completely is beyond us.

In Christ, however, it is a different story; the gospel, at its heart, is about new beginnings, a fresh start not of our own making but made possible by the grace of God. However frustrated you may be at your inability to live the life you want to, never lose sight of that fact: the life-changing power of God in Christ that is always striving to bring its new creation to perfection.

Reclaimed, renamed, retrained

You are a chosen race, a royal priesthood, a holy nation, a people who God has set apart so that you may declare the goodness of him who called you out of darkness into his wonderful light. Once, you were not a people – now you are the people of God; once you had not obtained forgiveness – now you have received mercy. (1 Peter 2:9-10)

When I was a boy I often used to walk around the mudflats of Essex, spotting birds or simply enjoying the peace of the countryside. Although I prefer rugged cliffs and sandy bays, there is nonetheless something haunting about those desolate places, a peace and tranquillity to be had there rarely found elsewhere. Close to nature it all may seem, yet much of the land thereabouts would not be accessible but for human intervention, the bulk of it having been reclaimed earlier last century with the help of Dutch engineers skilled at land reclamation. For example, what we today call Canvey Island was, not so long ago, simply an area of mud exposed at low tide, and, but for the sea wall that surrounds it, would swiftly revert to that.

There is a parallel to this in the Christian life, made clear in those words from the first epistle of Peter. By his grace, God has reclaimed us from the stranglehold of our old nature, he has renamed his people, and he is constantly at work within us, helping to reshape and redirect our lives. Once again, it is a continuing process, the way of self constantly threatening to engulf us. Yet, thanks be to God, though we must play our part, the final victory is not down to us but to him.

The rising sun

The sun will rise over us from heaven, to shine on those sitting in darkness and in the shadow of death; to guide our feet into the way of peace. (Luke 1:78-79)

There's something wonderful about dawn, isn't there? It speaks of new beginnings, a fresh start – another day set before us, full of promise and opportunity. It is precisely ideas such as these that lie behind the wonderful words of Zechariah in Luke's Gospel; words that capture something of the wonder, joy and hope associated with the coming of Christ. Here was one who would bring joy where there was sorrow, hope where there was despair, love where there was hatred, and peace where there was division; not just a fresh chapter in history but also the possibility of a similar renewal in every human life that can only be compared to the rising of the sun; a new dawn!

That is what God offers to you and me today, to anyone and everyone willing to turn to Christ; a fresh start, a new day, and though darkness may sometimes seem to threaten once again, this sun will never set, but go on shining for all eternity.

Peace

Inner peace

The peace of God

My legacy to you is peace – that's what I give you – my very own peace, unlike anything the world can offer. Don't let anything disturb or distress you, then. Put your heart at rest and fear nothing. (John 14:27)

A common marketing ploy today seems to be to promise peace of mind. Take out a pension plan or an insurance policy and you can put your worries behind you. Go on holiday to the sun and get away from it all. Buy a new car, washing machine or stereo system and take the stress and strain out of life. Anything and everything, it seems, promises us a more relaxed and happy existence. Sadly, however, statistics don't bear this out. We may have more leisure time and money today than previous generations, and we may enjoy all the latest hi-tech gadgetry, yet we live in a world where stress is rife and where countless people yearn for a sense of inner peace. Peace, like happiness, cannot be bought; indeed, the quest for money, possessions and status is often what destroys the little peace that we have.

We can find a degree of peace in this world in the sense of briefly getting away from it all, but for the Christian real peace comes ultimately from another source – from an awareness of God's love made real through the inner presence of his Holy Spirit. We cannot create such peace ourselves, but we can cultivate it through making time for God, creating a space in our lives for prayer and reflection, and being open to what he would do within us. Such peace involves letting go and seeing life from another perspective than that typically adopted, but it also means taking hold of a prize greater than anything the world can give – a peace that passes understanding.

One day at a time

Anxiety weighs down the human heart, but a good word cheers it up. (Proverbs 12:25)

I recently came across two wonderful quotations. The first was from Corrie Ten Boom: 'Worry does not empty tomorrow of its sorrow; it empties today of its strength.' The second was from William R. Inge, one-time Dean of St Paul's: 'Worry is interest paid on trouble before it falls due.' What wisdom there is in those words, yet how hard we find it to act upon them. We know that worry is futile, not only failing to achieve anything but actually undermining our ability to face life's problems, yet sometimes we just can't seem to help ourselves. To a point, that is natural, however sure our trust in God. When our welfare is threatened, or our loved ones are in any kind of danger, we would be less than human not to worry about it. Yet to worry about what might happen when there are no grounds to fear it, to fret about possibilities rather than certainties, is foolhardy. There is time enough to deal with these if and when they arrive without facing them several times over beforehand.

Few things have the power to crush the human spirit like worry, yet the irony is that most of the things we worry about never materialise and those that do are often less awful than we imagine. For the Christian there is the added confidence that, even when our worst fears are realised, God will be there to support us. Nothing can destroy the future he holds for us; don't let worry destroy the present.

Making peace

Peacemakers

Blessed are those who promote peace, for God will call them his children. (Matthew 5:9)

A while back, a nightly news bulletin featured one of the most moving stories I've heard in a long time. It was just a few days after the appalling suicide bombing of an Israeli wedding reception had left several people dead and countless others maimed and injured – men, women and children, one moment enjoying a family celebration and the next caught up in the most unspeakable carnage. Few incidents better sum up the depth of hatred between Jew and Arab, the level of atrocities on both sides seeming to know no bounds.

The story I have in mind, though, was very different. It concerned the father of a young man killed in an accident. Distraught with grief, the father agreed to donate his son's organs to a hospitalised patient in urgent need of a transplant. Nothing extraordinary about that, you might think, except that the donor was an Arab and the patient an Israeli! 'I wanted my son's death to bring life,' explained the father, 'whether it be to Jew or Arab.' The contrast could hardly be more poignant nor the example more challenging. A small act but a massive gesture that, for a few hours at least, spoke of peace and reconciliation. Would we have acted the same in that man's place? I wonder. Our situation may be far removed from his, but in innumerable ways we have the opportunity every day to act as peacemakers or to perpetuate the things that cause division. We can show forgiveness or nurse grievances, swallow our pride or thrust ourselves forward, admit mistakes or refuse to bend, make the first move or resist every advance. All of us have the opportunity in our daily relationships to work for harmony and reconciliation, but few of us take the opportunity as often as we should. Which are we: peacemakers or peace-breakers?

Power of God,
_____ its transforming nature _____

see also Strength in weakness; Sovereignty and wonder of God

A changed man

Peter sat outside in the courtyard, and a servant-girl approached him saying, 'You also were with Jesus the Galilean', but he denied it before them all, saying, 'I've no idea what you're talking about'. He went out to the porch, where another servant-girl saw him, and she said to those gathered there, 'This man was with Jesus of Nazareth.' He denied it once again, with an oath, 'I do not know the man.' Shortly afterwards, the bystanders came up and confronted Peter, 'There's no doubt that you also are one of them, for your accent gives you away.' Then he began to curse and swear, 'I do not know the man!' At precisely that moment, the cock crowed, and Peter remembered what Jesus had said: 'Before the cock crows, you will deny me three times.' He stumbled outside and wept bitterly. (Matthew 26:69-75)

A few months ago my wife attended a reunion of former classmates. She found it a fascinating experience. A few had hardly altered but the majority had changed beyond recognition. In our verses today, we encounter a man in whom there was to be a truly remarkable change. We meet him first as an ordinary fisherman going about his daily business, but following the call of Christ he quickly emerges as the leader of the Apostles. All that, though, must have rung somewhat hollow on that awful night when, just as had been predicted, he denied Jesus three times.

Yet, when we turn to the book of Acts, what a different story we find. It is Peter, in Acts 2, who boldly speaks out for Christ on behalf of the Apostles following the baptism of the Holy Spirit. Later, when his persistent testimony lands him in hot water with the authorities, he responds, 'Make up your own minds whether it is right in God's eyes to obey you rather than him. The fact is we cannot help but speak concerning everything we have seen and heard' (Acts 4:19-20). From one afraid to be associated with Christ, Peter had changed to one proud to bear his name; from one whose only thought had been his own safety to one heedless of the cost of discipleship. Here is an astonishing testimony to the way Jesus is able to change lives. The change in us may not be quite so dramatic, but the message of Peter's story is clear: if Jesus could change *his* life, he can change anyone's!

A God of surprises

You will have heard of my former conduct within Judaism – how I vigorously persecuted and laid waste the Church of God and how I progressed in Judaism beyond most of my contemporaries, defending the tradition of my fathers with a fanatical zeal. But when the one who had set me apart in my mother's womb graciously chose to reveal his Son through me, calling me to proclaim him among all nations, I did not consult with flesh and blood. I went into the regions of Syria and Cilicia, though I was unknown by sight to those in Christ in the churches of Judea. All they had heard was this: 'The one who was previously persecuting us is now preaching the very faith he aimed to destroy!' And they glorified God concerning me. (Galatians 1:13-16, 21-24)

Imagine what it must have felt like being a Christian at the time Saul was sweeping through Judea, intent on destroying the Church. Assuming you had clung on to your faith despite the knowledge that it might cost you your life, what would your prayer have been? Would it have been for grace to bear martyrdom with courage, or perhaps for Jesus to return and establish his kingdom, or maybe for Saul to be struck down? It might have been for all or any of those, but what you probably wouldn't have prayed for is what actually happened – that Saul, the arch-persecutor of the Church would become, arguably, the greatest ambassador it has ever had. Such a thing, you would have thought, was surely too much to ask for.

Throughout the scriptures, God has a habit of springing surprises, working in ways that defy human expectation or understanding, and so it continues today. A situation may seem beyond hope, a person beyond redemption, a problem beyond solution, but in each case that is to reckon without God. Never, ever underestimate his capacity to catch us unawares; what may seem impossible to us is always possible with him!

God's part

He said, 'The kingdom of God is like this: as if someone would scatter seed on the earth, and would then sleep and rise night and day; the seed would sprout and grow though that person has no idea how. The earth bears fruit without any further assistance; first a blade of grass, then an ear and then a full head of corn within the ear.' (Mark 4:26-28)

I will never forget the first time I tried my hand at horticulture. I had recently started at college, and my mother had given me some trad-escantia cuttings from home. It seemed impossible that those spindly stems with just a couple of leaves attached could ever grow into new plants but, obediently, I planted them and placed them on a windowsill, more in hope than expectation. To my surprise, a couple of weeks later they had developed roots and, before I knew it, they had formed thriving bushy plants that went on to grace my mantelpiece for the remaining four years of my college course. In that, alone, is a demonstration of God's creative power, but we can apply the principle far more widely. So often, he works behind the scenes in ways far beyond our imagining. Though we cannot see it, let alone understand how it happens, he takes the most unpromising of materials or situations and creates out of them something unrecognisable from that with which he started. If life were entirely in our hands, our future destiny shaped solely by our own efforts, what a sorry state of affairs it would be. If we had to tackle the problems we face without any assistance, or respond to God's call in our own strength, how bleak the prospect would seem. Thank God, in his sovereign power he is able to work without any other assistance to fulfil his will and accomplish his purpose!

The Lord of life

Jesus said, 'Remove the stone', but Mary, the sister of the deceased, exclaimed, 'Lord, there is already a stench because he has been dead for four days.' Jesus said to her, 'Didn't I tell you that you will see the glory of God if you believe?' So they took away the stone. He cried with a loud voice, 'Lazarus, come out!' The dead man came out, his hands and his feet bound with strips of cloth, and his face wrapped in a cloth. Jesus said to them, 'Release the bindings, and let him go.' (John 11:39-41a, 43-44)

'What wouldn't I give to believe!' When it comes to resurrection and eternal life, I've heard words like those countless times. Even the most avowed atheist or agnostic would like to believe there is something after this life; that death is not the end. Yet most, if they do not laugh derisively at such an idea, shake their heads wistfully at any suggestion it might be true.

So it was, quite understandably, for the family of Lazarus. They had watched him die and seen him sealed in his tomb; and with that, all hope had gone. Yet, suddenly, here was Jesus, ordering that the stone be rolled away, and, all at once, there was Lazarus before them, alive and well. It was a sign of things to come, a pointer to the empty tomb and the ultimate triumph over death in the resurrection of Christ – not just revival this time but resurrection, life for all eternity; and with it the promise of new life for all who follow him. We do not understand how it can be or what form that life will take, but, thankfully, it does not depend on our faith, but rests solely with Christ – the one who alone can say, 'I am the resurrection and the life.'

Lovingly restored

Have nothing more to do with all these things: rage, anger, malice, slander, abusive language and deceitful behaviour, for you have renounced the old self with its associated practices and become a new person, your minds being renewed into the likeness of the one who created you. (Colossians 3:8-10)

Not far from my home lies Hestercombe Gardens, in terms of horti-cultural history one of the most important landscape gardens in the country. Amazingly, until a few years ago, it was a derelict wilderness, its very presence forgotten. Then a local man, reading up about the area and recognising its importance, resolved to restore Hestercombe to its former glory, setting up 'Friends of Hestercombe' and mort-gaging his house to raise funds to begin the task of restoration. Today, just a few years later, the gardens bring delight to numerous visitors, and a grant of over £5000,000 has just been awarded by the Lottery Commission to help fund the next stage of work.

We can draw parallels here with our own lives, for although we are often far removed from what God intended us to be, he is constantly at work to restore and remake us. Although we may despair of ever changing, God never gives us up as a lost cause. He is continually striving to recreate us in the likeness of Christ – a transformation that, thank God, depends not wholly upon our own efforts, important though those are, but upon his grace.

A master touch

The centurion sent friends with a message for Jesus, saying, 'Lord, do not trouble yourself further, for I do not deserve to have you come under my roof. That's why I didn't presume to come to you in person. Just speak the word, and let my servant be made well. Like you, I am a man set under authority, with soldiers under me. I tell one, "Go", and he goes, and another, "Come", and he comes. Similarly, I say to my slaves, "Do this", and they do it.' When Jesus heard this, he was astounded, and turning to the crowd that followed him, he said, 'I tell you truthfully, I have not found any faith to equal this, even in Israel.' When the messengers returned to the house, they found the slave restored to health. (Luke 7:6b-10)

It wasn't a big job – just a few screws to be removed so that an old wooden partition could be taken out. All right, so the threads were a little worn, but I was confident that I could finish the task in no time. If nothing else, it would save the builders – who were fitting a skylight in the attic – a little time, if not save us a little money. Four hours later I was still hard at it, sweat dripping down my chin, blisters raw on my hands. It was time to admit defeat and let the experts take over. Two minutes later, the job was done! The lesson is clear enough. Sometimes we need to recognise that we need help.

So it was with the Roman centurion who asked Jesus to heal his slave. He was a man in authority, used to giving orders, accustomed to getting things done, but this time he recognised the need for a higher authority, someone who could do what he couldn't. There are times when we need to do the same. We should not underestimate the gifts that God has given, for there may often be times when the answer to our prayers lies in our own hands, dependent on us using those gifts as God directs. At other times, though, we need to recognise our impotence, and throw ourselves entirely upon the power of God. Pray for his guidance in getting the balance right.

A new heart

These are the words of the Lord God: I will give them a different heart and put a new spirit into them; I will take the heart of stone out of their bodies and give them a heart of flesh. Then they will conform to my statutes and keep my laws. They will become my people and I will become their God. (Ezekiel 11:17a, 19-20)

In December 1967, Dr Christiaan Barnard performed the first human heart transplant at Groote Schuur Hospital in South Africa. It was an operation that stunned and enthralled the world, few having believed it could ever be achieved. Today, it is almost a routine operation. In the early days, life expectancy for the donee was relatively short; today, such surgery means a new beginning and a fresh chapter in life. The words of Ezekiel are figurative rather than literal, yet the transplant they speak of is no less dramatic – if anything, it is more so – for what the prophet is talking about is people being changed not physically but spiritually. Can it really happen? Not according to worldly wisdom. 'A leopard cannot change its spots,' we say. 'Once a thief always a thief.' It's hard as life goes by not to share such a cynical view of the world.

The people of Ezekiel's day felt much the same, greeting his words with scepticism if not outright scorn. Quite simply, they'd heard it all before. Experience had taught them that they would go on making the same mistakes in the future as they had in the past. Ezekiel, though, believed differently, confident that God had the power to change people deep within. His words were, of course, to find their fulfilment in the coming of Jesus and the gift of the Holy Spirit. Through Christ, the work of renewal has begun; work that will continue until the day we are united in the kingdom of God. Never lose sight of that promise. Never forget what God has done or what he shall yet do.

Praise and worship

see also Sovereignty and wonder of God

A fitting response

He rescued me from the slippery pit, out of the mud and the mire; he set my feet on a rock and gave me a sure footing. He has put a new song on my lips, a song of praise to our God. (Psalm 40:2-3)

Imagine going to a concert or a play in which the most superlative performance was given but after which the audience got up and left in stony silence. Or imagine going to a football match or some other sporting event in which the crowd sat motionless, with no sign of emotion or involvement whatsoever. It's unimaginable, isn't it? Each of these excites passion and appreciation, not only inviting but expecting some kind of response. To applaud, chant, cheer, leap out of one's seat – each denotes how much the event means to those experiencing it.

So it is with God. After everything he has done for us can we remain silent? In the light of his inexpressible love, his innumerable gifts and his inexhaustible grace, can we do anything less than respond? Of course not! Here is the essence of worship – a spontaneous outpouring of praise, thanksgiving, love and wonder; a way of telling God how much it all means to us. Is that what worship means to you? Is that your motivation behind these few moments you have set aside for prayer and reflection? It should be, and if it's not then maybe it's time you reminded yourself once again of who God is, what he has given, and what he continues to give.

Praise where praise is due

You are worthy, O Lord our God, to receive glory and honour and power, for all things were made by you, their creation and existence down to your will. Worthy is the Lamb that was slain to receive power and riches and wisdom and strength and honour and glory and blessing! (Revelation 4:11; 5:12)

It's always nice to receive praise, isn't it? Or is it? Actually, I think there are times when it is the last thing we want. When we've done something well, given of our very best, then praise is indeed welcome and we feel justifiably disappointed if it is withheld. If, though, someone offers it to us when we know it to be undeserved, then we feel patronised, embarrassed, and even angry. As we rightly say, 'Praise where praise is due'.

With God there is never any question as to that. We owe all we are to him, all that is and all that ever shall be arising from him. He is the giver of life now and life to come, the power behind the universe, the provider of all our needs. So it is, similarly, with Christ – he offers life to all, hope and healing to a broken world, love that words cannot begin to express. He doesn't *need* our praise any more than God does, but both welcome it as an expression of our commitment, a token of our gratitude and a sign of our faith. We do not offer that praise because we have to, or because it is expected of us, but simply because it is appropriate, the natural response to everything we have received; the only response that will do.

Songs of praise

I will sing of your devoted love for ever, O Lord; my mouth will declare your faithfulness to the end of time. Come, let us lift up our joyful songs to the Lord; let us make a glad sound to the rock of our salvation! Let us come gratefully before him and make a joyful sound to him with songs of praise! Come, let us bow down and worship, let us kneel before the Lord our creator, for he is our God and we are his people. (Psalm 89:1; 95:1-2, 6-7a)

There are few areas within the life of the Church more divisive than music. Whereas issues of doctrine typically divided Christians in the past, today music seems to be one of the chief causes of discord. For some, traditional hymnody is like a distant planet, unexplored and presumed barren. For others, modern choruses are anathema, representing froth rather than substance, superficial emotion rather than faith rooted in history. The polarisation that can develop around this never ceases to amaze me. Of course we each have our preferences, just as we all have our own tastes in music, but is one inherently better than another? Some songs may be linguistically more polished than others and some tunes may be catchier, but as far as God is concerned that counts for nothing. What matters is the sincerity with which we sing, and whether our lives measure up to our words. As David reminds us, our songs are sung not for our own benefit but as an offering of worship to God. Whether it is a chorus or a hymn, a chant or an anthem, what matters is that we sing to the Lord. Without that, our songs are meaningless and our time is wasted.

Prayer

Asking in faith (*see also* Faith: Asking in faith)

Asking in prayer

Ask, and it will be given to you; search, and you will find; knock, and the door will be opened for you. For whoever asks receives, and whoever searches finds, and to whoever knocks, the door will be opened. Would any among you, should your child ask for bread, give a stone? Or if asked for a fish, would you give a snake? If then, you who are flawed, know how to give good gifts to your children, how much more will your heavenly Father give good things to those who ask him! (Matthew 7:7-11)

'Seek and you will find.' At least that's what Jesus tells us. It sounds good, doesn't it? And it is, no question. Yet, like most attractive promises, we need to be aware of important qualifications, for what Jesus was offering here was not a blank cheque, a guarantee that whatever we look for in life will be ours if only we pray hard enough. On the contrary, many will seek after goals like status and success, fame and fortune, but never find them. The seeking Jesus has in mind is of a different kind – a search for meaning, for truth, for God. It is more than the perennial quest for happiness, though that is part of it. It is more than a striving after personal fulfilment, though that too is an integral aspect. It is a prayerful search for the infinite, the root and goal of our being, the purpose behind the universe and life itself; a journey of discovery that reaches its destination in Christ.

Seek in that way, openly and honestly, and, like the wise men long ago, you will find. Open your life to him and you will discover life in abundance, the answer to your deepest needs, the one before whom we too, as the magi before us, can only fall down on our knees in worship.

Praying in faith

While Peter was kept in prison, the Church prayed earnestly to God for his safety. The very night that Herod intended to send for him, Peter, bound with two chains, was sleeping between two soldiers, a watch also being kept at the front of the prison door. Suddenly, an angel of the Lord appeared and a light filled the building. Touching Peter on the side, he woke him, saying, 'Get up quickly!' The chains fell from his wrists, and the angel said to him, 'Fasten your belt and put on your sandals.' He did so. Then he said to him, 'Wrap your cloak around you and follow me.' Peter went out and followed him. He went to the house of Mary, the mother of John Mark, where many had gathered in prayer. When he knocked at the porch door, a maid called Rhoda came to answer. On recognising Peter's voice, she was so overjoyed that, instead of opening the door, she ran back inside and announced that Peter was standing at the gate. They said to her, 'You've taken leave of your senses!' She was so insistent that it was him that they said, 'Perhaps it's his angel.' Meanwhile Peter carried on knocking; and when finally they opened the door and saw him, they were amazed. (Acts 12:5-9a, 12-16)

Ask any Christian what they find hardest in the Christian life and they will probably say prayer. We find it hard to give prayer proper time and harder still to find the words for what we want to say, but perhaps most difficult of all is coming to terms with the many times when we do not seem to receive an answer or when the answer given is not quite what we hoped for. Faith tells us one thing, experience another, and eventually it is experience, often all too painful, that tends to win the day. There was a time, perhaps, when we would have asked for something, fully confident that God would grant it, but as the years pass and that fails to happen, we find it increasingly hard to keep on believing. As a result, our prayers become mechanical, offered more out of duty than expectation.

Yet God does hear and does respond, our failure to hear his answer often due to our failure to listen or to the straitjacket we sub-consciously set upon him. It may be that his answer is 'no', or 'not yet', but it may also be that he has already answered 'yes', if only we can throw off the shackles of doubt and bring ourselves to believe it.

Reversing the roles?

Tread carefully when you enter the house of God. Better to draw near and listen than to offer the sacrifice of fools, for they cannot keep themselves from doing evil. Never be in a hurry to talk and do not let your heart speak hastily before God, for God is in heaven and you are upon earth. So, then, let your words be few. (Ecclesiastes 5:1-2)

How many of us, if we went to hospital for a consultation with a specialist, would refuse to listen to the diagnosis, insisting that we know better? Which of us, if we had to call out the AA, would tell the mechanic how to do his or her job? Or, again, how many of us, if by some mischance we found ourselves on trial in the high court, would presume to advise our barrister as to the best way to conduct the case?

In all of these situations, to stick our oar in and refuse to bow to a greater authority would be the height of folly, yet the words of Ecclesiastes warn us that we can often be guilty of doing something very similar when it comes to God. We claim that he is sovereign over all, ruler of heaven and earth, and Lord of space and time, but so often, having done that, we calmly proceed to present him with a personal wish list, without the slightest sense of incongruity. 'Grant me this', we say; 'do that', 'do the other', as if we fully expect him to be at our beck and call.

The problem is that some passages in scripture concerning asking in faith appear, on a superficial reading, to encourage such an approach, but think about the implications were that true: it would be tantamount to putting ourselves in God's place! Of course there will be times when something matters so much to us that we will beg him to listen, and of course there will be times when he readily does so, but if God is who we say he is, surely the right approach in prayer has to be to listen to what he wants before listing what we desire. Prayer is not finally something we do, but something he invites us to share in. Lose sight of that, and we're in danger of losing sight of him.

Faithfulness in prayer

A life of prayer

Epaphras, from among your number and a servant of Jesus Christ, sends greetings. He is always wrestling on your behalf in prayer, asking that you may stand firm, mature and fully assured of the will of God. (Colossians 4:12)

'I'll pray for you.' Countless individuals must have made that promise innumerable times across the years, but what does it actually mean? Sometimes it is little more than a platitude; a suitably pious-sounding way of avoiding the need to offer any more concrete help. Usually, though, we offer it in all sincerity, but, despite our best intentions, fail to act upon it. We mean to pray, but there are so many needs to pray for and so little time in which to do it. Meaningful prayer tends to go out of the window, reduced to a few cursory and general words. Contrast that with the tribute paid by Paul to the man at the centre of our reading today: Epaphras, a man who was 'always wrestling in prayer' for the Philippians. Of all his gifts, this, in Paul's opinion, was what made Epaphras stand out – his dedication to prayer.

So what can we learn here? First, for Epaphras prayer wasn't a casual take-it-or-leave-it activity; it was part of his life, a privilege and responsibility he wrestled with day by day. It wasn't a vague activity, either. He knew whom he was praying for, what he was praying about and why he was praying. Equally, prayer wasn't simply concerned with his own affairs or his immediate circle. It reached out to others, concerned with their needs and ultimate welfare. Finally, and most important, he acted upon his prayers. 'I can personally testify,' Paul went on to say, 'that he works tirelessly, both for you and for those in Laodicea and Hierapolis.' What exactly he did, we are not told, but it is clear that Epaphras didn't leave it all to God; he played his part in ensuring his prayers were answered. 'I'll pray for you.' It's a wonderful promise if we really mean it. How many of us actually do?

Ingredients of prayer

Honest prayer

O God, smash the teeth in their mouths! Rip out the fangs of the lions, O Lord! Let them disappear like water that trickles away; let them be trodden underfoot like grass and wither away. Let them be like a slug putrefying in their own slime, like a stillborn child that never sees the light of day. The faithful will rejoice when they see vengeance done; they will wash their feet in the blood of the wicked. Then people will say, 'Surely virtue is rewarded; there is indeed a God who judges the earth.' (Psalm 58:6-8, 10-11)

When did you last hear a sermon on a text like that! Frankly, I'll be astonished if you ever have. We rightly find such sentiments offensive, and the very idea that we might call these words prayer is utterly repugnant. Yet not so fast, for passages like this still have something to teach us. I don't claim that they're a paradigm of prayer – far from it – but what they do show is a remarkable candour before God. David, the writer of this Psalm, was clearly angry and frustrated; annoyed at the fact that evil seems to prosper, annoyed at the way he'd suffered because of it, and most of all annoyed that God appeared to be doing nothing about it. That's how he felt, so that's what he said.

Was that right or wrong? You tell me. If we're thoroughly fed up with life, what point is served by dutifully offering our thanksgiving? If we're consumed by doubt, how genuine is it to praise God for his purpose? There's a danger of simply going through the motions in prayer, telling God what we think he wants to hear rather than expressing our true feelings. More damaging still, we can assume that prayer requires a special sort of language, almost a technical expertise, if God is to hear us, and that some matters cannot be aired. Personally,

I believe God prefers an honest prayer, no matter how shocking, to one that is divorced from the heart. I'm not saying he will applaud our feelings, still less that he will answer as we would like, but he will respond nonetheless, and, if we listen, then we will learn and be equipped to grow, both as people and in faith.

A prayer from the heart

When praying, do not pile up empty words in the way the Gentiles do, imagining they will be heard because of their eloquence. Do not copy them, for your Father knows everything you need before you even ask him. Pray instead like this: Our Father in heaven, may your name be honoured, your kingdom come and your will be accomplished, on earth as in heaven. Give us the things we need and forgive our debts as we also have forgiven our debtors. Do not bring us into temptation but rescue us from evil. (Matthew 6:7-13)

Towards the end of my time at secondary school, I wrote what I considered to be one of my best essays, so it was with some excitement that I presented it to my English teacher, fully expecting an enthusiastic response. I was to be disappointed, his only observation being, 'It's a bit long-winded, isn't it.' You'd have thought I might have learned my lesson after that, but a few years later at theological college I received back an assignment from my Old Testament tutor with the following terse appraisal: 'Pompous and verbose.' If you've waded through this book you may well share his sentiments! Many of us use more words than necessary to get our point across, and that can be especially so when it comes to prayer, not because of any innate wordiness but because we somehow feel we must spell everything out if God is to answer us. We've probably all sat through services in which the prayers are longer than the sermon, or through prayer meetings that seem to go on for ever.

Contrast such experiences with the simple model of prayer given by Jesus, and his equally direct advice on the subject. God knows what we need, Jesus tells us, even before we ask him, prayer being for our benefit rather than his. It's the thought rather than the words that matters most to him. Of course, words have their place but we should never get hung up on them, still less worry that God will not hear us if we don't get them right. Indeed, it's worth asking whether we fail to hear him answer sometimes because we're too busy speaking to listen!

The Spirit's part in prayer

Partners in prayer

In the same way, the Spirit identifies with us in our weakness. We do not know how to pray or what to pray for, but the Spirit pleads on our behalf with entreaties that are beyond words, and the one who searches our hearts knows the Spirit's mind, because he intercedes constantly on behalf of the saints seeking the fulfilment of God's purpose. (Romans 8:26-27)

A while back, I was asked to speak at an event for Christian leaders on the subject of personal prayer. The invitation came as something of a surprise, for although I have written innumerable prayers, I still consider myself anything but an expert on the subject. Like the vast majority of Christians, prayer does not always come easily to me, nor am I as disciplined about it as I should be. If my spiritual well-being and relationship with God were entirely down to me, frankly it wouldn't be up to much. Thankfully, it's not; neither for me nor any one of us.

The Holy Spirit articulates our thoughts to God, even when we find it impossible to do so. More than that, Christ himself is constantly interceding on our behalf, bringing our unspoken needs and requests before God. Prayer may start with us but it doesn't end there. However much it may sometimes feel like it, we are never alone when we attempt to pray. That's not to encourage casualness or complacency, for prayer is ultimately given for our own benefit as much as God's, but if you can't quite find the right words, and if you genuinely can't find the time you'd like to give, don't punish yourself, your prayer will get to him nonetheless.

When prayer seems unanswered

Persevering in prayer

He said to them, 'Imagine going to a friend at midnight and saying, "Friend, lend me three loaves of bread, for one of my friends has turned up and I haven't a scrap to feed him", only to receive the answer, "Stop bothering me; the door's fastened and we're all in bed; I'm not getting up to give you anything." I tell you, even though friendship may not be a sufficient spur to rouse your friend to help you, sheer persistence, if nothing else, will persuade him to get up and give you whatever you need.' (Luke 11:5-8)

At first sight, the teaching of Jesus on prayer can seem confusing. On the one hand, he tells us not to go in for long-winded prayers as if God will hear us because of our many words; on the other, he urges us to persist in prayer until God hears and answers. There is, though, no contradiction here. The injunction to keep things simple still stands – after all, God knows our needs before we ask him, so we hardly need to labour the point. On occasions, however, God chooses for a variety of reasons not to answer our prayer immediately, or is unable to do so. It may be that we need to demonstrate our resolve, or that the time to grant our request is not yet right, or perhaps that we are asking for the wrong thing. Whatever the reason, this parable tells us not to lose heart; still less to worry that God might grow impatient with us. Unlike the friend at midnight, God is always anxious to meet our needs, at any and every moment. If the answer doesn't seem to come, make no mistake, there is good reason.

The silences of God

The Lord was passing by, and a gust of wind arose, so strong that it shook the mountain and shattered rocks before him, but the Lord was not in the wind. After that came an earthquake, but the Lord was not in the earthquake, and after the earthquake came fire, but the Lord was not in the fire; and after the fire there was simply the sound of silence. When Elijah heard that, he hid his face in his cloak, went out and stood at the entrance of the cave. Then a voice came to him that said, 'Why are you here, Elijah?' (1 Kings 19:11b-13)

The story of Elijah's encounter with God on the slopes of Mount Horeb has inspired countless sermons and innumerable prayers, not to mention the celebrated hymn, 'Dear Lord and Father of mankind, forgive our foolish ways'. What, though, is the story all about, and what, in particular, is the significance of the 'sound of silence', or the 'still small voice', as other translations put it?

There are probably several equally valid answers to such questions, but one that occurred to me rereading these verses is that perhaps this incident has something to say concerning those times when God seems far away. Elijah looks for God in the mighty wind, surely a sign of his power, but no, he is not there. He looks again in the mighty earthquake, but again, no. Then there is the fire, reminiscent of the cloudy pillar that guided the people of Israel, and you can almost imagine Elijah thinking, 'This must be him!' – but yet again it isn't. Then, just when the prophet may have been giving up hope, there comes that voice like a gentle whisper – so unpretentious, so insignificant, you could almost miss it. Was this God's way of telling Elijah he is present in the ordinary and mundane moments of life even when it doesn't look like it? I may simply be clutching at straws here, but I like to think there is a grain of truth in such an interpretation, for, let's face it, occasions when God is dramatically at work are few and far between. The fact is that he is equally present in the humdrum business of daily life, even when we struggle to catch sight of him; perhaps there most of all.

Unanswered prayer

I call to you, O Lord my rock: do not refuse to listen, for if you keep silent I shall be like those who go down into the depths. Hear my entreaty as I beg you for help, and as I lift up my hands towards your dwelling place. (Psalm 28:1-2)

It was a frustrating business. We'd been connected and were enjoying a good chat when suddenly a fault developed on the line and although I could still hear my friend, he could no longer hear me. It felt suddenly as if I was talking to myself. On other occasions like this, the roles may be reversed, so that we are suddenly unable to hear the person we are speaking to even though they continue to hear us. Both scenarios can find an echo in prayer: one day we are blissfully aware of God's presence and the next it's as though we've been cut off; either our words unheard, unregistered, or the reply being blocked somewhere.

So it was, on more than one occasion, for David. In Psalm 28, he cries out to God, begging him to listen, patently aware that an answer does not always appear forthcoming. In Psalm 22, his prayer is even more poignant: 'O my God, I cry to you by day, yet you do not answer; and by night, yet find no relief' (verse 2). Those who have never had such an experience in prayer are fortunate indeed. Yet, for David this was not the end of the story. In both cases, he ends his psalm with an outpouring of praise, an expression of trust and thanksgiving, for it becomes clear that God has not only heard him but also responded. If ever you feel, then, that the 'line has gone dead' and your prayers are unheard, remember what David went through but what he also found to be true. The testimony of scripture is that ours is a God who always hears and who will always finally answer.

Questions of faith

All to the good

We know that all things work together for good with those who love God, who have been called according to his purpose. (Romans 8:28)

There's no getting away from it – life is a strange paradox. At times it all goes smoothly, bringing joy and fulfilment, but, at others, it brings tragedy and sorrow, leaving us searching for answers, hopelessly bewildered as everything we put our trust in is turned upside down. How do we make sense of it? Can faith offer a solution? Some maintain that God plans everything down to the very last detail. They may be right but, personally, I believe the answer is more complex; that God constantly needs to adapt his plans as time and again they are frustrated. Yet, though life may be impossible to understand at the time, when we come to look back it is often possible to discern God's hand at work, taking even the most terrible of moments and weaving them into his sovereign purpose. In that, rather than any simplistic sense, we can truly say that all things work together for those who love God.

Faith and understanding

Lord, my heart does not look above itself nor do I lift my eyes higher than I can hope to see. I do not dwell on matters beyond my comprehension, too wonderful for me to fathom. No, I see myself instead as a weaned child, as one whose mother has set its soul at rest. That's what my soul's like: a child gently soothed by a mother's love. (Psalm 131:1-2)

Space, so the experts tell us, is circular. Travel out into the furthest reaches of the universe and, if you keep on going for long enough, you will eventually return to where you started. Frankly, that makes no sense to me whatsoever, for if space has any kind of boundary, then what lies behind it? Surely, more space! Yet how can something go on and on, without ever reaching an end? That, too, seems to defy all reason. The whole concept of infinity is truly mind-boggling. The fact, though, that I can't get my head round it doesn't alter the truth; it simply highlights the limitations of my mind.

There is a lesson here when it comes to questions of faith. While I would never for a moment encourage Christians to avoid wrestling with complex issues relating to belief, I would equally urge caution in rejecting truths simply because we cannot understand them. There comes a point when we have to admit the limitations of our intellect – our inability, in this life at least, to fathom the deepest realities of life. Baffling questions, such as the existence of suffering and evil, can all too easily lead us to question everything, but we need to learn to live with paradox. In the words of George Rawson's great hymn:

> We limit not the truth of God
>   to our poor reach of mind,
>   by notions of our day and sect,
>   crude, partial and confined . . .
> Who dares to bind to his dull sense
>   the oracles of heaven,
>   for all the nation's tongues and climes
>   and all the ages given?
> That universe, how much unknown!
> That ocean unexplored!
> The Lord has yet more light and truth
>   to break forth from his word.

The key to it all

Remember, then, what you have received and heard; observe it and repent. If you fail to keep watch, I will come upon you like a thief at an hour that you will have no way of knowing. Those who triumph will be clothed in white robes, and I guarantee that their name will not be erased from the book of life; I will acknowledge them before my Father and his angels. All who have ears to hear what the Spirit is saying to the churches, let them listen. And to the messenger of the church in Philadelphia, write this: These are the words of the holy and true one, the one having the key of David, who opens so that no one can shut and shuts so that no one can open. (Revelation 3:3, 5-7)

Have you ever lost or forgotten your house key? It's infuriating, isn't it? You can look through the letterbox, peer through the window, but you just can't get inside. If you're lucky, a neighbour or friend has a key; if not, you have to force the lock or smash a window to get in. For many, much of the Bible and the Christian faith feels rather similar – it gives a tantalising glimpse of a world they want to be part of, but which they cannot seem to get into. How can we believe in a loving Creator, they ask? What is meant by eternal life? Where and what is God? Even the most committed of us struggle to answer questions such as these. It has rightly been observed that no one has ever been argued into the kingdom of heaven. Even those of us who are Christians struggle to make sense of much in the scriptures, not least in the pages of the Old Testament. If we agonise over the problems and questions, valid though they may be, we will never reach a point of commitment and forever find ourselves on the outside looking in, and there is no way this time of forcing the lock to gain entry.

Ask questions, yes; search for answers; but remember finally that the truth lies not in expansive theories or human wisdom but in the love of God revealed on the cross; in Christ crucified and risen – the key to it all!

Life's riddle

O Lord, how long must I cry to you for help before you will listen? How long must I cry, 'Violence!' before you will save? Why do you let me witness wrongdoing and endure trouble? Destruction and aggression are all around me; conflict and disputes spring up everywhere. The law is watered down such that justice has no chance of winning through. The righteous are surrounded by wickedness, and so justice is perverted. (Habakkuk 1:2-4)

I like the book of Habakkuk. There's something hugely refreshing about the honesty with which it tackles the enigmas of life. No pious acceptance here that every event must somehow be God's will; no tortuous attempt to find a spiritual explanation for whatever happens – for this prophet the world presents deep puzzles for which he seeks some answers.

Those who find his questions disturbing may prefer to gloss over them, turning instead to the less controversial passages that follow, but to do that is to bury one's head in the sand. Avoiding the issues helps no one, for the challenge does not go away. Simplistic answers are equally unhelpful, in the end doing more harm than good. Personally, I believe God prefers an honest cry of confusion to a faith that deals with life's riddles by sweeping them under the carpet.

Light in our darkness

Job resumed his discourse, saying, 'If only I could go back to the way things were, to those days when God watched over me; when his lamp shone over my head and I walked by its light through the darkness. If it could be like when I was in my prime, when God encircled my tent; when the Almighty was still beside me and my children surrounded me; when my footsteps were awash with milk, and the rock gushed out streams of oil for me! Now my soul is empty within me; despair holds me each day in its grip. My bones are racked night after night by a remorseless pain. God himself has cast me into the mire, discarded like dust and ashes.' (Job 29:1-6; 30:16, 19)

The book of Job is one of the more unusual books of the Bible. It does not offer memorable promises or assurances of blessing. It does not deal with mighty deeds or glorious conquests. Instead, it wrestles with the age-old problem of suffering, and it does so in what is, at times, a brutally stark manner. Whatever else, the book does not pull its punches, Job speaking his mind with a frankness that can shock the unsuspecting reader. It is, though, perhaps for this reason that many have found the underlying message of Job so helpful, for it tackles a universal conundrum with a startling honesty. There are no pat answers, no simplistic attempts to explain the inexplicable. Instead, there is a blunt admission that some things in life are beyond our comprehension. We cannot and do not always understand the way God works.

Yet we are not left entirely high and dry. Despite the traumas he endured, Job ultimately found his faith deepened and his awareness of God enriched. The journey was undeniably painful, but he emerged stronger and wiser for it. The mystery is not fully resolved, yet some sense is made of it: out of darkness God brings light; out of evil, something good; out of despair, hope. If that was true for the writer of Job, how much more so is it true for us today in the light of the suffering and death of Christ!

Living with doubt

They brought the child to him. Seeing him, the spirit immediately convulsed the boy, and he fell to the ground, rolling about and foaming at the mouth. Jesus asked the father, 'How long has this been happening to him?' And he said, 'From infancy. Many times it has hurled him into flames or water, to destroy him, so if there is anything you can do, for pity's sake help us.' Jesus said to him, 'The question is, can you do anything – all things are possible for the one who believes.' And immediately the father of the child cried out, 'I do believe; help me deal with my unbelief!' (Mark 9:20-24)

'I believe in God, the Father Almighty, creator of heaven and earth . . .' The opening words of the Apostles' Creed have been accepted and repeated across the centuries as a summary of the faith of the Church. And most of us most of the time are happy to add our voices to those who have gone before us. Yet there are times when it's not that simple, when we find ourselves wracked with doubt. To make things worse, such moments are often compounded by a sense of guilt. The result can be a lonely struggle in the wilderness, crushed by a sense of isolation, failure and shame.

Yet, we are not the only ones to feel this way. Remember Thomas, nicknamed 'doubting Thomas' for his refusal to believe without proof. Above all, remember the father in the story above and his frank confession of where he stood. It wasn't that he didn't believe; it was just that there were some things he struggled to accept. Doubt may come to us all, however secure in faith we appear to be. Do not fear it, for it is not something to be ashamed of. Believe, rather, that God is able to take and use your questions to lead you into a deeper understanding of his purpose and a richer sense of his love. Do this and you will discover that doubt is often an essential part of the journey of discipleship rather than an obstacle to progress.

Questions and answers

If you cry out for insight, and raise your voice for understanding, if you seek for it as for hidden treasures – then you will understand the fear of the Lord and find the knowledge of God. For the Lord gives wisdom; from his mouth come knowledge and understanding. (Proverbs 2:3-6)

Many of us will recall the radio quiz shows *What's My Line?* and *Twenty Questions*. It's fun to work out the answer through a process of deduction, even though the questions themselves may be very simple. Such games are, in fact, a microcosm of life, for the chief way we learn anything is through asking questions. At the time of writing, my daughter Kate is at that stage of repeatedly asking 'Why?' about anything and everything. It can be exhausting, even infuriating at times, but it is an essential part of growing up and the sign of a healthy enquiring mind.

Sadly, when it comes to faith some Christians feel guilty about asking questions, almost as though they feel they are being disloyal or sinful in entertaining them. Many feel that they must unquestioningly accept every item of Christian doctrine and dogma. Such unthinking acceptance, however, is a dangerous business, not least because Christians themselves cannot agree about what should and shouldn't be accepted, as witnessed by denominational and theological divisions, and other splits over worship and church practice. Words have different nuances and events can be interpreted in various ways; few things are as clear-cut as they might seem. We all see some of the answers but no one sees them all. Far from discouraging questions, I believe God wants us to ask them, so that our minds may be stretched and our understanding of his loving purpose may grow. That doesn't mean that we should reject what we cannot make sense of, nor that we should set up scientific or human wisdom as the yardstick by which all is measured, but it does mean that we search and keep on searching for deeper understanding and greater enlightenment, always open to the new insights that God waits to reveal.

Shutting our ears

Stephen, being full of the Holy Spirit, gazed up into heaven and saw there the glory of God and Jesus standing at his right hand, and he said, 'Look! The heavens are open and I see the Son of Man standing at the right hand of God.' Then they cried out with a loud voice, and shut their ears, and, in one mind, they rushed upon him. (Acts 7:57)

Have you ever been banned from a church? I have. It was many years back, during my time as a student, and I was preaching in a church in one of the Welsh valleys. My theme was Jonah and the whale, and as part of my exposition I enthusiastically went into the various scholarly interpretations of the story, ranging from affirmations of its literal truth to the suggestion that it might be a parable designed to counter bigotry and intolerance. I went away feeling the sermon had gone rather well, but a few months later I was summoned into the principal's office to learn otherwise. Not only had my words caused offence, but on no account was I ever to return there again!

Should I have aired theological debate in a sermon? Probably it was the wrong time and place. That experience brought home to me, however, how easily people close their ears to what they'd rather not hear. Don't think I'm condemning, for I'm as guilty as any. We all have opinions from which it is hard to shift us, however open we may think ourselves to be. Like those who listened to Stephen as he testified to his faith, we shut out anything that challenges our preconceived ideas, preferring to silence it rather than face its challenge. It may be, of course, that our point of view is right all along; it may equally be that it is wrong or in need of modification. Unless we are willing to listen, we will never know.

A tough decision

Everything is allowable for me, but not everything is valuable. All things are permissible, but I will not allow anyone to dictate to me. Watch out, though, in case exercising your freedom should put a stumbling block in the way of the weak. (1 Corinthians 6:12; 8:9)

Was it a goal or wasn't it? The 'goal' scored by Geoff Hurst in England's victory against West Germany in the 1966 World Cup final must be one of the most frequently shown clips and widely debated incidents in the annals of sport. Even today, with the aid of slow-motion replays and computer simulation, nobody can be completely sure, so what hope did the unfortunate referee have on the day? Yet, of course, he had to come to a decision.

There are often moments like that in daily life; moments when we are faced by the need to decide even though the right choice is far from clear. So it was for the Corinthians in the days of the Apostle Paul, the decision facing them whether it was permissible or otherwise for Christians to eat meat previously dedicated to idols. Paul's answer, essentially, was that it depends on the circumstances – what's right in one situation may be wrong in another. There is a warning here that we would do well to heed. Occasionally issues may be clear-cut, but there are times also when it is unwise to be dogmatic. We may prefer living with moral and ethical certainties, but that is not always the way of Christ.

The unseen hand of God

You are the one who drew me from my mother's womb and who led me to safety at her breast. I was dependent on you from birth, and since my mother bore me you have been my God. Do not be far from me, for trouble is at hand and I have no one to help me. You have rescued me from the horns of wild oxen. I will proclaim your name to my kinsfolk and I will praise you among the congregation. All who fear the Lord, praise him! For he did not spurn or despise the suffering of the downtrodden; he did not hide his face from me, but responded when I cried to him. (Psalm 22:9-11, 21b-23a, 24)

'Life must be lived forwards, but it can only be understood backwards.' So remarked the Danish theologian, Søren Kierkegaard, and there's a lot of truth in his observation. So often we cannot make sense of our existence one day to another. We look for a purpose but see only a riddle. We try to see where God's hand is at work but draw a blank. We cry out for help but none seems forthcoming. At such times, faith can be tested to the limit, as we struggle to understand why God seems remote and unmoved by our plight. Yet, as is so often the case in life, time can make all the difference. Weeks, months, even years later, we look back and we recognise with amazement how God was at work in our lives just when we were least aware of it. Experiences that seemed cruel, situations that looked bleak, days that felt hopeless, turn out to be formative moments in our journey of faith, leading us forward to new insights and horizons.

Remember that next time you feel God has forgotten you. Remind yourself that, though you may not see it now, the time will surely come when everything fits into place and you realise that God's unseen hand has been leading you safely onwards, through the good and the bad.

Where is your God?

Tears are my food day and night, while people keep on saying to me, 'Where is your God?' (Psalm 42:3)

Where is your God now? Has anyone ever asked you that? They may not use those words exactly but they mean much the same thing. People ask the question for a variety of reasons. Some are only too eager to do faith down, looking for any and every opportunity to say, 'Look at that, I told you so.' Others have a very different motive, having begun to explore the claims of Christianity for themselves and maybe even tentatively committed themselves to Christ, only to find their faith shattered by experiences they cannot make sense of. Sometimes, and hardest of all to cope with, it may be *us* posing the question ourselves, unable to reconcile what we see in the world with the things ·we believe. Are there any easy answers at such times? Well, if there are, I don't know of them.

Yet there is an answer of sorts, and like so much in our faith, it comes back to the cross of Christ. As he hung there in agony, there were some gathered to gloat, some watching in disbelief, and even Jesus himself asking why God had forsaken him. The scribes and elders called out in mockery, 'He trusts in God; let God come and deliver him if he so wishes', or, in other words, 'Where is your God now?' It seemed proven beyond doubt that the God Jesus trusted in simply wasn't there, and yet we know that he was there most of all, reconciling the world to himself, opening the way to life for all. We will still be asked sometimes 'Where is your God?'; we will still occasionally ask it ourselves, and we will still struggle to answer it satisfactorily, for we are by no means sure how exactly to relate the cross to our own experiences of suffering or the ills of our world, yet we hold on to the conviction that even when we can least see him God can be most powerfully at work.

Why?

Why, O Lord, are you so distant? Why do you hide yourself from me in my hour of need? My God, my God, why have you abandoned me? Why are you so far from helping me, from heeding my groans? I cry to you by day, O God, but you do not answer; and by night, but gain no respite. Why did I not die at birth, expire when I was brought from my mother's womb? Why do those consumed by despair continue to see the light of day, and why is life given to the bitter in soul who long for death only for it not to come? (Psalm 10:1; 22:1-2; Job 3:11, 20-21a)

Of all the mysteries of life and faith, none is harder to reconcile than the problem of suffering. How is it, we ask, that a supposedly loving and caring God can allow so much pain and misery to rack our world? Across the centuries scholars have wrestled with that conundrum yet failed to come up with a satisfactory solution. It is all too easy to offer pat answers that serve only to add to the misery of those wrestling with inexplicable suffering.

The book of Job was written precisely to counter such simplistic responses, flatly contradicting the received wisdom of the time that suffering was God's punishment for sin and that a godly life goes hand in hand with health, happiness and prosperity. Yet, no alternative theory is offered in its place. That would have risked repeating the mistake. What Job offers instead is the ultimate conviction that even when we cannot begin to understand, and even when life flies in the face of all we believe, God is nonetheless there.

──────── Self-denial and sacrifice ────────

see also Discipleship: Cost of discipleship; Serving others

The extra mile

If anyone decides to sue you and take your coat, let them have your cloak as well, and whoever forces you to go one mile, go with them a second also. Give to whoever begs, and do not turn away anyone wishing to borrow from you. (Matthew 5:40-41)

The sign was quite specific: Taunton 84 miles. Still a long way to go, then, but having driven over one hundred miles already, at least we were over half-way home. I set the milometer to nought so that I could keep track of our progress and ploughed onwards, hoping that the children would stay asleep in the back. Thirty miles further on (I'd counted every one!) and another sign: Taunton 59 miles. To our dismay, another five miles had crept in somewhere and, to cap it all, Kate had woken up and started screaming in protest!

To go further than one expects is never easy, even if it's only a car journey, but when Jesus spoke to the crowd in the Sermon on the Mount he had in mind something far more demanding than that. A Roman soldier had the right, in law, to compel any subject to carry his armour and accessories for one mile – no more, no less. It was a heavy physical load to bear, but in Jewish eyes what was worse was the way it brought home their status as an occupied nation, an enslaved people. Yet here was Jesus telling them not just to do what was required but to go far beyond it, to fall over themselves to help. That advice applied not just then but is equally valid now. Don't just do what you have to do, Jesus tells us; look whenever you can to do more; to do that little bit extra; to put yourself out for the sake of others. It's not easy advice, is it? Most of us prefer to serve ourselves before thinking of anyone else. But the way of Christ is the way of sacrifice, of giving without counting the cost, of always being ready to go the extra mile.

The first and the last

Then the mother of the sons of Zebedee approached him with her sons and, kneeling before him, she asked him to do her a favour. He responded, 'What is it you wish for?' She answered, 'Say that these two sons of mine will sit with you in your kingdom, one at your right hand and one at your left.' Jesus answered, 'You don't know what it is you are asking. Are you able to drink the cup from which I am about to drink?' They said to him, 'We can.' He continued, 'You will indeed drink from that cup, but to sit at my right and left hand is not mine to grant; it is for those for whom my Father has prepared it.' Overhearing this conversation, the remaining ten disciples were incensed at the two brothers' behaviour. Jesus, however, beckoned them across to him and said, 'You are well aware that the rulers of the Gentiles and those who are elevated to positions of authority lord it over their people. Don't let it be like this among you; for who-ever wishes to be great among you must be your servant, and whoever wishes to be first among you must be your slave.' (Matthew 20:20-27)

Reading this account, it is hard not to think of modern-day parents thrusting their precocious children into the public eye through talent shows, beauty contests and the like. Were James and John similarly pushed forward by a doting, domineering mother? Well, not exactly, because for one thing they were grown men, well capable of speaking for themselves. It is more likely that they got their mother to speak on their behalf, voicing a concern held by all of the Apostles as to whether their loyalty would be rewarded, but one that each was embarrassed to ask about outright.

Before we shake our heads in disapproval at their pushiness, we do well to ask ourselves if we are any different. Is our faith wholly altruistic, concerned solely with the service of Christ, or is there more than a hint of safeguarding our ultimate destiny, guaranteeing future blessing in the life to come? There is probably an element of that in everyone's faith, but we are called to serve Christ for his sake rather than our own, to seek his kingdom rather than our welfare. If faith becomes just another way of putting ourselves first, then it is time to think again, for whatever else it may be, it is not faith at all.

Made for sharing

Some give unreservedly, yet grow richer for it; others keep back what is due, yet end up suffering want. A generous person will find enrichment and the one who brings refreshment to others will be refreshed in turn. (Proverbs 11:24-25)

Do you remember the old advertising slogan, 'Quality Street, made for sharing'? It had a point, didn't it, for, like most pleasures, a box of chocolates is indeed all the better for being shared. To enjoy something on one's own simply doesn't bring the same satisfaction; it somehow feels more like indulgence, selfishness or greed. In much the same way as a problem shared is a problem halved, so a pleasure shared brings double the happiness. It's not just true of chocolates but of most things; in fact of people in general – we are all made for sharing. Receiving may bring happiness but giving brings a far greater joy; a jealously guarded possession loses its lustre yet one that is shared with others finds its sparkle polished anew every day. Generosity of spirit is a rare quality that doesn't come naturally to many of us, yet it is one of the most precious gifts we can ever have. Learn to let go of what you have, to share from your little or your plenty, and you will discover what enrichment really means.

Self-service?

Brothers and sisters, you were called to freedom. Make sure, though, that you do not use that freedom to indulge the flesh, but, in love, become servants of one another. (Galatians 5:13)

We live today in a self-service world. Whether we're popping in to our local supermarket, filling up at the petrol station or eating in a canteen, the chances are that we will serve ourselves, and our only contact with a member of staff will be to pay the bill. All this, of course, reflects the wishes of consumers who, by and large, enjoy having the freedom to choose what they buy and value not having to queue too long to buy it. I would be the first to endorse those benefits, yet I can't help thinking sometimes that this trend reflects an underlying and less desirable facet of human nature, which arguably has become more apparent over recent years in Western consumer society as a whole: the idea of putting self before all others, looking after number one.

To find people willing to give up their time voluntarily for others is becoming increasingly difficult. Many once-flourishing charitable movements, for example, committed to serving the community, are now struggling to survive. This is not down purely to greed and self-interest; hard economics makes it necessary for many couples to work long hours simply to pay the mortgage and make ends meet, thus yielding little time for anything and anyone else. Yet most of us, if we are honest, could still afford a little more time, interest, support and money than we are willing to give. As Christians, we are called to serve others, putting their needs before our own. Can we claim to have responded to that challenge, or are we children of our time: self-service Christians?

Serving others

see also Discipleship, cost of: Faith in action; Self-denial and sacrifice

The litmus test of faith

When the Son of Man comes in his glory, together with his angels, he will sit in state on his throne, with all the nations gathered before him, and he will separate people one from the other as a shepherd separates the sheep from the goats, putting the sheep to his right and the goats to his left. Then the king will say to those on his right, 'Come, those who my Father has blessed — inherit the kingdom prepared for you from the foundation of the world. I was hungry and you gave me something to eat, thirsty and you gave me a drink, a stranger and you made me welcome, naked and you clothed me, sick and you visited me, in prison and you had time for me.' Then the righteous will answer, 'Lord, when did we see you hungry and give you food, or thirsty and give you a drink? When did we see you a stranger and make you welcome, or naked and clothe you? When was it that we saw you sick or in prison and visited you?' Then the king will answer, 'I tell you the truth, whenever you did it to the least of your brothers and sisters, you did it also to me.' (Matthew 25:31-40)

Do you remember your first chemistry experiment at school? Almost certainly it involved a piece of litmus paper, dipped into a test-tube of liquid to see if it turned red or blue, indicating acid or alkali. There is something of that test in the words of Jesus concerning the sheep and the goats, only this time the test concerns something very different – how faithfully we have responded to Christ.

What are the distinguishing features we should look for? Doctrinal soundness? Faith that can move mountains? Gifts of the Spirit? An impeccable record of church attendance? Not according to this parable, they're not. What counts, rather, is whether we have responded to people in need; whether we have shown our faith in action, expressing through our care and compassion the love of Christ. That, we are told, is the litmus test of Christian discipleship. Of course, we need to consider such words in the light of Christ's teaching concerning mercy and forgiveness, but we should not use that to evade or tone down their challenge. Faith may not *depend on* works but it ought to *result in* them, at least in part. The warning here is not so much that Jesus will reject us but that, through turning our back on others, we may find that we have rejected him.

SERMON HOOKS

OHMS

Whatever you do, do it with all your being for the Lord rather than any person, since you know that you will receive an inheritance from the Lord as your reward. You serve the Lord Christ. (Colossians 3:23-24)

What does it mean to call Jesus 'Lord'? On the one hand, it means to honour him, to give him our praise and adoration, as summed up by the popular chorus 'Jesus, we enthrone you'. But it means more than that. It has something of the idea encapsulated in those four letters above: letters that stand, of course, for 'On Her Majesty's Service'. Admittedly, when they are stamped on formal correspondence the initials are largely figurative: the Queen has no direct interest either way in our tax affairs, electoral intentions or other such matters. Yet, the efficient administration of such things is essential to the smooth running of any kingdom. No doubt the Queen would be highly gratified by the unbridled devotion of all her subjects, especially in an era when the monarchy is coming under ever-closer scrutiny, but I have no doubt also that what matters most to her is not adulation but service in its broadest sense.

I suspect the same may be true with Jesus. Of course, worship is vitally important, but if we leave it there, as we can so easily do, then it doesn't mean all that much. To call Jesus Lord, to honour him as king, ultimately means one thing: reaching out to the world 'on his majesty's service'!

Remembering the poor

All they asked was that we should continue to remember the poor; precisely what I was determined to do. (Galatians 2:10)

We are told that in Britain, over the last twenty years or so, the rich have grown richer and the poor have grown poorer. If that's true here, it's all the more true in the world as a whole, the gap between the 'haves and the have-nots' having widened to enormous proportions. The figures are truly staggering: well over three-quarters of the world's resources are enjoyed by less than a third of its total inhabitants. Is this simply a matter of academic concern? For anyone who claims to follow Christ the answer must be no. Throughout his ministry Jesus showed what Archbishop David Sheppard termed, in the title to his controversial book, a bias to the poor; and his words show that a concern for the poor is not just an optional part of discipleship but integral to it; an inescapable challenge to all who would follow him.

So it was that the early Church, racked by a time of controversy concerning the relationship of Jews and Gentiles, came up with one simple requirement – to remember the poor. Yes, there's a danger of seeming patronising, or of giving to charity to salve our consciences, but there's a much greater danger of using such reservations as an excuse to avoid the challenge and forgetting the poor altogether. Forget their needs and the gospel seems strongly to suggest that we have forgotten Jesus as well.

Righting wrongs

When you spread out your hands in prayer, I will hide my eyes from you; even if you offer many prayers, I will not listen. Your hands are full of blood; wash and make yourselves clean. Take your evil deeds out of my sight! Stop doing wrong, learn to do right! Seek justice, encourage the oppressed. Defend the cause of the fatherless, plead the case of the widow. (Isaiah 1:15-17)

In my garden is a small area that for a few months every year is overrun by fungi. The reason is very simple: it sits next to an old tree stump that has long since died but that I have been unable to dig out. I can treat the area with fungicide as much as I like, dig up the fungi until the cows come home, but it will make no difference – the problem will always return unless I succeed in tackling that root cause.

There are parallels here with world hunger and poverty. It has increasingly been recognised in recent years that the only way to resolve the growing gap between rich and poor, and to give what we call the Third World real hope, is to address the underlying factors of inequality. Short-term relief is vital but more needs doing if we are to see anything approaching a genuine solution. So where does that leave us? Are we left powerless in the face of impersonal economic forces or international government bureaucracy? Not at all! Ordinary people can make their voices heard. Through the way we shop or invest our money, the causes we support and the products we boycott, through more direct measures – such as petitioning our MP or lobbying multinational companies – we can call for change. The Jubilee 2000 campaign was a classic example of what can be achieved through concerted effort. Should Christians involve themselves in such matters? Isaiah reminds us that a hunger for justice and a commitment to the poor is not an optional extra in the Christian faith but a responsibility at its very heart.

Salt of the earth

You are the salt of the earth; but if salt is adulterated, how can its saltiness be restored? It no longer has any use, fit only to be thrown out and trampled underfoot. (Matthew 5:13)

The salt of the earth – how often have you heard that expression used of someone? What a wonderful compliment it is! To be somebody who adds that little bit extra to life, who brings help and happiness to others, who is trustworthy and dependable – what higher praise can there be? So would people describe us in those terms? They should do, according to Jesus. We should be those who exhibit precisely such qualities; those whose way of life makes people sit up and take notice.

Of course we can't please everyone all the time, and there will always be those hostile to the Christian faith who have little time for us. Yet the principle holds nonetheless. Faith is not simply about ourselves: our own welfare, security and happiness. It's about making a difference to the world we live in, helping to change lives, showing compassion and offering love. If we're not doing that, then it's time to ask ourselves some serious questions.

Small world

Anxious to save face, the lawyer asked Jesus, 'Ah yes, but just who is my neighbour?' 'A man was travelling on the Jerusalem–Jericho road,' answered Jesus, 'when he was ambushed by bandits, who beat him up and made off with all he had, even his clothes, leaving him critically ill. A little later, a priest happened to be passing that way. When he saw the unfortunate fellow, he gave him a wide berth and hurried on past. Similarly, a Levite chanced upon him, he too keeping at a safe distance and moving hastily on his way. A Samaritan came by next, and the moment he spotted the man he rushed to his aid. Deeply concerned at his plight, he tended his injuries, salving them with oil and wine. Then, placing the man on his donkey, he took him to an inn and continued to look after him for the rest of the day. Next morning, he handed the innkeeper two denarii, with the instruction, "Take good care of him. I'll settle the bill when I return, so don't worry about the cost." What do you reckon: which of these three proved to be a neighbour to the man set upon by bandits?' 'The one who had compassion on him,' answered the lawyer. 'Then off you go and do the same,' said Jesus. (Luke 10:29-37)

'It's a small world.' Today that seems more true than ever. We can travel across the globe in a matter of hours, watch events live by satellite from thousands of miles away, and talk to people in distant continents almost as if they are in our own front room. That fact brings enormous blessings but also new responsibilities and demands. 'Who is my neighbour?' the lawyer asked Jesus. The answer was anyone and everyone.

Two thousand years ago that challenge must have seemed daunting enough; today it is massive, for suddenly every person in every country has become our concern; every disaster, our disaster; every*one* our neighbour. When floods strike Bangladesh, we know; when famine hits Sudan, we know; when students are massacred in Tiananmen Square, we know. Day after day, pictures of emaciated children confront us as we sit down to our meal of plenty; of the homeless as we sit in the warmth and comfort of our homes; of the poor as we enjoy an ever-rising standard of living. All these are our neighbours in today's small world. Charity may begin at home but it cannot end there. By ourselves, of course, we cannot put all the world's ills to right, nor respond to every place of need, but neither can we turn our backs and pretend that they are none of our business. 'Which of these,' said Jesus, 'was a neighbour to the man?' 'The one who showed him mercy,' came the answer. 'Go and do likewise!'

Sorrow and despair

see also Adversity, faith in; Hope

The God of all comfort

Comfort, comfort my people, says your God. He has sent me to comfort all who mourn, to decorate them with a garland of beauty instead of ashes, the oil of joy instead of sorrow, and a spirit clothed in praise instead of cloaked in despair. As a mother comforts her child, so will I comfort you. (Isaiah 40:1a; 61:1b, 2b-3; 66:13)

There are many joys in being a parent, and one is the privilege of being able to comfort a child in times of distress. It is astonishing how a sobbing, hysterical child can, in just a few moments, be laughing and smiling once more, simply through the reassuring warmth of a mother or father's embrace and words of reassurance. 'Let's kiss it better,' we say, and, although it's nonsense, it works! The pain doesn't necessarily go away, but the child knows that he or she is loved.

If *we* can do that for *our* children, how much more can *God* do it for *us*, as we see time and again in the scriptures, not least in the words of the prophet Isaiah. Ours is a God who loves us more than the most devoted parent; who grieves when we grieve and suffers when we suffer. He doesn't lightly allow us to be hurt but, like any good parent, he knows that it is the price of true freedom and the necessary corollary to experiencing joy and pleasure. Yet he always cares, always longs to encircle us in his arms, and, whatever we may face, he promises always to be there to bring us comfort. In the words of the Apostle Paul: 'Glory be to the God and Father of our Lord Jesus Christ: the God of all comfort, who comforts us in all our suffering so that we can comfort those experiencing any kind of suffering with the comfort God has given us' (2 Corinthians 1:3-4).

The valley of tears

After this, they went to a spot called Gethsemane. 'Sit here while I pray,' Jesus instructed his disciples. Taking Peter, James and John with him a little further, he suddenly became distraught. 'I am so crushed by grief that it's killing me,' he told them. 'Remain here and keep a lookout.' Going on by himself a few steps more, he prostrated himself before God, asking if there was any way he could be spared the ordeal before him. 'Abba, Father,' he pleaded, 'nothing is beyond you, so take this cup away from me. Yet don't do what I want, but what you have to do.' (Mark 14:32-36)

'I shouldn't be feeling like this. I know it's wrong but I just can't help it.' I've lost count of the times I've heard comments like that from people feeling guilty about being depressed or miserable. The idea that they've anything to be ashamed of is ridiculous, of course, yet there are subtle pressures in the Church today that can make us feel we should banish all negative thoughts from our minds. Much modern worship focuses upon themes such as joy, praise and celebration, to the exclusion of other emotions, and this emphasis seems to be reinforced by verses like Philippians 4:4, which states: 'Rejoice in the Lord always; again I say it: rejoice!' If we're not careful, the sorrowful and downhearted can feel excluded, even to the point of regarding their feelings as a sin. They feel that they should somehow be able to rise above sorrow; that, even though they are not immune from tragedy, it should not hit them in quite the same way that it does non-believers.

That is one reason why the story of Gethsemane is so important, for here we see God identifying himself with human sorrow. 'My heart is ready to break with grief,' said Jesus; or as the *New International Version* puts it, 'My soul is overwhelmed with sorrow to the point of death.' Here is a reminder that God himself, through Christ, has shared in our blackest, bleakest moments. He is a God who not only understands what grief and heartbreak mean but who also empathises with those experiencing them. Above all, he is a God who stays close to us through such times and who, finally, will bring hope after despair, laughter after tears and joy after sorrow.

The wilderness of despair

Calling two of his disciples, John sent them to the Lord to ask, 'Are you the one we've been anticipating or should we await someone else?' Now Jesus had just healed many of diseases, afflictions and evil spirits, and given sight to many who were blind. He replied, 'Go and report to John the things you have seen and heard: how the blind see again, the lame walk, lepers become whole, the deaf hear, the dead are raised, the poor hear good news. Blessed is everyone who has no problem understanding this.' (Luke 7:19, 21-23)

There are days when life seems utterly bleak. We listen to the news and it is another catalogue of disaster, tragedy, hatred and violence. We look around us, and we see greed, division and selfishness. We look within, and where once there was faith now there is doubt.

It felt like that for John the Baptist in the days following his arrest. Having spent his ministry as a voice in the desert, he found himself in a different sort of wilderness: the wilderness of despair. Had all his efforts been for nothing? Had he been taken in, naively putting his faith in a sovereign purpose that simply didn't exist? Was Jesus an impostor, not the Messiah after all? No wonder John sent messengers to Jesus seeking reassurance, asking what exactly was going on. Only then the message came back: news of a different sort, good things happening, signs of hope, new beginnings, new life. What that news meant to John back in the darkness of his cell we are not told, but I imagine it was all he needed to hear, giving him strength to face his imminent death with a quiet and calm assurance, the knowledge that God's will would triumph. His story is a reminder to all who find themselves in the wilderness of despair: stop and look again, for there, in the apparent barrenness all around you, you will see the seeds of God's kingdom, the proof of his love, bursting into new and irrepressible life.

— Sovereignty and wonder of God —

see also Power of God, its transforming nature

A glimpse of glory

An angry-looking storm cloud approached from the north as I watched: a massive cloud from behind which light seemed to shine and from within which leapt bolts of flame, inside of which in turn glowed what looked like amber. At the heart of the cloud appeared to be four living creatures, at the centre of which coals seemed to blaze like flaming brands and flashes of lightning. Gazing in wonder at these living creatures, I saw a wheel beside each of them, this taking the shape of a wheel within a wheel, while above their heads stretched what resembled a dome, glistening. Over the heads of the living creatures there was something like a dome, shining like cut glass. Finally, over this dome sat what I took to be a throne, resplendent as sapphire, ensconced on which appeared to be a human being. The spectacular sight can only be compared to a rainbow bursting through a bank of cloud, yet even this gives just some idea of what it was like to glimpse the glory of the Lord. (Ezekiel 1:4-5a, 13, 15, 16b, 22, 26, 28)

The more established we become in our faith, the more fixed our picture of God can become. It's not that we consciously let this happen; it's simply that we settle into a rut – and the deeper we sink, the harder we find it to escape. The vision that once fired our imagination becomes blurred; the sense of God's love and power that previously excited us becomes just another article of faith.

Just occasionally, however, something happens that brings God sharply back into focus. That's what happened to the prophet Ezekiel, carted off to exile in Babylon. For him and his fellow Judeans it must have been a desperate time. How could God allow it to happen? The experience was deeply disturbing, but the divine encounter that resulted from it was to change Ezekiel's life for ever, for through his extraordinary, mind-boggling vision he came to realise that God was far greater than he had ever dared imagine, more wonderful than the mind can even begin to fathom!

The God beyond us

My thoughts are not your thoughts, neither are your ways my ways, says the Lord. For as the heavens are higher than the earth, so are my ways higher than your ways and my thoughts higher than your thoughts. (Isaiah 55:8-9)

When did you last feel a sense of awe in the presence of God? How long is it since you caught your breath in wonder as you offered him your worship? It may be that such moments are still frequent but, if my experience is anything to go by, you may find that they have grown fewer and farther between. Partly that happens because we simply don't find time to worship as often as we should; partly it's because over-familiarity dulls our senses. See anything breathtakingly beautiful once and we gaze in amazement. See it several times and the chances are we'll pass it by without a second look.

Whether we're talking of a beautiful view or a sense of God's majesty, it can take a fresh pair of eyes to stir our imaginations once more and help us recapture that first-time sense of wonderment. For me, that fresh pair of eyes is given in those wonderful words of the prophet Isaiah. They are a constant reminder of the sheer 'otherness' of God whose greatness is beyond words, whose awesomeness defies expression; who is more powerful, more caring, more gracious, more good than the human mind can ever comprehend. Glimpse that, and once more we find ourselves catching our breath in sheer amazement and kneeling in joyful worship.

A God both near and far

You, Lord, are enthroned high over all the earth, exalted above all gods. Your constant love is higher than the heavens and your truth reaches up to the skies. To you be glory, O God, high enthroned in heaven. Let your glory illuminate the earth. (Psalm 97:9; 108:4-5)

'So near, yet so far.' How often have we heard that expression used to sum up people's feelings when they have nearly, but not quite, achieved a certain goal? With God we can use that expression in a different sense, 'near' and 'far' no longer being mutually exclusive but two points in a single spectrum. On the one hand, the Bible portrays God as the sovereign Creator, the ruler of space and time, mighty and mysterious, beyond human comprehension – one to be served with fear and trembling. On the other hand, he is a God who draws near, who walks and talks with his people and who has shared our humanity in the person of Christ. It is a wonderful paradox, both aspects of God's nature vital to recognise if we are to have a balanced picture of who he is. We need a sense of his transcendence so that we do not end up shaping him in our image but we need also an awareness of his immanence if faith is to have any bearing on our life.

So, what sort of picture do we have of God? Do we still feel a sense of awe in his presence, a feeling of privilege that we are able to come before him? We should do. Yet, do we also see him as an intimate friend, involved in every aspect of our life, genuinely interested in our hopes and fears, joys and sorrows? Ours is a God whose greatness is beyond expression; yet a God also who delights to hear our prayer, who longs to bless us and who is passionately concerned about our lives – a God both near and far!

A god of our own making

Their idols are silver and gold, fashioned by human hands. They have mouths, yet cannot talk; eyes, yet cannot see. They have ears, yet cannot hear; nostrils, yet cannot smell. They have hands, yet cannot feel; feet, yet cannot walk; no sound comes from their throats. Those who make them become like them; and so does everyone who trusts in them. (Psalm 115:4-8)

Of all the offences against God it is possible to commit, few are censured more frequently in the Old Testament than the worship of idols. Throughout its pages a succession of leaders and prophets pour scorn on anybody foolish enough to pay homage to an inanimate object fashioned by human hands, and, reading their scathing condemnations, it is tempting to imagine we could never make a similar mistake, the very idea unthinkable.

Yet such self-righteousness is ill advised, for though we would never consciously consider worshipping a man-made idol, there are insidious ways in which we do just that. The idols of our time are not carved in wood or moulded in metal, but they are no less real – money, success, power, sex, these are just a few of the modern-day 'gods' which hold sway today. And though we may not like to admit it, *we* may figure more prominently among their devotees than we care to admit. All too easily we shape our understanding of God to fit with what we want to believe. The result may seem more comfortable to live with, but in the final analysis it offers nothing for, quite simply, we are left with no God at all.

Here, there and everywhere

Where can I evade your spirit? Where can I flee from your presence? If I soar up to heaven, you are there; if I make my bed in Sheol, you are there. If I sail on the wings of the morning and settle at the uttermost limits of the sea, even there your hand will lead me, your right hand holding me firm. If I say,

'Surely darkness will steal over me, night will envelop me', darkness is not dark to you; the night is as bright as day; for you both dark and light are the same. (Psalm 139:7-10)

'We seek him here, we seek him there, those Frenchies seek him everywhere. Is he in heaven? – Is he in hell? That demmed elusive Pimpernel?'

So run the famous lines of Baroness Orczy concerning the renowned character of her novels: the so-called Scarlet Pimpernel. Come what may, the dashing hero invariably turns up at the right time and the right place; no one and nowhere, it seems, beyond his reach. Such, of course, is the prerogative of fictional heroes.

With God, though, it is no fiction. He is the one before and beyond all, yet the one who is with us, here and now; the ruler over space and time, yet the one constantly by our side. No one is outside his love, nowhere beyond his grace, no situation outside his concern – not even death itself can separate us from his sovereign purpose in Christ. Whether you see him or whether you don't, whether you sense he is close or feel he is far away, remember this: he is here, there and everywhere.

In light inaccessible?

Moses said, 'Show me your glory, I pray.' God answered, 'I will cause all my goodness to pass before you, and I will pronounce my name, "The Lord", in your hearing. I will be gracious to whom I will be gracious, and I will be merciful to whom I would show mercy. However, you cannot see my face, for no one can see my face and live.' (Exodus 33:18-20)

Recent years have yielded some stunning pictures of the planets in our solar system, most particularly Mars and Jupiter, revealing details about them never seen before. Such pictures, however, wonderful though they are, have only served to highlight the vastness of space and the massive limitations on our ability to explore it. Most of our solar system is millions of light years away, so even if we sent out a space probe today to distant stars, it would not yield any information for centuries to come. So much of the universe is tantalisingly inaccessible, and can only be understood through piecing together the various clues given us.

In a sense, the same was true for the Israelites when it came to God. He appeared remote in his holiness, awe-inspiring in his sovereignty; a God who inspired fear as much as love. If he could be known, it was only at a distance; not in the sense of a living and daily personal relationship. For us, all that is different thanks to Christ. In him, God has shared our humanity, becoming one with us. Through him, he has broken down whatever keeps us apart. From him, we receive life – the very life of God himself. He is the same God as before, enthroned in splendour over all, yet a God whom we can know as a friend and companion, whom we can relate to one to one and whom we can approach in confidence, knowing that his nature is to love and forgive. In contrast to that warning given to Moses, we not only see God in Christ but, through doing so, we also discover the way to life in all its fullness.

The mighty acts of God

Come and see what God has done, how awesome his works on our behalf! He turned the waters into dry land so that his people might pass through them on foot. Come and rejoice in him. He rules for ever by his power, his eyes watch the nations. How wonderful are the works of the Lord, pondered on by all those who delight in them. They are majestic and glorious; his righteousness endures for ever. He has gained renown through his awesome deeds; the Lord is gracious and rich in mercy. (Psalm 66:5-7; 111:2-4)

What is it that makes someone famous? The answer, of course, lies in the special things they have done, the scale of their achievements, the way they stand out from the ordinary. The adulation accorded to modern-day stars can come very close to worship, and in a sense there is a parallel here to our worship of God, for at its heart this is about the great things he has done. To this day, Jewish worship revolves around past events: deliverance from Egypt, the crossing of the Red Sea, manna in the wilderness – and nowhere is this celebration of God's mighty acts more evident than in the psalms. 'Sing a new song to the Lord, for he has done marvellous things' (Psalm 98:1a). Or, as Psalm 136:3-4 puts it: 'Give thanks to the Lord of lords, for he alone does great wonders.'

If the psalmists could write like that all those years ago, then how much more cause have we to rejoice today, for we can celebrate the coming of Christ, the history of the Church and our personal experience of the Holy Spirit! Take time to remember what God has done, in the world, the Church and your own life. Reflect on his mighty acts – all he has done, is doing and has yet to do – and so let us echo the psalmist once more in declaring: 'The Lord has done great things for us and we are glad!' (Psalm 126:3)

Stillness and quietness

A pause for thought

Martha was preoccupied with her many tasks; so she came to him and asked, 'Lord, doesn't it matter to you that my sister has left me to do all the work by myself? Tell her to lend a hand.' But the Lord answered her, 'Martha, Martha, you are fretting and distracted by many things; only one thing is really important. Mary has chosen that more important thing, and it will not be taken away from her.' (Luke 10:40-42)

We live today at breakneck speed, rushing here, there and everywhere, yet forever chasing our tails. Despite having labour-saving gadgets such as our grandparents could only have dreamed of, we are part of a society ravaged by exhaustion and burn-out as we attempt to cram yet more activity into our already overcrowded lives. The material rewards are many, yet spiritually most of us are hopelessly impoverished.

We need sometimes to pause and ask ourselves where we are going and why. We need to consider the deeper things of life and to reflect on what actually matters most. Unless we pause to think now, we may reach the end of our days only to discover that we have frittered our lives away on much that is ultimately empty and meaningless trivia.

Stepping back, stepping forward

He told his disciples to get into the boat and go on ahead of him to Bethsaida, on the other side, while he dismissed the crowd. After taking leave of them, he went up on the mountain to pray . . . In those days he went out to the mountain to pray; and all night he continued in prayer to God. (Mark 6:45-46; Luke 6:12)

Have you ever heard of Henry the Hermit or St Cuthbert? Both are associated with the magical coast of Northumberland. St Cuthbert made his home on Lindisfarne, otherwise known as Holy Island – a small rocky outcrop connected to the mainland by a narrow causeway that for most of the day is submerged by the sea. Henry was even more of a recluse, spending his days in prayer and meditation on an island some distance offshore. Few of us will feel called to quite such an austere way of life, but we can learn something from their example, for there are times when we too need to get away from it all, if only for a few moments, in order to hear God's voice. It's not that he's removed from the daily round of life – far from it – but sometimes pressures can build up in such a way that they obscure his presence. When writing *Daily Prayer*, for example, there were many times when I struggled for inspiration, becoming increasingly agitated when none was forthcoming. At one time, I would have soldiered on regardless, spending hours and even a whole day on one paragraph, yet getting nowhere. Experience, though, has taught me to get up and walk away; to take a stroll in the garden, or to reflect on a different passage, or simply to spend a few moments doing nothing. Through stepping back, I am able to step forward.

It is noticeable that Jesus himself, at key moments in his life, made time for quietness, drawing away from the crowds, spending time alone high in the hills so that he could focus on the presence of God, away from the innumerable pressures and demands put upon him. It is not always easy to do that, I know. When the children are screaming and there's a pile of washing-up to see to, when there's another meeting to attend and another deadline to meet, stepping back can seem a luxury we can ill afford. Yet, the fact is, it's a necessity; a step we sometimes need to make if we are to have any hope of progressing further.

——— Strength in weakness ———

see also Power of God, its transforming nature

Against all odds

The Philistine [Goliath] said to David, 'Am I a dog, that you approach me with sticks?' and he swore at David using the name of his gods. 'Come on,' he taunted, 'attack me, and I will give your flesh to the birds of the air and to the beasts of the field.' But David responded, 'You confront me with sword, spear and javelin, but I confront you in the name of the Lord of hosts, the God of the armies of Israel, whom you have defied.' When the Philistine advanced towards him, David darted forward to do battle with him. Reaching down into his bag, he took out a stone, slung it, and struck the Philistine on the forehead; the stone sank into his forehead, and he collapsed face downwards on the ground. (1 Samuel 17:43-45, 48-49)

It's always pleasing, isn't it, when a midget turns the tables on a giant. Whether it be a non-league football team defeating its Premier League relations, a village store fighting off competition from an out-of-town supermarket, or a local pressure group resisting the plans of a multinational company, our hearts warm to tales of the underdog come good.

Little wonder, then, that the tale of David and Goliath has stood the test of time, told and retold by countless generations across the years. Their celebrated encounter is a classic example of the underdog coming out on top, triumphing against all the odds. There can be few plots more extensively used by writers throughout the centuries, but what makes this story so wonderful is that it is not fiction but fact. It offers an enduring testimony to the way God is able to help each one of us measure up to the obstacles we face and, no matter how great they may be, to emerge victorious over them.

Boasting in weakness

He has said to me, 'My grace is enough for you, for my power is made perfect in weakness.' Therefore, I will gladly boast of my weaknesses that allow the power of Christ to work within me. I am more than happy to endure weakness, abuse, privation, persecution, and misfortune for the sake of Christ; for the weaker I am, the stronger I become. (2 Corinthians 12:9-10)

What does it mean to talk about strength in weakness? The idea sounds nonsensical, a contradiction in terms, and, wrongly understood, it is precisely that. If we imagine that every frailty is in fact a source of power, every Achilles' heel the secret of some Herculean endowment, then we are in for a rude surprise. No weakness in itself is something to be proud of. What matters is how we deal with it: whether we persist in attempting to prove ourselves, or whether we recognise our ultimate dependence on divine grace. God, and God alone, is able to turn weakness into strength. The more we understand that, the more he is able to work within us.

A constant source of strength

I labour and I struggle, exploiting the mighty strength of Christ at work within me. (Colossians 1:29)

Have you ever watched the television series *World's Strongest Man*? My son used to be fascinated by it, sitting glued to every programme in virtual disbelief. His interest was understandable. Whereas I struggle to pick up a heavy suitcase, these heavyweights pick up a massive block of solid concrete as though it's a mere pebble, toss tractor tyres as if they are playthings, and tow a mighty juggernaut as though it's a Dinky toy. It's all impressive stuff, which few of us could ever hope to match.

There's one source of strength, however, that we all have access too, and that is the power of God, or, as Paul describes it, the mighty strength of Christ. We may not be able to hoist a car with our bare hands but, through faith, we can move mountains! We can take on impossible odds, we can persevere in adversity, we can help to shape lives and even transform the world, not in our own strength but with God's help. It is, of course, a very different sort of power than that which can be cultivated through exercise and body-building routines, yet it is ultimately a greater power than any, for it comes from the one who brought the very universe into being.

Never underestimate what God can do, and never forget what he can do through you.

No contest!

The Lord's word to Zerubbabel was this: Not by weight of arms or brute force, says the Lord of hosts, but by my Spirit. (Zechariah 4:6)

In the right corner: Hercules; in the left corner: Mr Bean! It's an incongruous thought, isn't it, a greater mismatch hard to imagine; yet it is no greater than the situation that faced Israel in the days of Zechariah. After many years exiled in Babylon, they had returned to rebuild Jerusalem and restore the temple, but what hope did they realistically have? Compared to the numerous other countries that surrounded them, let alone the mighty empires of their day, they were puny, with scarcely a hope of defending themselves should they be attacked. So it had been for the bulk of their history; a small country surrounded by marauding giants. Humanly speaking, they had no chance, but the words of Zechariah were not about human things but about God and what he could do through his Spirit.

The situation was not so different for the Apostles gathered together on the day of Pentecost. How could they possibly fulfil the call of Jesus to make disciples of all nations? The answer, of course, is that *they* couldn't, but *God* could! *Without* him, they were powerless; *with* him, all things were possible. We need to remember that today when we feel up against it. When we look at the needs of society and feel over-whelmed by our inability to respond, when we are faced by apathy concerning the gospel and wonder how we can even begin to share our faith, we need to recall and trust his promise that we will find true strength: 'Not by weight of arms or brute force, says the Lord of hosts, but by my Spirit.'

Rising to the challenge

The Lord said, 'I have witnessed the misery of my people in Egypt; I have heard their cry at the hands of their taskmasters. Yes, I know how much they are suffering, and I have come down to deliver them from the Egyptians, and to lead them out of that country to a fine and extensive land; the land of the Canaanites, Hittites, Amorites, Perizzites, Hivites, and Jebusites, flowing with milk and honey. The cry of the Israelites has reached my ears and I have seen how the Egyptians oppress them, so come, and I will send you to Pharaoh to bring my people Israel out of Egypt.' But Moses retorted, 'Who am I that I should go to Pharaoh and bring the Israelites out of Egypt?' God answered, 'I am with you.' (Exodus 3:7-12a)

When did you last face a challenge that seemed completely beyond you but from which there was no escape? Anyone who has been in such a situation will have at least some insight into how Moses must have felt when God turned up in a burning bush ordering him to confront Pharaoh and demand the release of his people. It was a lot to ask of anyone, but for someone like Moses, by all accounts nervous and hesitant in speech, it was little short of purgatory. This was one request he could do without! The trouble was, God apparently couldn't do without him.

The verses above are but the start of one of the most astonishing conversations between God and man recorded in scripture. On the one hand, we have the sheer humanity of Moses, coming up with reason after reason why he was the least suitable candidate for the job, and, on the other, we have God countering every argument with an unanswerable riposte. It's hard not to feel sorry for Moses as finally he is almost browbeaten into submission, but it's equally impossible not to be inspired by the way that, having finally risen to the challenge, God provided him with all the resources he needed, and more besides. Remember, then, next time you face an apparently impossible challenge, that though it may be beyond *you*, it's not beyond *him*!

From small beginnings

From you, Bethlehem of Ephrathah, small though you may be among the clans of Judah, shall emerge one who is to rule in Israel, whose roots go back into history, from the earliest of times. Therefore, he will give up his people only until the time when she who is in labour bears a child; then the remnant of his people will return to their kinsfolk in Israel. He will stand and feed his flock in the strength of the Lord, in the majesty of the name of the Lord his God. Thus, they will live in safety, for at that time his greatness will extend to the ends of the earth; and he will be the man of peace. (Micah 5:2-5a)

'Every oak has been an acorn.' 'Small is the seed of every greatness.' 'Great weights hang on small wires.' 'Great engines turn on small pivots.' These are just some of the innumerable proverbs reminding us that unpromising beginnings need not be a barrier to success; a theme that similarly runs throughout the Old Testament, from Moses taking on the might of Egypt to David killing Goliath, from Elijah triumphing over the prophets of Baal to Daniel facing up to the terrors of the lions' den.

The prophet Micah adds one more unforgettable picture to the list in the little town of Bethlehem. It is hard today to appreciate how extraordinary it must have seemed to hear God's promised Messiah associated with this insignificant town, notwithstanding its associations with King David. Jerusalem, surely, was the only place fitting for someone of such stature! In human terms, this may have been true, but not in God's. As so often before and since, God proves himself to be a God of the unexpected. In his kingdom the first invariably find themselves last, and the last first.

You can do it!

I can do all things through him who strengthens me. (Philippians 4:13)

'I can't do it.' How often have you made that excuse when faced with a difficult and demanding challenge? Occasionally it may be justified but, more often than not, the truth is that we either don't want to do what's asked of us, or fear we may make a fool of ourselves if we attempt it. The task in question may well be within our capabilities, but we would rather not risk finding out, just in case it's not. Yet, unless we are prepared to face such situations head on, to have a go and never mind the consequences, we will never realise our true potential, held back instead by half-formed fears and uncertainties. Two old sayings make the point well: 'Nothing ventured, nothing gained' and 'Nothing succeeds like success'.

Temptation

see also Lent

Cut it out!

If your right eye is your weak spot, pluck it out and throw it away; it is preferable for you to lose one part of your body than for the whole of it to be thrown into hell. And if your right hand is your weak spot, cut it off and throw it away; it is preferable for you to lose one part of your body than for the whole of it to go to hell. (Matthew 5:29-30)

We'd done a good job – or so I thought. We'd scrubbed the walls until every last trace of mildew was gone and then applied two layers of mould repellent before decorating once again; surely this time our problems were at an end. Yet, three months later, we were back to square one, the walls black with mould, the room dank and stale. Where had we gone wrong? The answer, of course, is that we hadn't tackled the root problem: the lack of a damp course and adequate ventilation. Without that, we could redecorate as often as we wanted to and it would make no difference.

That experience helped me understand what Jesus was talking about in those somewhat puzzling words of the Sermon on the Mount. Would any of us really mutilate ourselves in the way he suggests? I hope not, for what Jesus was doing here was using the typical rabbinic device of hyperbole to get across the importance of his point. If you want to conquer your weaknesses, he is saying, it's no good simply papering over the cracks. You have to tackle the root cause of the problem; otherwise it will repeatedly resurface. It's not finally a part of the body we need to cut out but those things in our lives that expose our weaknesses. Ignore those and, for all our good intentions, we're asking for trouble.

A disfigured masterpiece

So God created humankind in his likeness – he made both male and female in his own image. God looked at all he had made, and was satisfied that it was good. The Lord God commanded the man, 'You can eat freely of any tree in the garden except the tree of good and evil; the day you eat of that you shall die.' When the woman realised that the tree not only offered attractive and appetising food but was also able to make one wise, she took one of its fruits and ate; and she gave some of it to her husband, who was with her, and he ate too. Then their eyes were opened, and they understood that they were naked; and they sewed fig leaves together to make loincloths for themselves. (Genesis 1:26-27; 2:16-17; 3:6-7)

The act shocked the nation: an internationally renowned painting wantonly vandalised by a knife-wielding madman in a frenzied and motiveless attack. What once had been a priceless masterpiece was suddenly a shredded piece of canvas hanging forlornly from its frame; a pathetic reminder of what should have been.

A similar act of desecration lies behind the creation stories in Genesis, only on a much broader scale, for we are talking here not about a human creation but God's, not about an abstract masterpiece but human lives. God made us in his likeness, each one of us designed as a unique and precious masterpiece, but such is our nature that we disfigure that creation, our faults and failings rendering the initial design almost unrecognisable. Remember this next time temptation comes: remember that each time we succumb we are not just betraying ourselves – we are destroying the work of God's hands, the people he intended us to be.

A moment's madness

As the afternoon was drawing on, David got up from his couch and, taking a stroll on the palace roof, he happened to spot from there a woman taking a bath; a woman who was very beautiful. David sent someone to find out who the woman was. The report came back: 'She is Bathsheba, daughter of Eliam, the wife of Uriah the Hittite.' So David sent messengers to summon her, and she came to him, and they made love. (2 Samuel 11:2-4a)

'On guard!' According to Hollywood at least, words such as those used to precede sword fights in years gone by. It would have been considered lacking in chivalry not to give one's prospective opponent due warning and time to prepare for battle. Unfortunately, when it comes to temptation the attack is often very different. It comes without warning, unsought, unexpected; nine times out of ten taking us by surprise.

So it was for David. One moment he was reclining on his rooftop enjoying the afternoon sun, and the next he was planning illicit sex. A great and devout king he may have been; it counted for nothing – like a moth drawn towards a candle he was unable to resist the pull of temptation. In one moment of madness he made a mistake that was to haunt him for the rest of his life. We cannot excuse David's actions, but we can learn from them. Like those swashbuckling 'heroes' of old, real or imagined, we too must be 'on guard'.

Resisting temptation

Joseph was fine-looking and attractive, and in time his master's wife cast her eyes on Joseph and said, 'Make love to me.' But he refused and said to her, 'I need to consider my master. He has no worries concerning the affairs of his household, having entrusted its administration into my hands. My authority here is second only to his, and he has withheld nothing from me except you, since you are his wife. How, then, could I repay him with such wickedness, and sin also against God?' Although she made insinuations to Joseph every day, he refused to lie beside her or even to be with her alone. (Genesis 39:6b-10)

Temptation comes in many shapes and forms. For some it is sex, for others money; for some drugs, for others power. All of us have our Achilles' heel – a vulnerable spot where temptation unerringly strikes – and though we may resist for a time, it is hard not to succumb when faced by temptation's repeated assaults.

The same must have been true for Joseph, faced by the flirtatious advances of Potiphar's wife – he would have been less than human had he felt no stirring within him. Yet however attracted he may have been, he did not succumb, because he knew that to do so would be to compromise everything he believed. Sold into slavery he may have been, rejected by his own brothers, and faced with an uncertain future in a foreign land; it didn't matter – the principles that underpinned his life and the faith that sustained these still held good. For Joseph, the all-important factor was not what he desired but what God required. It is a principle that all of us, faced with temptation, do well to follow.

Slipping back

Thus says the Lord: If people fall, do they not get up again? If they go astray, do they not return to the right path? So why are my people continually backsliding, forever falling away? . . . We need to pay ever more attention to everything we have heard, so that we do not let it slip. (Jeremiah 8:4-5a; Hebrews 2:1)

The other day brought an unexpected and unwelcome surprise. On what ostensibly was the first day of spring we had some of the heaviest snow of the year; the streets briefly covered by a treacherous layer of slush that made walking difficult. What should have been a pleasant stroll became a tortuous journey, everyone picking their way gingerly in case their feet should go from under them.

At least, though, the danger was clear, so everyone knew to take extra care. There are times on the road of Christian discipleship when the going becomes slippery yet with no outward indication of the fact. Instead of being like snow it is more like black ice. We can be progressing serenely along our way, sure of our footing and confident of reaching our destination when, before we have time to realise what's going on, we find that we have taken a tumble and slipped over. Our confidence is shaken and our faith undermined such that we are uncertain where to take our next step. It all happens so easily and quickly. If we are not to find ourselves sliding back, we need to be vigilant and awake to the things that might cause us to fall. Most of all, we need to focus on God and seek his guidance, for he finally is the one who can direct us safely along our path.

An unwitting mistake

You know my folly, O God; there can be no hiding my wrongs from you. (Psalm 69:5)

'Robot Wars' pyjamas! – it was just what we were looking for, so we hung them on the pushchair and continued our look round the store. Some time later and several shops further on, we looked down in horror, for there were the pyjamas, still hanging where we'd put them earlier. Somehow, we'd paid for everything else but clean forgotten about these, walking away with them, security tag and all! Luckily, I was able to rectify my mistake, hurrying back to the shop to settle up, but that experience brought home to me how easy it is inadvertently to make a mistake. A moment of carelessness, a word thoughtlessly spoken, or simply a case of sheer forgetfulness such as mine, and we can find we've done wrong though it was the last thing on our mind.

Is it right to call such errors sin? Not in a pejorative, judgemental sense, no, yet unintended mistakes can be as destructive as any premeditated wrongdoing. They are also, by definition, the hardest mistakes to avoid, since we do not even know we are making them. Perversely, we can be harder on ourselves over our unintended blunders than God will ever be. Where he, as always, is ready to forgive, we chastise ourselves for not having seen the pitfalls. Such concern may be understandable and, if it helps avert repeating our errors, it has a place, but we will never eliminate every misjudgement from our lives.

In this, as in everything, we depend on his grace – a grace that knows us and loves us as we are.

Waste disposal

Put to death whatever is earthly within you: sexual immorality, depravity, lust and other evil desires, including greed, which is a form of idolatry, because the wrath of God will come on account of such things. You once followed ways such as this, in your former way of life, but now you must get rid of all such things – anger, wrath, malice, slander, and abusive language from your mouth. (Colossians 3:5-8)

What is the most exciting vehicle on today's roads – a fire engine, police car or ambulance, perhaps; a digger, crane or car-transporter; or perhaps a Porsche or BMW? When my son was a little boy there was one vehicle that ranked higher than any of these: the municipal waste disposal truck. Each collection day, we had only to say the magic words 'Bin lorry!' and Samuel would be there, eyes glued to the front window as he watched the lorry's progress with rapt attention. Waste disposal – hardly a thing to get excited about, you might think, and yet, of course, without it our streets would soon become clogged with rubbish resulting in all kinds of threats to health and public safety. When waste is allowed to accumulate, the consequences can be dire.

This leads us to what Paul was striving to get across to the Colossians, as indeed in so many other of his letters. He had spoken a little earlier of the grace and mercy of Christ, but here he breaks off for a moment, in case his words might be misconstrued. Don't use that goodness, he says, as an excuse to ignore the build-up of undesirable characteristics in your life. Don't let thoughts and deeds that have no place gain a foothold once again, for if you do they will poison from within the new life you have found in Jesus as surely as rubbish left to accumulate will contaminate its surrounding environment. We may not be able to identify with all the vices Paul lists, but there are probably a few we can relate to well enough. Get rid of them, says Paul, before they get rid of you! Don't let them gain a hold, or you may find that though God has time for you, you no longer have time for him.

Time

see also Christian festivals

God's timing

The fullness of time

In the fullness of time, God sent his own Son, born of a woman and born under the law, so that we who were subjects of the law might be redeemed, and, through adoption, become his children. (Galatians 4:4-5)

Some people claim that there could have been no more opportune moment for the coming of Jesus than the time God actually chose. The Roman empire, they argue, brought unparalleled peace and stability, an opportunity to travel as never before, and an intermingling of cultures that brought an openness to new ideas – just the sort of world in which the gospel could quickly spread. It's a beguiling argument, but it doesn't work, for the fact is there are many other times in history for which an equally strong case could be made. If Jesus had come today, for example, how much more of an impact might he have made? Using modern technology, he could have relayed his message around the world in seconds. Instead of preaching to small crowds on the hillside, he could have addressed whole nations live by satellite. Surely, if any era qualifies for the label 'the fullness of time', it should be the twenty-first century!

Yet God didn't choose this or any other date we might suggest – he chose that day in the reign of the Emperor Augustus when Mary and Joseph had gone to Bethlehem to be taxed. We cannot say why, for we do not know the workings of God's mind. His timing is of his choosing, no one else's. There is a lesson here concerning not just the birth of Christ but the whole of life. We may wonder sometimes why our prayers are not answered as quickly as we would like. Equally, we may find that God is calling us to grasp the moment when we want to hang back, reluctant to commit ourselves. Advent reminds us that God's timetable and ours may not be the same, and it asks us if we are ready to put his timing first.

Wise use of time

Patience, patience

It is better to be patient in spirit than proud in spirit. (Ecclesiastes 7:8)

The meeting was going on longer than expected, and I was growing increasingly impatient. 'Get to the point!' I felt like saying, but of course I didn't say anything; I just sat there stewing. At last, I was on my way home, but what was this? – a slow driver ahead of me, tootling along as though he had all the time in the world, and such was the nature of the road I had no chance of overtaking. Again, there was nothing for it but to grit my teeth as my blood rose to boiling point! I got past eventually and put my foot down, hoping to make up for lost time, but it was no good, for more obstacles were to follow: first, a set of road-works, then a diversion, and so it went on – patience frayed to the limit.

Was it worth getting so worked up? Of course not. When I eventually arrived home, my head ached, my hands were tense and my mind in a whirl; several hours spoiled for the sake of a few minutes. All too easily, life is like that. We rush from one thing to the next, one eye on the clock, begrudging every wasted moment, yet in trying to save a few seconds we end up frittering away far more of our lives. We need to learn that every moment is God's gift, whatever we are doing, and to make the most of each one while we have it.

This is the day

This is the day that the Lord has made; let us celebrate and rejoice in it. (Psalm 118:24)

The other day I was looking back at a holiday scrapbook compiled by my mother when I was 9 years old. It had been my first proper holiday and it was fascinating to recall moments long since past. It's good sometimes to look back just as it's good also to look forward, yet we must take care, for both have their dangers. If we're not careful, we can end up so preoccupied with the past or the future that we overlook the blessings of the present. We strive in the first half of our lives to achieve first this, then that, only in later years to look back to the good old days and wish we'd made more of them while we had the chance.

What we need to learn is to enjoy each moment, recognising all it has to offer. Give thanks for the past, by all means; anticipate the future, of course; but never forget that *this* is the day the Lord has made – don't let it pass you by.

A time for everything

There is a season for everything, and a time for every activity under heaven: a time to be born, and a time to die; a time to plant, and a time to uproot; a time to kill, and a time to heal; a time to pull down and a time to build up; a time to cry and a time to laugh; a time to grieve and a time to dance; a time to scatter stones and a time to gather them; a time to embrace and a time not to embrace; a time to seek and a time to lose; a time to keep and a time to throw away; a time to tear and a time to mend; a time for silence and a time for speech; a time to love and a time to hate; a time for war and a time for peace. (Ecclesiastes 3:1-8)

Time's a funny thing, isn't it? One moment we can feel down in the dumps and the next on top of the world; today life can seem full of trouble but tomorrow it may appear full of promise. Our experience is always changing and life is constantly moving on. In some ways that is a sobering prospect, reminding us all too starkly of our mortality, yet where would we be without the variety that the passing of time brings: the passing of the seasons, the birth and growth of a child, the anticipation of a special event and, of course, our hope in Christ.

The secret, with time, is knowing how to respond to it; understanding what mood or action is appropriate for a particular occasion. Should we put the past behind us or hold on to it? Should we grasp the nettle or admit defeat? Should we stand up for our principles or be ready to bend? We face a host of questions like these every day, and no answer is uniformly correct. We need to seek God's guidance and help, for he is the one who holds all time in his hands; the one who in all the changes and chances of this life will not change.

Time's paces

Lord, you have been our home across the centuries. Before the mountains were formed and before you fashioned this world we live in, from eternity to eternity you are God. You return us to dust, saying, 'Back to what you once were, you mortals!' A thousand years are like a passing day in your sight, as short-lived as the night-watch. Our fleeting span is seventy years, perhaps eighty if we are strong; throughout they are filled with struggle and sorrow, here today and gone tomorrow. Teach us to make the most of our days and so to discover the secret of inner wisdom. (Psalm 90:1-4, 10, 12)

There comes a time in our lives when it dawns on us that we are not as young as we used to be. Whereas the future once seemed to stretch out indefinitely, suddenly it appears all too short, the time left to fulfil our dreams far less than we thought. Time and tide, as they say, waits for no one.

It would be easy to move from here to a maudlin self-pity, but instead the psalmist turns to focus on God whose eternal nature stands in such contrast to our own transience. In the context of faith, the passage of time should not be seen as the years running out so much as life moving on, one more step along an unfolding journey in which there is always more to be discovered and new joys to be experienced. Of course, we will sometimes remember the past with a tinge of regret, and look to the future with a degree of anxiety, but we should also recognise each day as God's gift, and live every one of them in the assurance that nothing will ever separate us from his love made known in Christ.

Trust

Daring to trust

There was a certain disciple in Damascus by the name of Ananias, and the Lord spoke to him in a vision, saying, 'Ananias.' He answered, 'I'm here, Lord.' The Lord said to him, 'Get up and go to the street known as The Straight, and there look in the house of Judas for a man called Saul of Tarsus. He is praying at this very moment, and in a vision he has seen a man called Ananias enter and lay hands on him so that he might recover his sight. But Ananias protested, 'Lord, I have heard from many people about this man, about all his cruelty to your saints in Jerusalem, and how he has come here now with authority from the chief priests to arrest all those who confess your name.' (Acts 9:10-14)

What would you do if you sensed danger looming? The answer is obvious: you'd do everything possible to avoid it. Should you be the adventurous type, it's possible that you might flirt with it for a moment but, if you felt your life was on the line, you'd ultimately want to ensure your own safety. That, no doubt, was paramount in the mind of Ananias, having heard that Saul, persecutor of the Church, was in town. Quite simply, he was keeping his head down until the danger had passed, hoping against hope that he would not hear the fateful knock on the door summoning him to imprisonment and almost certain death. Imagine his surprise, then, when another summons came, calling him to seek out this man who struck fear into the heart of every Christian, and to knock on his door! It was asking a lot, to say the least!

Would you have obeyed that call, or would you have made excuses to evade it, dismissed it as ridiculous, looked the other way? Had Ananias done any of those, who can say how different the history of the Christian Church might have been? It took his faith and courage to finish the transformation of Saul, enemy of the faith, into Paul, its greatest ambassador. When God asks you to step out in faith, will you have the courage, like Ananias, to say yes?

God is able

Then in a blinding rage, Nebuchadnezzar ordered Shadrach, Meshach and Abednego to be brought in; so they were brought before the king. Nebuchadnezzar said to them, 'Is it true, Shadrach, Meshach and Abednego, that you do not serve my gods or worship the golden statue I have had erected?' Shadrach, Meshach and Abednego answered the king, 'O Nebuchadnezzar, we have no need to answer to you concerning this matter. If any god is able to deliver us from the fiery furnace, then it is our God, and he will deliver us from your hand, O king. But if not, let us tell you this, O king, we will not serve your gods and will not worship the golden image that you have set up.' (Daniel 3:13-14, 16-18)

The story of Shadrach, Meshach and Abednego is one of the great biblical classics, an unforgettable tale of courage and the triumph of good over evil that has captured the hearts of countless generations. Yet, as with all classics, there is a danger that familiarity may inure us to the full impact of the underlying message. We read the story, knowing the outcome of events – for Shadrach, Meshach and Abednego there was no such luxury. They staked all in the faith that God would deliver them, risking death itself rather than compromising their convictions.

Have we that same conviction of God's purpose? Do we have even a fraction of their astonishing trust? They knew that whatever trials they might face and whatever conspired against God's purpose, nothing finally could thwart his purpose. Remember that next time you feel up against it, the demands of life too great and your resources to meet them too small. Remember that we too can say with confidence, 'If any god is able to deliver us then it is our God.'

The moment of truth

The day dawned when the Lord planned to take Elijah up to heaven in a mighty wind. Elijah and Elisha were about to set off from Gilgal, and Elijah said to Elisha, 'Stay here; for the Lord has sent me to Bethel.' But Elisha said, 'By the Lord's life and yours, I will not leave you.' So they went down to Bethel together. A company of prophets there approached Elisha, saying, 'Are you not aware that the Lord is going to take your master from you today?' 'I'm aware of it,' he replied; 'say no more.' (2 Kings 2:1-3)

To take responsibility for our lives and make our own decisions is a difficult and, at times, painful business, yet it is an essential part of reaching maturity. As children, we rely on parents for guidance, or, failing these, perhaps a close friend, another member of our family, or a teacher at school. Eventually, though, both they and we need to let go if we are to make our own way in the world.

In the case of Elisha, dependence was rooted in his friend and mentor Elijah, but suddenly his world fell apart as he found himself faced with the prospect of having to go it alone. No wonder he didn't want to talk about it. In his words and actions we see someone desperately trying to deny reality. Yet, when the critical moment came, he found God had prepared him to meet the challenge.

An unhealthy sense of dependence can attach itself not only to people but also to God, such that we expect him to give us clear instructions in every situation. I've even heard of Christians earnestly praying as to what they should eat for breakfast: seriously wondering whether God prefers them to have cornflakes or shredded wheat! There is, of course, a place for seeking his will, but we can take it too far. He offers us the help and instruction we need but he has also given us common sense, which he fully expects us to use.

Taken on trust

Gideon said to God, 'To test whether you will indeed deliver Israel by my hand, as you have promised, I am going to put a fleece of wool down on the threshing-floor. If there is dew only on the fleece and the ground is entirely dry, then I shall know that you will deliver Israel through me, just as you have said.' Sure enough, that is what happened. When Gideon rose at dawn the next day and squeezed the fleece, he wrung enough dew from it to fill a bowl with water. Then Gideon said to God, 'Please don't lose your temper with me; permit me to speak again. Allow me to make one more trial with the fleece. This time may the fleece alone be dry and the ground be covered all over with dew.' And that night God did exactly what he asked. Only the fleece was dry; the ground everywhere was wet with dew. (Judges 6:36-40)

Few things are more difficult than living by faith. The idea sounds wonderful, but when it comes to the moment of decision most of us prefer certainties to promise. If that's true in our human relationships, it's equally so in our dealings with God. Which of us at some time or other hasn't asked for a sign: some clear, unmistakable indication that we have understood his will correctly and taken the right path? Such an attitude is perfectly natural – but it is not faith. It betrays, ultimately, a lack of assurance in God's sovereign purpose – a purpose that, for our own well-being, we must learn to take on trust.

Wholeness and healing

The last resort?

A woman, who for twelve years had endured a persistent haemorrhage and who had suffered greatly at the hands of numerous physicians, spending everything she had in the process yet getting worse as a result rather than better, heard about Jesus. Pushing through the crowd, she touched his robe, saying, 'If I can only touch his clothes, I will be healed.' (Mark 5:25-28)

I read this week the powerful story of a woman's battle against breast cancer. She had endured radical surgery, together with radio- and chemotherapy but to no avail; the disease was still progressing. Finally, she turned in desperation to alternative medicine, travelling across the world to Mexico to find a cure, and today, several years later, she is alive and well to tell the tale. It does not follow that natural remedies guarantee a cure, but this woman's despair drove her to explore a last resort that, in her case, proved successful.

The story in Mark is very similar, only this time the last resort was Jesus. She had tried everything else and spent a fortune in doing so; he was her last hope. Her faith was not disappointed. How often do we treat Jesus as a last resort? How often do we turn to him in prayer only when we've exhausted every other option? In so many aspects of life, it only occurs to us to seek his help when every other door has closed to us. We cannot guarantee, of course, that our prayers will be answered as we wish; it is often patently not so. Many seek healing, for example, but are not made well. What we can guarantee, however, is that we will find strength, support, peace and wholeness no matter what we face. Don't leave Jesus as a last resort. Don't turn to him in prayer when all else has failed. Bring your needs to him and let his renewing grace touch your life.

Picking up the pieces

I had become like a broken pot but you heard my pleas when I cried out for help. The Lord is close to the broken-hearted and he saves those who are crushed in spirit. He mends the broken in spirit and tends their wounds. (Psalm 31:12b, 22b; 34:18; 147:3)

What would you do if you smashed a prized ornament? The answer, of course, depends on the extent of the damage but the chances are that you would try to pick up the broken fragments and glue them back together. Consider, though, if it was a clay flowerpot you had dropped; what would you do then? Almost certainly, you would sweep up the shards and discard them without a second thought. It is only when something means a lot to us that we attempt to repair it.

All of which helps us to appreciate the testimony of psalms like those quoted above. Like David in Psalm 31, we too can feel battered and broken by life, shattered beyond repair. Can God possibly care enough about us to spend time rebuilding our lives, putting the pieces back together again? It seems impossible, doesn't it, yet God does precisely that. However long it takes, however painstaking a process it may be, he is always looking to heal and renew us, to make us whole. No matter how broken we may be, we are never beyond his restoring touch.

_____ Will and purpose of God _____

see also Guidance; Faithfulness of God; Judgement of God

All in God's time

When they had brought them, they had them stand before the council. The high priest questioned them, saying, 'We gave you strict orders not to teach in his name, yet here you have filled Jerusalem with your teaching and you are determined to bring this man's blood on us.' But Peter and the Apostles answered, 'We must obey God rather than any human authority.' Then a Pharisee in the council named Gamaliel, a teacher of the law, respected by all the people, stood up and ordered the men to be put outside for a short time. He said to the council, 'Fellow Israelites, consider carefully what you propose to do to these men. I urge you to keep away from them and let them alone; because if this plan or this undertaking is of human origin, it will fail; but if it is of God, you will not be able to overthrow them – in that case you may even find you are fighting against God!' (Acts 5:27-29, 34-35, 38-39)

Don't jump to conclusions – we have been told that time and again, yet sometimes we just can't seem to help ourselves. Instead of giving time for cool and calm reflection, we succumb to the knee-jerk response, the instinctive reaction, usually based more on our personal likes and dislikes than the merits of a given situation. So it was for the Apostles in the early days of the Church as they sought to proclaim their new-found faith to their fellow Jews. Few were willing even to consider their message, such was their hostility towards anything to do with Jesus. Their sole desire was to silence the Apostles by any means possible. One man, though, was different: the Pharisee Gamaliel. Where others jumped in to condemn, he urged caution. Time will tell, he argued; the will of God shall ultimately triumph.

We can push that argument too far, of course, using it to justify the status quo as God's purpose, yet there is nonetheless enormous wisdom in it. Before we rush in to criticise what is new and unfamiliar, before we rubbish anything that does not fit in with our preconceptions, we should stop and ask whose response this reflects: our own or God's? If it is the former, then we should stand back, take time, and give God the chance to confirm what he thinks rather than what we assume his response will be.

The best-laid plans

Come now, you who say, 'Today or tomorrow we will go to such and such a town and spend a year there, doing business and making money.' You do not even know what tomorrow will bring. What is your life? For you are a mist that appears for a little while and then vanishes. Instead you ought to say, 'If the Lord wishes, we will live and do this or that.' (James 4:13-15)

Even the best-laid plans, they tell us, go to waste. It is, though, in the nature of humankind to look ahead. We want to know what life has in store, we feel the need for a clear sense of direction, and we do everything in our power to ensure that the future measures up to our expectations.

There is no shortage of encouragement to such a way of thinking. Pension firms urge us to plan for retirement, insurance companies offer cover against each and every eventuality, whilst banks and building societies offer us all manner of investment schemes that promise bumper tax-free pay-outs ten, fifteen, twenty-five years into the future. All of course have their place for those who can afford them, as part of a sensible stewardship of their resources, but neither these nor anything else can guarantee the future. We never know what tomorrow may bring. Whilst it is necessary in life to look ahead it is also vital to live each day as it comes, valuing it for what it is, and being open to what it may bring.

God's active word

'I am God, and there is no other. I am God and there is none like me, pronouncing the end at the beginning and speaking at the dawn of time of things yet to be done, proclaiming, 'My will shall prevail, and I will fulfil my purpose. I have spoken, and I will make it happen; I have planned, and I will accomplish it.' (Isaiah 46:9-10, 11b)

Look at the label on any medicine and you will see there a list of active ingredients. Without them, your prescription would be useless, a mere placebo. In the words of Isaiah, we are pointed towards active ingredients of a different sort, the prophet able to speak with conviction of the ultimate fulfilment of God's purpose because he knows that when God says he will do something he does it. There is never any question of him saying one thing and doing another, making a promise and then forgetting to honour it. He is wholly dependable, a God in whom we can put our trust.

That truth is supremely fulfilled in Christ, God's living Word.

Through him, God acted decisively in human history, wonderfully and unmistakably putting his words into practice! He didn't just wish the world well and then leave people to get on with their own affairs. He didn't simply tell us what we need to do and then expect us to struggle on as best we can. He didn't give fine-sounding promises that remained only promises. He revealed love in action, through the Word made flesh; a Word that continues to be active today, in our lives and in our world. Through him, we know indeed that what God has pledged to do, he will accomplish!

It's a promise!

Was I vacillating when I wanted to do this? Do I make my plans according to ordinary human standards, ready to say 'Yes, yes' and 'No, no' at the same time? As surely as God is faithful, our word to you has not been 'Yes and No'; but in him it is always 'Yes'. For in him every one of God's promises is a 'Yes'. For this reason it is through him that we say the 'Amen', to the glory of God. (2 Corinthians 1:17-20)

How many of us can put our hand on our heart and say we have never broken a promise? I doubt anyone could make such a claim. It's not that we intend to go back on our word – not usually anyway; more that circumstances alter, unforeseen eventualities arise, or we are simply unable to deliver on our pledge. The Apostle Paul knew this as well as any, his second letter to the Corinthians revealing that they had taken him to task for failing to honour his promise to visit them. Yet, there is one, he says, whose promises are never broken, whose word is utterly reliable, and it is to him that Paul suddenly turns, almost in mid-sentence, bursting into a joyful celebration of God's faithfulness. What God has said he will do, shall be done – we have his word.

Return to sender?

As the rain and snow come down from heaven and do not return until they have watered the earth – making it blossom and sprout, and giving seed to be sown and bread for food – so it is with the word of my mouth; it will not return fruitless, but will accomplish my purpose and achieve that for which I sent it. (Isaiah 55:10-11)

I'd posted my letter and was waiting eagerly for a reply, each day growing increasingly impatient at the delay. 'What could be keeping them?' I wondered. How much longer would it be? Three weeks later the letter arrived – not the letter I was anticipating but the one I had sent with a curt message scribbled across the front: 'Return to sender. Address not known.' Life can be like that sometimes, can't it? We think we've done something, only to find it's gone wrong. We believe we've completed a job only to discover it needs doing all over again.

With God, it's different. What he says he will do, he does. What he accomplishes is accomplished once and for all. We may frustrate him, impede him, even oppose him but, ultimately, his will shall be done. Hold on to his promises, trust in his word, for neither will return to him empty.

Rough justice

The Lord is slow to anger but great in power, and will most certainly not overlook the guilty. Who can stand before his righteous anger? Who can endure the heat of his fury? The Lord is a sure stronghold in a day of trouble; he keeps safe those who seek refuge in him, even though a flood surges around them. He will obliterate his adversaries and pursue his enemies into darkness. Why, then, do you hatch plots against the Lord? He will put an end to it; no adversary will rise up twice. (Nahum 1:3, 6a, 7-10)

The book of Nahum is not an easy book to read, its theme one of undisguised glee at a catastrophe about to befall the enemies of Judah. Yet if we see beyond the prophet's apparent vindictive delight, his words carry an important message, for the point he makes is that justice will finally be done. That must have taken some believing for his hearers, since for generations the people of Judah had suffered under the mighty yoke of the Assyrian empire. Sure enough, however, within a few years this seemingly impregnable dynasty was to collapse, as a new superpower, Babylon, emerged to take centre stage in the ancient world.

In recent years we have seen events just as remarkable in the destruction of the Berlin Wall, the end of the Cold War, the removal of apartheid, and the successive overthrow of dictatorial regimes the world over. All this is not to say that everything in this life works out as it should, for there are times when it manifestly does not. Yet at the heart of our faith is the conviction that God is actively involved in human history, striving to establish his kingdom despite everything that conspires to frustrate his purpose.

Taking it on the chin

All the people, high and low, approached the prophet Jeremiah and said, 'Ask the Lord your God to show us where we should go and what we should do.' The prophet Jeremiah said to them, 'Fair enough, I will pray to the Lord your God as you ask, and I will pass on to you whatever answer the Lord gives. I will hold nothing back from you.' They responded to Jeremiah in turn, 'May the Lord be a steadfast and implacable witness against us if we do not act exactly as the Lord your God indicates to us through you. Whether it is welcome or unwelcome, we will obey the voice of the Lord our God to whom we send you, so that it may go well with us; we will obey his voice.' (Jeremiah 42:1b-2a, 3-6)

When did you last ask somebody for a straight answer? More important, when did you last seriously reflect on an answer that went against what you wanted to hear? We don't like being told to do something we'd rather not do and we resent advice that undermines our established opinions. The same is true when it comes to God. Although we may say, 'Your will be done', most of us are probably like those who approached Jeremiah, asking him to seek God's guidance for the future. They sounded sincere enough, and they probably were, but when Jeremiah delivered God's answer, suddenly a very different attitude became evident. 'You are lying!' they said; 'The Lord our God has not sent you to forbid us from making our homes in Egypt. Baruch, son of Neriah, has turned you against us so that we may be put in the power of the Babylonians, and that they may kill us or deport us to Babylon' (Jeremiah 43:2b-3). Their response was perfectly understandable, for, faced by Babylonian occupation, they preferred to shape their own future rather than have it imposed upon them. In consequence, they dismissed anything they didn't want to hear.

We talk much in the Church today about seeking God's will but often it is more about shaping God to our will than letting his will shape us. The truth is that he doesn't always fit in with our expectations, and his guidance may be anything but welcome. It is at such times that faith is tested, and shown to be genuine or otherwise. Are we any more willing than the people of Jeremiah's day to listen to what God wants to say to us?

Wisdom of God

The beginning of wisdom

Happy is the one who finds wisdom and who acquires understanding, for wisdom profits more than silver, and brings gain better even than gold. She is more precious than jewels, and nothing you might name can compare with her. Long life is in her right hand, and in her left are riches and honour. Her ways bring pleasure, and all her paths bring peace. She is a staff to those who lay hold of her, a source of happiness and security to those who hold her fast. (Proverbs 3:13-18)

What do Plato, Aristotle, Darwin, David Attenborough, Monty Python, and the writers of Proverbs and Ecclesiastes have in common? The answer is that all have explored questions concerning the meaning of life, albeit in very different ways! How did life start? Why are we here? What does the future hold? We need wisdom to grapple with questions like these, but what is wisdom and how do we find it? For some, the answer lies in academic study. Others claim it is through the university of life. Others still maintain that the solution is to let go of the world and lose oneself in mystical speculation. According to the author of Proverbs, however, the answer is much simpler: 'The fear of the Lord is the beginning of wisdom' (Proverbs 1:7; 9:10) – a contention echoed in Psalm 111:10. Gain insight into the ways of God, and we will discover the true meaning of life.

Does this leave a place for the intellect, the wisdom we can gain through study and daily experience? Of course it does. The range of topics covered in Proverbs is surprisingly down to earth, yet do not confuse the message given there with mere worldly wisdom. Faith, thank God, is concerned with the daily stuff of life, but it brings to this a new dimension and a different perspective that often stands accepted wisdom on its head – a different kind of wisdom exemplified in the folly of the Cross, through which true meaning is found for all.

Daring to be different

God saw that the earth was corrupt and filled with violence. And God said to Noah, 'I have seen the wickedness of humankind, and how the whole earth is violated because of them. I have resolved, therefore, to destroy them along with the earth. Make yourself an ark of cypress wood; make rooms within it, and cover it inside and out with pitch. Noah did just this, precisely following God's instructions. (Genesis 6:11, 13-14, 22)

Few of us like to stand out from the crowd, least of all when it involves being different. The occasional foible is one thing, eccentricity quite another. No one likes being thought odd. When Noah, though, set to work building an ark in the middle of the wilderness he must have looked exactly that – a strange character if ever there was one. We can scarcely imagine the ridicule he must have endured day after day as he laboured on his extraordinary enterprise with no sign of rain, let alone flood.

Noah, though, was no stranger to being thought different, for, as the book of Hebrews (11:7) reminds us, his righteousness set him apart from others; his determination to stay true to God, whatever the pressures to the contrary; a rarity in his time just as it is in ours.

Given all that, it is tempting to suggest he had the last laugh, but I suspect laughter was the last thing on his mind after the tragedy that followed. The story of Noah is not about saying 'I told you so' to a cynical and hostile world. It is rather about having the courage to be different in the hope that someone, somewhere, may perhaps take notice.

Witnessing to Christ

Grasping the moment

Running up to the chariot, Philip heard [the eunuch] reading Isaiah the prophet, so he asked him, 'Do you understand these words you're reading?' The eunuch answered, 'How can I possibly do that unless someone explains them to me?' And he urged Philip to come up and sit with him. The eunuch asked Philip, 'Tell me, who is the prophet talking about here? Does he refer to himself or someone else?' Then Philip, beginning with that passage of scripture, talked to him about Jesus. (Acts 8:30-31, 34-35)

The question caught me entirely by surprise. I was on a train journey during my time as a theological student, when suddenly a young man sitting opposite me, spotting the textbook I was poring over, leant across and asked me what I made of Jesus. Have you ever had an experience like that, asked out of the blue to summarise what your faith means to you? If you have, then, like me, you may well have found yourself caught on the hop, unable to make the most of the opportunity. Contrast that with the story of Philip and the Ethiopian eunuch. For years, the eunuch had been searching the scriptures seeking enlightenment, recognising that they pointed to something truly special yet unsure quite how to interpret them. Philip found himself in the right place at the right time but, more important, he turned out to be the right person, using the God-given moment to win this man to faith. Interested enquiry rapidly turned into enthusiastic commitment, and all it took was a willingness to get alongside and bear witness to Christ.

How, then, should we apply this today? I don't think it's about memorising words of testimony until we have them off pat – that will cut little ice with anyone. Nor would I advocate immersing ourselves in statements of doctrine, creeds, or other kinds of theological jargon, in the hope that we can trot them out parrot-fashion whenever the need arises – that would prove even more counter-productive. What is important is that we take time to reflect on our faith, and to ask ourselves honestly what Jesus means to us and what difference he has made to our lives. Do that and, when the opportunity comes to speak out for Christ, we shall not be found wanting.

Introducing Jesus

The woman left her water-jar and returned to the city. She said to the people there, 'Come and see a man who told me everything I had ever done. He cannot be the Messiah, can he?' (John 4:28-29)

We will all, at some time or other, have been in a situation when a friend or acquaintance says to us, 'Let me introduce you to so and so'. This can, of course, be nothing more than a formality, an expected social nicety, but it can mean a great deal more. A simple introduction can lead to a fascinating encounter and even a lasting friendship as two people move from being complete strangers towards getting to know each other.

Consider this in relation to the example of the Samaritan woman in John's Gospel. She did not introduce people to Jesus in the strict sense of the word, but her words had much the same effect, inducing those she told about him to meet Jesus for themselves – to talk with him and enter into a personal encounter. The result? 'Many Samaritans from that city believed in him, because of the woman's testimony' (John 4:39). There is an important lesson here when it comes to Christian testimony. We can try sometimes to argue people into faith, imagining that we need to answer all their questions before they can come to belief. What is actually required is something far simpler: merely to introduce people to Jesus – to ensure that they know of him and about him. We must do our part; the rest is down to him.

So much more to share

On the first evening of the Sabbath, the disciples having assembled to break bread, Paul preached to them and, conscious that he was due to depart the next day, he talked on past midnight. Now there were a number of oil lamps in the upstairs room where they had gathered and, as Paul continued still longer with his sermon, a young man called Eutychus, who was perched on a window sill, sank into a torpor and fell from the third storey, and was assumed to be dead. Paul rushed down and cradled him in his arms, saying, 'Don't be alarmed. He's still alive!' And he went back upstairs, broke bread, and, having eaten this, once more talked at length until dawn broke, after which he finally departed. (Acts 20:7-11)

When did you last hear a boring sermon? We've all sat through them, haven't we, and in my case I've probably preached a few as well! I doubt, though, that we've ever been involved in a situation quite like that recorded in Acts 20. Here we see none other than the Apostle Paul as the archetypal preacher who doesn't know when to stop, going on so long, in fact, that one of his unfortunate listeners dozes off, keels over and falls out of an upstairs window! Whether the sermon was dull we are not told – the mishap is charitably put down to the room being over-warm – but had I been sitting there beyond midnight I think my eyes would have glazed over too. What is truly astonishing, however, is that when the young man turns out not to be seriously injured, or even dead as first feared, Paul gets back to his feet and carries on with his sermon! Is that thick-skinned, or what!

So what lay behind this mammoth homily? It wasn't that Paul liked the sound of his own voice; it was rather that the good news bubbled up within him so that he felt compelled to share it! His example isn't one I would recommend following too closely, but we all need something of that enthusiasm. If we had even a fraction of Paul's irrepressible desire to share our faith, what a difference we could make.

Something to share

Then they summoned them in again and ordered them not to speak or teach at all in the name of Jesus. But Peter and John responded, 'You must decide for yourselves whether it is right in God's eyes to obey you rather than him. The fact is that we cannot help speaking about the things we have seen and heard.' (Acts 4:18-20)

What is the first thing you do if you have a bit of good news? Unless you're very different from me, I expect your immediate reaction is to want to share it. Whether you've just got engaged, had your first child, earned promotion, come up on the premium bonds, or won a dream holiday, the natural and instinctive response is to rush round to a loved one, pick up the telephone or put pen to paper. Such is our excitement we may even end up sharing our news with a complete stranger. To keep it to ourselves just doesn't seem right.

What, then, of the greatest news of all, the message of Christ? Do we burn to share that? Do we find we simply can't stop ourselves talking about it sometimes? That's what Peter and John found, in the days of the early Church. They knew the risks of speaking out and if they had entertained any lingering doubts these must surely have been dispelled by their reception at the hands of the chief priests and elders. Yet, despite every effort to silence them, they knew that they could not keep quiet. The problem we have today, of course, is that the gospel is not news in quite the same way; most people are aware of the Christian message even if they have little knowledge of what it is actually all about. We are confronted by a world convinced that it's old hat, and a world in which what's news today is forgotten tomorrow. We will not get far standing on our soapbox and quoting the Bible at people, nor through reciting parrot-fashion the creeds or central tenets of faith. We need to take a leaf out of the Apostle's book and tell of the things we have seen and heard; in other words, to share what faith means to us and what Jesus has done in our life, and to do that honestly, naturally and spontaneously.

Sowing the seed

Jesus told the crowd many parables, including this one: 'A farmer went out to sow and, as he did so, some seed fell by the wayside, and the birds swooped down and devoured it. Other seed fell on rocky ground, where there was little soil and, though it sprang up quickly because the earth was so shallow, when the sun rose, it was baked and withered away, since it had no root. Other seed fell among thorns, which, as they grew, choked the seedlings, so that they yielded no grain. Other seed fell into good soil and brought forth grain, shooting up, increasing and yielding thirty- and sixty- and a hundred fold.' And he said, 'Let those with ears to hear listen!' (Mark 4:2-9)

What's the most important lesson to be drawn from the parable of the sower? Is it that our lives need to be like fertile soil, receptive to the word of God, so that we bear a rich harvest to his glory? It could be, for there's no doubt God wants to see this in our lives. Is a more important message that we need to beware of temptations that may insidiously destroy our faith before we realise what is happening? It could be this, too, for there's no denying how real and dangerous temptation can be. Could it be that the underlying theme is to guard against shallow discipleship, a faith rooted in a superficial and emotional response rather than grounded in body, mind and soul? That's certainly an important point, for how many people commit themselves to Christ for a moment in a surge of enthusiasm, only swiftly to fall away? We can even argue that Jesus is telling us that some people will never respond to the gospel no matter how often they hear it. True perhaps, though it would be foolish to judge the state of another's soul. The truth, of course, is that all of these points are equally valid.

Yet there is a further lesson in his words which is, perhaps, more important than any, and that, quite simply, is the need to sow. The seed may be the object of the story, but the sower has first to sow it, and for 'sower' read 'us'. We are the ones called to spread God's word, the responsibility of proclaiming the good news of Christ entrusted to us.

We cannot guarantee the results of our efforts but one thing is certain: unless we sow the seed, whatever the ground, there will be no harvest.

Speaking their language

Standing in the middle of the Areopagus, Paul said, 'People of Athens, I perceive that you are deeply religious, for as I walked by I couldn't help noticing your objects of worship, among which I spotted an altar on which was inscribed "To an unknown god". What you worship as unknown, I now proclaim to you. The God who created the world and all things in it, the Lord of heaven and earth, does not live in shrines made by human hands, nor is he served in the sense of being dependent on anyone. Rather, he gives breath and life to all things. He created all nations that live on earth from a common ancestor, and he established the times and limits of their existence so that they will search for God and, should they grope after him, eventually find him – although ultimately he is not far from any of us. In him we live, move and have our being, as indeed some of your own poets have said, "For we also are his offspring."' (Acts 17:22-28)

If someone were to regale you with Einstein's theory of relativity, how long would it be before you excused yourself? Unless you happened to be a physicist, I expect you would look for the earliest opportunity to escape. The subject may be fascinating to experts, but to most of us it is virtually another language. Communication is about speaking to people in terms they can relate to.

This perhaps accounts for the astonishing success of the Apostle Paul throughout his ministry. Look at the way he addressed the people of Athens. As a Jew, his inclination must have been to talk of Jesus in terms of Old Testament prophecy, and, as a Pharisee, in terms of the Jewish Law; but he did neither, because he knew such concepts would mean nothing to his Greek listeners. He needed to speak to them in terms of their own faith and culture, and that is precisely what he did, quoting, in a masterstroke, from Epimenides and Eratus, two of their own poets – in other words, talking their language. Do we follow their example when we share our faith, or do we slip into the language of jargon? Effective testimony takes two things: a willingness to speak honestly about what God means to us, and a sensitivity towards those we are talking to, so that God may speak to them in turn.

Telling the news

As it says in scripture, 'No one who puts their faith in him will be put to shame.' For there is no differentiation between Jew and Greek; the same Lord is Lord of all and generous to all those who call on him. As it says again, 'Every-one who calls on the name of the Lord will be saved.' How, though, can they call on one in whom they have not believed, and believe in one of whom they have never heard? How can they hear without someone to proclaim him, and how can anyone proclaim him unless they are sent? (Romans 10:11-15a)

According to Stephen Pile's *The Book of Heroic Failures*, Hiroo Onoda, a lieutenant in the Japanese army, still believed he was fighting the Second World War until 10 March 1974, twenty-nine years after the war had ended! How did he not know peace had been declared? He was stationed on a remote island in the Philippines, and although 'Come home' letters had been dropped from the air, no one bothered to tell him in person that the war was over.

It's a remarkable story that takes some believing, but the principle behind it is clear enough and it is one we do well to heed as Christians. 'How can they call on one in whom they have not believed, and believe in one of whom they have never heard?' asked Paul, and, of course, they couldn't. Unless people are told about Jesus, they will never come to faith. There was a time when those words were a rallying call to mission overseas. Today, they are also a call to mission at home, for there are many here in our country who have little knowledge of Christ, their awareness limited to the few smatterings they may have heard in assemblies and religious instruction at school. The temptation is that we leave the telling to someone else – and the danger is that no one else will tell them! We may not all be sent as missionaries or evangelists, but we all have a story to tell and a faith to proclaim. Can we afford not to share it?

Words from the heart

While [Paul] was making his defence, Festus exclaimed, 'You've taken leave of your senses, Paul! All your learning has driven you insane.' Paul replied, 'I am not insane, most excellent Festus; what I am telling you is the truth and sound common sense. The king knows well enough about these things, which indeed is why I speak to him freely; for I am quite sure none of these matters escaped his notice, none of them having been done in a corner. King Agrippa, do you believe the prophets? I know that you believe.' Agrippa said to Paul, 'Do you think you can persuade me to become a Christian in such a short time?' Paul answered, 'Whether it take a short or a long time, I pray God that not only you but all who are listening to me today might become such as I am – except for these chains.' (Acts 26:24-29)

A few years ago a fascinating television documentary series asked the question 'What makes a great speaker?' Using archive film of great orators such as Lloyd George, Winston Churchill, Martin Luther King, Billy Graham and Donald Soper, suggestions were made as to the essential qualities for any speaker. These included posture, gestures and mannerisms, power and inflection of voice, well-chosen pauses, eye contact, tempo, repetition and humour. I watched those programmes eagerly, hoping that next time I delivered a sermon the congregation would leap to their feet in wild and spontaneous applause, and that before long crowds would be flocking to my church in their droves! Sadly, it never happened and, of course, I never seriously imagined that it would, truly gifted speakers being a rare breed.

One such speaker, however, was clearly the Apostle Paul. In part, this was due to his willingness to talk the language of his listeners, but he had another quality that we can all emulate – quite simply, a transparent sincerity. There was no artifice about Paul, none of what, in modern politics, we have come to refer to as 'spin'. In his trial before Festus and Agrippa, instead of toning down his message as many would have done in his place, he gave a frank and honest life history, telling of the personal pilgrimage that had led him to Christ. None of us will achieve anything like Paul achieved, nor speak with a fraction of his authority, but all of us can speak with sincerity, and if we do that, we may find that the results are far greater than we ever dared to expect.

Your God needs you!

How can they cry out to someone they have not believed in? How can they believe in someone they have never heard of? And how can they hear of him unless someone proclaims it to them? And how can anyone proclaim unless they are sent? (Romans 10:14-15)

If you had been out and about in the year 1914, you would have seen, wherever you went, a poster emblazoned with the words 'Your country needs you!' It was all part of the government's campaign to enlist new recruits to serve in the First World War and, incredible though it may seem to us today in the light of what we know about the horrors of that conflict, young men signed up in their thousands, eager to be part of this 'great adventure'. The reasons behind that are many: partly it reflected nationalistic fervour and partly dreams of glory and heroism, but perhaps the underlying reason – and one cleverly exploited by the poster – was the fact that all of us like to feel needed. This, more than anything, gives us a sense of worth and purpose in life.

So, when we read the words of Romans 10, we should catch our breath in praise and thanksgiving, for here we find God expressing his need of us! In Christ he has good news for the entire world, a message he wants everyone to hear and rejoice in, but in order to spread the word and make real his love, he depends on our contribution. It may be a cliché, and one that sounds quite incredible, but it is nonetheless true that God requires us to be his hands and feet, his eyes and mouth, his agents here on earth. Quite simply, your God needs you!

Word of God

The challenging word

God's word is dynamic and alive, sharper than any two-edged sword, penetrating so deeply it divides soul from spirit, joints from marrow; able to discern the thoughts and objectives of the heart. (Hebrews 4:12)

Seeking God's will, if we take it seriously, involves risks – the risk, first, that we may be disappointed by God's answer or lack of it, and the risk, second, that it may lead to more than we had bargained for. Sometimes, for reasons we don't understand, no clear guidance seems forthcoming, while at other times the answer God gives is very different from the one we'd hoped for, bringing an awkward, disturbing challenge that we would rather not hear. The question then, of course, is: are we willing to listen, or do we close our ears?

God's living word

For, as it is written . . . (Matthew 2:5b)

'As it is written' – those words run like a thread throughout the Gospel of Matthew and, indeed, throughout much of the New Testament, the message of the law and the prophets seen as fulfilled in the birth, life, death and resurrection of Christ. So what is it saying? On one level, it reinforces the theme we explored yesterday of God's word always being active, never exhausted until it has fulfilled its purpose. There is, though, a second truth that can be drawn from these words, which takes those observations a little further, for the fascinating fact is that the scriptures cited as being fulfilled were, more often than not, initially addressed to a very different situation in an altogether different time. Suddenly, though, with the coming of Christ, they took on new meaning; imbued with fresh power and fulfilled in a yet more wonderful way. God's word of old was speaking again to a new time and situation.

Countless generations across the years can testify to that same truth in their own lives, words of scripture initially concerned with events and people long past having leapt out of the page as though God was speaking directly to them. Here is the wonder of the Bible: that words so very old can seem so startlingly new. That is why we call it God's word, because, difficult though it may be sometimes to understand –

occasionally dry, often complex, frequently mystifying – God can none theless speak through it today to you, to me, to everyone.

The message that speaks for itself

Jesus did many other signs before his disciples that have not been recorded here, but these things have been written so that you might believe Jesus is the Christ, the Son of God, and that, through believing, you might have life in his name. (John 20:30-31)

I worked out recently that during my time in the ministry I preached well over a thousand sermons. That statistic brought home to me how many millions of sermons must have been delivered over the years, thousands more being added to that number every week. Do any say anything new? I doubt it. More important, I doubt any set out to do so, for the goal of every preacher is, or should be, simply to proclaim the age-old message of the gospel. Certainly, each will attempt to bring home afresh the significance of that message for new generations, and this may well involve exploring different approaches and angles, but ultimately the heart of what any may say will have been said many times before. Sometimes a sermon will succeed in its aim: challenging, teaching, instructing, inspiring. At other times, it will leave its listeners cold, serving more to obscure than to illuminate.

No doubt, the same has been true of the reflections in this book, some having brought home the wonder of God's grace, others having left as many questions as answers. No one has a monopoly on truth, still less the ability to fathom the full riches of the gospel. Thankfully, scripture's ability to speak does not depend on any human agency, however helpful this may be at times. It has spoken across the years to countless generations and continues to do the same today, still having the power to transform lives and win people to faith in Christ. We do our best to fathom and communicate its meaning but, thankfully, God does not depend solely on us – his word is able to speak for itself.

Rediscovering the word

While they were fetching the silver that had been brought into the house of the Lord, the priest Hilkiah discovered the book of the law of the Lord that had been given through Moses. Hilkiah said to the secretary Shaphan, 'I have discovered the book of the law in the house of the Lord'; and he gave the book to Shaphan who brought the book to the king and informed him, 'The priest Hilkiah has given me a book, and he read it out aloud to the king. When the king heard what was in the book of the law, he tore his clothes, saying, 'Great is the anger of the Lord, poured out on us because our forebears did not obey the commandments of the Lord or do what is written in this book.' (2 Chronicles 34:14-16b, 18b-19, 21b)

Reading the Bible today is something we take for granted, all too literally. We have all kinds of translations to choose from, and a host of material designed to help us better understand whatever passage we are reading. Most of us will have a Bible in our home, if not several, but how often do we make time to read it? In all too many households, the Bible is left to gather dust, serving more as a talisman than a word to live by.

If that is true for us, we do well to consider the reaction of Josiah when, early in his reign, the book of the law was discovered in the temple, having been hidden away there and forgotten for many years. A regrettable oversight, some might have called it, but not Josiah. For him it was a calamity that had immediately to be addressed, for in his eyes this neglect of God's word was tantamount to throwing one of God's most precious gifts back into his face. Are we guilty of doing the same today? A Bible sitting on the shelf helps no one; it's reading it that counts!

Studying the word

On the first day of the first month Ezra fixed the day for the departure from Babylon, and on the first day of the fifth month he reached Jerusalem, for the gracious hand of his God was upon him. For Ezra had committed himself to study the law of the Lord, and to put it into practice, and to teach its statutes and ordinances in Israel. (Ezra 7:9-10)

Few people if asked to list their top ten characters of the Old Testament would include Ezra in their choice. Despite having a book named after him, he fails to capture the imagination quite as characters like Moses, Samson, David or Isaiah do. Some have called him dull; others have gone even further and accused him of being largely responsible for the narrow legalism which came to typify Judaism at the time of Jesus.

Yet this is to overlook the very real contribution Ezra made to his nation at a formative time in its history, and to undervalue the motivation that lay behind it. As a scribe and priest, his overriding concern was to nurture the faith of his people, and he did this in the way he knew best: by reading, learning and acting upon God's words. He knew that if past mistakes were not to be made again, the people's relationship with God needed to be deepened, and one of the best ways of ensuring this was through reflecting on scripture. There is much we can learn today from his example of single-minded devotion to the study of God's word if we too would grow in faith.

You can say that again!

As I said to you before, I say to you once more, 'If anyone preaches any gospel other than that which we have received, a curse be on them!' (Galatians 1:9)

When I wrote *Daily Prayer*, the publication on which this book is based, I thought it would be a relatively straightforward job. I had plenty of material to adapt from my time in ministry and numerous new ideas mulling in the back of my mind, so a few months at most and I would be finished. Instead, the book took the best part of a year to complete involving innumerable hours' work. The reasons were many, but chief among them was a concern that I might end up repeating earlier material, inadvertently perhaps using the same reading, prayer or thought for the day. No, I'm not using that as an excuse to do just that here, but would it matter if I had done, for isn't there a sense in which we've been doing that anyway as Christians for the past two thousand years?

Of course the words haven't been precisely the same, but just think of the countless sermons that have been preached and Bible passages discussed over the centuries, all on essentially the same message. There will have been different approaches, different texts, and different nuances of interpretation, but essentially the concern of each has been to proclaim the good news of Jesus Christ. All this points us to the wonder of the gospel – that though we may hear it again and again, it still has the power to speak to us in new and challenging ways, and still has the power to change lives. I tried not to repeat myself word for word – not on purpose anyway – but I hope in a sense I have repeated myself on every page in testifying to the renewing life-giving power of God revealed in Christ. For here, if ever there was one, is a message that will be as fresh tomorrow and every day as the day it was first spoken; a message concerning which we can happily declare, without hesitation, 'You can say that again!'

Gospel message, essentials of

Keep it simple

We proclaim Christ crucified, an offence to the Jews and plain folly to others, but to those who have been called, whether Jews or Greeks, it is the message of Christ, the power and wisdom of God. (1 Corinthians 1:23-24)

Read the small print. I expect we've lost count of the times we've been told that, but I wonder how many of us actually do. When we receive a policy document through the post, or when a licensing agreement for our latest computer program pops up on the screen, how many of us sit down and read it through word for word? The fact is that not only is this usually interminably dull but more often than not it is also incomprehensible. Little wonder that efforts have been made in recent years to cut down on official gobbledegook, even if it doesn't as yet show!

It's not just officialdom, though, that can be guilty of verbosity; we can all fall into that trap. In fact, according to my editor, I do it all the time! As Christians, we're particularly prone, repeatedly slipping into language that may mean much to us but says nothing to those outside the Church. Worse still, we complicate the gospel with all kinds of dogmas, doctrines and creeds, insisting that this is sound and that unsound, one point a central tenet of faith while another borders on heresy. I don't doubt that there is sometimes a need for theological niceties or a place for religious jargon, but I suspect we would all do well occasionally to get back to basics.

That's what we see in the words of Paul to the Corinthians. Derided as a public speaker in comparison to the great orators of his day, and condemned by his fellow Jews for having supposedly blasphemed against his God, he didn't care. He summarised his message in one sentence; a sentence that says it all: 'Christ crucified . . . the power and wisdom of God.' Yes, of course that needs fleshing out, and what one person means by it may be different from the next, but it's there nonetheless, the heart of the matter in a nutshell. The success of Paul as a preacher speaks for itself, and it's a lesson we need to learn from. We often extol the virtue of a simple faith; sadly, we don't often practise it.

Index